Praise for

Amazon.com   Five Stars: A Must Read for All Who Have Experienced Loss. July 2003

Nimblespirit.com
"One of the most important lessons Schocket has for us is that the heart and psyche have their own timetable for grieving.

As Schocket takes us hour by hour through the first days of her grief – she describes actions and emotions that all of us have gone through. Yet there's something incredibly comforting in making the journey in one's armchair.

There are plenty of books on grieving but I know of no other author who narrates in the first person the shock, the ordinary compulsions like needing to have the living room dusted before guests arrive from the cemetery, and the terrible loneliness, as vividly and plainly as Schocket does.

My Life Closed Twice is inspirational, yet grounded in everyday experience; honest, yet compassionate. It speaks to us from the depths of grief but does not leave us there."

SENTINEL-TRIBUNE   Bowling Green. OH
"Witticism is sprinkled through her writing about everyday life, even in as mundane a tale as sending her husband to pick up tuna at the grocery."

CITY PAPER   Toledo, OH   Interview with the author.
What is the message of *My Life Closed Twice?*
"It's not a sad book. The beginning is sad but if you stick with it, you will find it rewarding. I think it says something new about loss. A woman told me it helped her cope with her divorce. There's a message in it – you may not be mourning a person, you may have lost your job – and you can learn from this."

Fred Giordano, Public Library Director (retired), NY
Over and above the poignant and heart-rending story of her losses and the ongoing challenge of managing grief, the author rendered the social history of her generation (and mine) accurately and engagingly.

Reader in California

"I was so profoundly moved by your book, the way you managed to take me into the epicenter of your grief and despair without either hopelessness or helplessness. Your book touched me because it offered so many practical pieces of advice. In many of the seemingly ordinary aspects of our lives, I suddenly saw the elements I treasure most: my young daughter bounding through the door after school right after I finished your book, moved me to tears.

I am currently pursuing a new career. Your book completely reinforced my feelings that even at this stage in life, I can embrace change."

The Compassionate Friends: Rockland County Chapter Newsletter

"The author refrains from preaching and tells her story as she experienced it. Many of us will readily identify with the feelings of the early stages of grief, which she expresses with remarkable honesty and insight.

Although her methods of coping may not be for everyone, she helps us understand that it is possible for someone with multiple losses to climb out of the abyss of darkness and learn to live again."

M. Seifert, Long Term Care Advisor, Maryland

"There is very little in grief literature on double loss. Ms. Schocket's book is an important and essential contribution. It is a "must" read for anyone who seeks a path to a meaningful life without their loved one.

Having lost my own 36 year old son, I felt that someone had taken me by the hand and put a comforting arm around my shoulder after reading "My Life Closed Twice."

Life goes on, albeit differently. Ms. Schocket's book shows us how and somehow puts it all in perspective. "

Additional reader comments:

"As the mother of a daughter who died at 21, and a wife whose marriage ended not by death but by divorce, I found a lot of comfort and hope in this book. There are no easy answers and we all are different but the author shows us what everybody finds out in time: that we do not know our inner strengths until they are tested and then we surprise even ourselves."

"Sandra Schocket's memoir brings the reader to the heart of a devastating grief. The people in her life are very well-drawn, and we come to know them and appreciate them, and ultimately grieve her loss. Yet her story is one of resilience. A very moving and well-written book."

My Life
Closed
Twice

Surviving a Double Loss

To Darcel,
Thank you —
Sandra Schocket

by Sandra Klamkin Schocket

Second Edition, 2004
ISBN 0-9760917-0-4
Previously ISBN 0-9710723-3-7

TX 5-772-706 2003

Library of Congress Control Number: 2004112982

Published by: Monroe Press
                 PO Box 662
                 Holland, OH 43528
                 monroe50@att.net
                 www.multipleloss.net

Designed by: Onscreen Designs, LLC
Printed and bound in the United States.

Poem 1732 *"My life closed twice"*. Reprinted by permission of the publishers and the Trustees of Amherst College from THE POEMS OF EMILY DICKINSON, Thomas H. Johnson, ed., Cambridge, Mass.: The Belknap Press of Harvard University Press, Copyright ©1951, 1955, 1979 by the President and Fellows of Harvard College.

Moon River
From the Paramount Picture BREAKFAST AT TIFFANY'S
Words by Johnny Mercer
Music by Henry Mancini
Copyright © 1961 (Renewed 1989) by Famous Music Corporation
International Copyright Secured
All Rights Reserved

Why Did I Choose you?
Lyric by Herbert Martin.
Music by Michael Leonard.
Copyright© 1965 (Renewed) HERBERT MARTIN and MICHAEL LEONARD
All Rights Controlled by EDWIN H. MORRIS & COMPANY, A Division of MPL Communications, Inc. and BJS MUSIC CORP.
All Rights Reserved.

To Sophie, the next generation

Part I.
MY LIFE CLOSED TWICE

Part II.
SO HOPELESS TO CONCEIVE

Part III.
A SLOW AND CAUTIOUS WAY

My life closed twice before its close –
It yet remains to see
If Immortality unveil
A third event to me

So huge, so hopeless to conceive
As these that twice befell.
Parting is all we know of heaven,
And all we need of hell.

—*Emily Dickinson*

Part I

My Life Closed Twice

The lives of 2,278,994 Americans ended in 1994, the year my new life began. My husband and son were two of the dead. They died in December within 24 hours of one another. I felt as if a meteor had fallen out of the sky aimed directly at me. There was no escape. My life became uncharted, as if I had stepped from my known world onto another planet. People have asked how I survived such a tragedy.

I shall give you a true accounting of events that unfolded as I remember them. To respect the privacy of people included, all of the names are changed except for the immediate family. The names of some places and institutions have been changed and some incidents have been condensed. I have changed too. This is my story.

Alarm

I t started out like any other Sunday—a bright blue December
day that would have gone unremembered if it had not split my
world into a before and after, like a page torn neatly down the
middle. It was the day my husband Jay, 59 years old, left home and
never returned. We lived a New Jersey mid-way life. We were mid-way
between New York and Pennsylvania, although closer to New York, mid-
way between young and old, although closer to old, and mid-way between
rich and poor, but a little closer to rich. We owned two cars, a house
with a front yard, backyard, pretty view of a stream and stone bridge,
and a dwindling mortgage. We thought of moving to a smaller place and
talked about retirement. Our life had reached a pleasant plateau, with
time to travel and grandchildren to look forward to.

Jay was a lawyer who specialized in corporate law. He was a pensive
man, quiet and deep, with a keen intelligence that was better suited to
mergers and acquisitions than courtroom drama. He became a lawyer in
1960 when there were fewer of them. The profession was 99 percent
white male and lawyer jokes were an oxymoron. Because he had no taste
for the courtroom, he entered a specialty where his goal was to keep his
clients out of court. His rare court appearances included representing his
mother after she was in a traffic accident and defending clients' children
who got speeding tickets or used fake identification in bars.

We were, in the 1960's and 70's, the rare dual-career couple. In my
neighborhood and even among my married college friends, I was the
only woman who had an occupation other than housewife and held a
paying job when my children were young. My interests, skills and

temperament did not lend themselves to full-time childcare and housework. Realizing this, I obtained a part-time job as a counselor to university students. As my career evolved, I eventually returned to the corporate world where I had started as a recent college graduate. In my current job, I work for a management consulting firm that provides "outplacement" services to corporate employees. This line of work did not exist until the early 1980's when corporations began to shed hundreds of thousands of employees, creating the opportunity for a new industry to fashion itself for the assistance of the victims. The independence and confidence that I gained from working all those years, in addition to the financial benefit, enabled me to be more self-sufficient in the new life I was about to undertake.

Through a household division of labor that had evolved, not always peacefully over the years, Jay was responsible for the laundry and the food shopping. He was a man of habit. He arranged his Sunday as he might prepare a sandwich with everything layered, stacking it up until it became a coherent whole. The structure of his Sunday depended on the season. On this December day, he went to the supermarket in the morning. "They run out of things in the afternoon," he told me, but I knew that the real reason had little to do with supermarket stock. As in thousands of households nationwide, he spent his Sunday afternoons in front of the television watching NFL football. Household chores, however cumbersome, would be completed by game time.

During the summer he was less concerned with bringing home everything on the list than he was in playing a morning of tennis. He took his chances with the store's supplies in the afternoon, occasionally grumbling that they were out of things. (Being as sharp as he was, I am sure he knew I didn't believe his excuses but he offered them anyway.) When I first convinced him that the marketing would be a good thing for him to do, he didn't exactly embrace this chore as an opportunity, but undertook it as he would a legal assignment, logically, objectively and with almost military precision. Other than eating, Jay's acquaintance with the kitchen was minimal. He could make instant coffee in the microwave oven, put together a cold cut sandwich or toast a bagel. Boiling an egg would have been a stretch. So shopping for food put him into new territory.

Feeling insecure about what to buy and not wanting to incur my wrath if he returned with the wrong item, he required me to make a detailed list of the merchandise he would have to purchase. If the list said two cans of tuna fish, he wanted to know what size cans.

"How many ounces?" he asked.

"How do I know how many ounces?" I replied, annoyance creeping into my voice. "Just buy two cans of tuna fish. You know what a can of tuna fish looks like." He bought only what was on the list, having no confidence to make substitutions if an item was not in stock. Until he developed that intuition, we often had heated disagreements about what he came home with. But he learned and eventually did a good job, even to the point of collecting coupons for bargains. He occasionally went overboard on sale items buying far too much of something that we had no need for. A colleague at work once confided that she had a basement full of toilet paper. Her husband, a high level scientist at a major corporation, was also the family shopper. He could not resist a sale on toilet paper and any markdown resulted in warehouse size inventories in her basement.

On this fateful Sunday, Jay's team, the New York Giants, who play in New Jersey, was playing the Cleveland Browns in the "late" afternoon game, which aired at 4 p.m. Eastern time. This schedule, contrived by the TV networks to attract more West Coast football fans, kept East Coast viewers in their seats from early afternoon until long after dark. Jay chose not to watch the first game, which left him a few empty hours in the early afternoon to work in the house. He did not enjoy handyman chores but when he undertook a job, he read a how-to book, bought all the right equipment and generally did the task well. He is the only person I know who learned to sail by reading a book. When we moved to a lake community, we bought a small sailboat. Jay went to the library, took out a book on sailing, read the principles of forward velocity, the specifics pertaining to the boat we owned, went out, rigged the boat and sailed off. Just like that.

His project for the day was to paint the laundry room, which had grown dingy over the years. He wore a funny white peaked painter's hat, which sits to this day on a table where he left it with the cleaned brushes and some paint thinner. By 4 o'clock, with all errands and chores complete, he had settled himself in front of the TV for relaxation, if the shouting, pounding, armchair-quarterbacking, and second-guessing that went on for three hours could be considered relaxation. He missed having sons at home. He would have liked companionship for the game, someone who would agree that they should have gone for the field goal instead of the first down. But I have little patience for prolonged football on TV. I'll watch the second half of the Superbowl game or the last game of the World Series and figure I've seen the result, why bother with the process. Just tell me how it all comes out - like reading the bottom line on an annual report or the jacket cover of a book that isn't worth the long haul. On this afternoon, I might have watched the third or fourth quarter with him, but the day never worked out that way.

Although I had planned to take a walk in the fading daylight, I chose instead to put my feet up on the couch and read the Sunday paper, I downstairs, he up in the cozy paneled TV room off the master bedroom. So it was that I was at home when, a few minutes later, Jay called to me from upstairs. "I'm sick to my stomach," he complained. I ran upstairs and found him lying on the bathroom floor. He hadn't fallen, but perhaps was too weak to stand and had to lie down. I thought at first he was reacting to a restaurant meal we had the night before. Then he said he had a bad pain in his chest.

I ran to the phone. My hands shook as I dialed 911. I went downstairs to leave the front door open for the rescue squad. Then I ran back up to see what I could do for Jay. I put a towel under his head and held his hand. Within five minutes, the emergency squad was at the door. They said we were lucky that they could respond so quickly. It was a quiet day and they were not busy. They instantly assessed his condition as a heart attack and hooked him to various machines and tubes. Shortly afterward they loaded him onto a stretcher. He was a big man, six feet two inches tall, 185 pounds. The technicians carried him down the stairs, struggling to angle the stretcher on the landing where the stairs turn sharply at the bottom. Then they moved easily through the wide front hall and out the front door. They stopped briefly on the lawn to position the stretcher before lifting it to the ambulance. I stood looking out the window at this brief tableau - the ambulance, the workers, the stretcher, my husband. "My life will never be the same," I thought as I reached for my coat and ran to my car.

It was the second time he had changed my life. I was just out of college when we met in New York, he a second year law student, I an underwriting clerk in an insurance company. He swept me off my feet with his worldliness. He had preceded me to New York by a year. Concentrating more on the city's good life than on torts and procedures,

he knew all the best jazz spots in Greenwich Village, how to get around the city by subway, and where to find the creamiest cheesecake at 1:00 a.m. We frequented a restaurant that used to be a speakeasy and still had the slot in the door where insiders peeked out to see which outsiders were eligible to enter. We ate paella and blintzes, and danced at the Rainbow Room in Rockefeller Center with its picture book view of Manhattan's twinkling nighttime skyline.

Tall and slim, with black hair that 35 years later showed only a few signs of gray, he was also a great dresser. And why not? His father owned a men's clothing store in Trenton, New Jersey, enabling him to outfit himself in the Ivy League classics that remained his lifetime choice long after the store had closed. At the time Jay finished law school, military service was required of all young men. Our generation was lucky. We slithered between the wars. Too young for Korea, too old for Vietnam, the military obligation primarily meant doing time. Jay had three choices: three years as an officer, two years as an enlisted man or six years in the Army Reserves. He chose the Reserves. Shortly after our marriage, he left for basic training where the eighteen-year-olds called him "the old man." (He was 25.) He hiked ten miles in poorly fitting boots, slept in the snow in a tent and became a clerk at Fort Dix in New Jersey, where he typed with two fingers, filling out overseas transfer forms. He polished his boots, peeled potatoes, learned to shoot a rifle and earned a sharpshooters badge. Following six months of active duty, he became part of New Jersey's Lightning Division. He attended weekly meetings to train him in his job as clerk. His two weeks of summer service were at Camp Drum in the scenic Finger Lakes region of upper New York State. He always came home with a tan. When his six years of military service were over, he earned an honorable discharge and a commendation from his commanding officer. Although the U.S. government did not consider him a veteran, he saved all his badges, insignia and even his dog tags.

Jay entered law practice in New Jersey, setting out on the route that led from unpaid law clerk, required at the time, to corporate attorney. He began his career at a small law firm in Newark, then started his own firm with a few colleagues. Much of his work seemed dull to me, dealing as he did with business rather than personal issues. "Couldn't you defend a notorious criminal or get million -dollar settlements for woman whose rich husbands have moved on to younger women?" I asked him. But he was good at what we did and happy in his chosen specialty. Later, he accepted a position as general counsel with a company that sold toothpaste that not only whitened the teeth of smokers but was also good for removing water stains from furniture. Being in a corporate job, the scope of his activity changed from local to national and even international. That job had some excitement to it, as far as I was concerned, and the work was something that I could understand, such as acquiring new products or working on trade agreements in Venezuela. We went to annual conferences of professional organizations at fancy hotels where CEO's in tuxedos, madras bow ties and red suspenders danced the hully gully at formal banquets. We rode to airports in limousines and were entertained by executives from corporations that wanted to make deals. But it all ended abruptly when a larger corporation acquired Jay's company and hired someone else to do his job.

He returned to private practice and we learned to live with different expectations. The pay wasn't as good but Jay was happier rid of the tyrannical boss who called at two in the morning and once tracked us down at a restaurant where we were celebrating our wedding anniversary to convey a bit of information that could easily have waited until morning. And this was long before mobile phones. He represented a client who was the first to sell pizza to Russians on the streets of Moscow. Later, still under Communism, the client opened the first American restaurant in Moscow. It became the gathering place for Pan Am flight attendants, American diplomats, journalists, business executives and anyone else who could pay in dollars. The menu offered veal chops, home fried potatoes, and apple pie, a touch of home that went a long way in austere Russia. Another client, a wine merchant, escorted us on an enchanting vineyard tour of France. We ate huge meals in country inns and I had my first taste of green wine. I wish I could tell you more about Jay's work but he rarely discussed it. He told me I wouldn't be interested. Eventually I stopped asking.

When I married my husband, I would have followed him anywhere, although following him to an emergency room had not occurred to me at the time. As I drove through darkened streets on the way to the hospital I had no concept of speed. I was daring, almost hoping that a police car would pull me over. "My husband had a heart attack and I'm rushing to the hospital," I would say. "Sorry, ma'am," the young officer would reply, "follow me." And off I would go with police escort. It did not happen until later that same week. This time I arrived without incident, turning off the quiet road at the large EMERGENCY sign. Saint Agatha's is a local hospital run by the Sisters of the Sorrowful Mother. In contrast to their mournful name, the nurses are pleasant, cheerful and helpful. The floors are immaculate and shiny beyond the dreams of a 1950's housewife. The halls smell of mint. Having raised two boys, I was not a stranger to the Emergency Room.

I first went to Admissions where I had to register Jay and was then directed to the ER waiting room. The room was large and square, and everything in it - walls, floor and furniture - was green. A man sat with his wife and an older woman in one corner. The TV was turned off. A few well-used magazines were tossed on a table. I tried to read one but could not concentrate. By the time they let me see my husband, an internist had already examined him. She had called a cardiologist, Dr. Siegel. He was a young Doctor of Osteopathy who had recently joined an established cardiology practice. The doctors told me I had saved Jay's life by calling the emergency squad so quickly. Jay was suffering a major heart attack and they had already administered TPA, a clot-dissolving medicine. The next 24 hours would be critical. Jay was awake and aware of all that was going on around him. I held his hand for a while.

"That feels good, " he said softly. He wanted to know everything that was happening. "Why does it hurt so much?" he asked.

"Because you're having a heart attack," I told him trying to sound calm and matter-of-fact although I probably looked anxious and nervous. After a few hours in the emergency room, he was taken to a critical care unit on an upper floor.

The waiting room on that floor was empty except for a young dark-haired woman who was using a telephone on a table in the corner. I was surprised to see that it was not a pay phone but a regular telephone such as one would have at home, only an older model. The TV was on for no one to watch. The woman finished her call and left the room. When I went to the table near where she had been sitting I saw that she had left the telephone directory open - to the classified listings of funeral homes. A large clock on the wall read 7:15. Only three hours since our ordinary life was so brutally shattered.

I had to phone the family. Our older son, Barry, at 30 was a cheerful, kind man - the extrovert of the family. Married for a year and a half, he and his wife Ellen lived in suburban Maryland, not far from Washington,

DC. Barry had finished his graduate courses in clinical psychology and was in the final stages of writing his dissertation, another step on the long road to becoming a psychologist. He worked part-time as a counselor at a methadone clinic in downtown Washington. Ellen, a nurse, had completed her master's degree in Public Health Administration the previous spring and shortly afterward started a new job as an administrator for a large home-healthcare agency.

Andy, four years younger than his brother, lived in Virginia where he was a graduate student in American history. At 6 ½ feet, Andy had long been taller than his father and brother although they were also more than 6 feet tall. All three were slim and bore a strong family resemblance, which I did not share. "You give birth to them and they end up looking exactly like your husband," a friend used to say whose sons also looked nothing like her. Barry and Andy maintained a close relationship. They visited one another frequently and spent hours on the phone discussing sports, jobs, and what was going on in their lives.

The waiting room was still empty as I took out my telephone card to make the calls. I asked the hospital operator how to make a credit card call. "That won't be necessary," she said. "You just dial the call." I was amazed; free long-distance calls. The bill for Jay's 24 hours at Saint Agatha's was $14,000 so I guess the cost of a few phone calls was built in. I called Barry first. No one was at home. I spoke to the answering machine, leaving the message that Jay had suffered a heart attack and I was calling from Saint Agatha's. That message, words on a mechanical instrument, would end Barry's intact world, where parents were stronger and wiser, the helpers not the helped. He would return home from a pleasant evening out with his wife to find a blinking red light, a danger signal telling him to listen to the words that would alter his life.

Andy also was out. He shared a house with another young man and I was reluctant to leave a message on the machine. I called Jay's younger brother Larry, a physician in Denver. He was concerned, but not surprised, by Jay's heart attack. Their father had a disabling heart attack at 61 and died of a massive attack two years later. The brothers were opposite in their approach to health. Jay smoked, enjoyed hamburgers and doughnuts, and although an active athlete when young, had settled into a more sedentary life in his 50's. He had not had a medical checkup in years. Larry gave up his pipe years ago; his low-fat, low sugar diet is a model of moderation; he is fit and trim and monitors his cholesterol levels more frequently than an astronaut. Speaking as a doctor rather than a relative, Larry explained the physiology of a heart attack and the steps that would likely follow. "They will perform an angiogram," he told me, "to determine the exact location and amount of damage. Later on he will probably undergo angioplasty." This is a procedure where doctors insert a catheter into the blocked artery and inflate a tiny balloon that squeezes open the blockage.

Larry said he would speak with Dr. Siegel the next day about Jay's condition and prognosis. I felt reassured. It was helpful to have someone to speak with. Time passed slowly in the waiting room. I picked up a six-month-old magazine, leafed through it, then another. The phone rang. Who would be calling a hospital waiting room at that hour on a Sunday night? After a few rings, I answered, expecting a wrong number. It was Barry. He and Ellen had returned home, heard the phone message and tracked me down. He had already spoken with Andy and the two of them would come the next day.

By 9:30, Jay's condition was stabilized and even improved. The nurses told me to go home and get some sleep. I could call at 6:00 a.m. on Monday for an update. Arriving home after 10:00, I realized I had not eaten since lunch. Unlike some who eat more under stress, my desire for food disappears when I am nervous. A cup of tea and a hastily defrosted roll from the freezer were my dinner that night. There was also my work to think about. I was scheduled to lead a workshop at 9:00 the next morning. From the hospital, I had left a message on the answering machine of a co-worker in charge of workshops, saying my husband was seriously ill and I would call the office early Monday morning regarding work that day. I assumed she would get the message and try to arrange for a backup. It is usually very difficult to find a last-minute replacement so in my message I said that if Jay's condition had stabilized by morning, I would try to come in for the afternoon.

As insurance I knew I would not need, I set the alarm for 6:00 a.m., slept fitfully and was awake long before daylight. The news from the hospital was encouraging. Jay continued to be stable and they expected him to be out of the critical care unit by evening. He would then go by ambulance to Highmount Memorial, a larger hospital where cardiac surgery is performed. I felt tremendously relieved and even hopeful that he would make a full recovery. The nurse said I could visit for a few hours that morning. I called my office around 8:00 to see if they had recruited someone to replace me. "Where are you?" asked the officious office manager who answered the phone. "You are supposed to be here to do a workshop this morning," she said. I was not surprised by her response. She was a tough woman with little compassion for human frailties or transgressions. Her stern reprimand could bring secretaries to tears. Although not my boss, she once scolded me for wearing a sweater and slacks to work on a half-day before a holiday, a day on which we were planning to move files and hang pictures. "Didn't you get my message? My husband had a heart attack. He's in intensive care at Saint Agatha's." She apologized. The woman on whose machine I had left the message was out of town so the office hadn't heard. I said that if other staff members could fill in for me during the morning, I hoped to be there by noon. "You're a trouper," she said.

Although hospital visiting hours did not start until 10:00, the nurses at Saint Agatha's are uniformly kind in allowing exceptions. When I arrived before 9:00, Jay was awake and in less pain than he had been in the day before. His face looked drawn and anxious and he needed a shave. He was uncomfortable and sore. He shared a small room in the critical care unit where he was attached to various machines with many tubes that moved fluids in and out. Boxes blinked with numbers while they measured and controlled vital body functions. He wanted to know how sick he was and how long he would be in the hospital. He had not been in the hospital since we were married. He had been amazingly healthy, traveling to South America and Russia without so much as a stomach ache. Never a broken bone, no chronic conditions. I told him about my conversation with his brother and he seemed reassured that, having survived the night, he was on his way to recovery. I sat with him for a few hours and spoke with the doctor who said that he had responded well to treatment and, as planned, would be moved to the larger hospital that evening. When I left the hospital just before lunch time, I was encouraged by Jay's condition. I was also relieved that our sons would be there in a few hours to be with him. Having them to talk with, to reassure and comfort me would lessen the stress I felt inside.

My feet felt lighter as I walked to the parking lot. I drove toward my office on a route built for farmers to deliver their produce to market. Usually clogged with cars during rush hour, the road was not busy at this time of day. By noon I was at work. After the tremendous anxiety of the previous day, being at work was a relief. I was in familiar surroundings, doing something where I was in control — for people I could help. For the next three days I would work with a small group of job-seekers. I would guide them in the process of preparing themselves to re-enter the job market and I hoped they would leave feeling confident about their prospects.

Other staff members had taken shifts as instructors of the group during the morning session. They had told the participants, who had lost their jobs the previous week, that I would be late because of a family crisis. The attendees barely seemed to notice that I was late, wrapped up as they were in their own problems. Not knowing the system, they probably assumed that workshop leaders are interchangeable, which in a sense we are. The programs are designed to be the same, whether delivered by a woman in New Jersey or a man in California. We bring our personality and favorite stories to the presentation, but the core information we provide is consistent.

The participants had finished venting their anger toward their employer, an insurance company, expressing their shock that a company to which they had given such loyalty and devotion could let them go without even a day's notice. One day they assumed they were valued employees, the next they were told to pack up their belongings and head for the door. They were devastated. Allowing time for people to talk about their hurt is a necessary part of an outplacement workshop. Some groups are so angry that, given the time, they would spend the whole morning bemoaning their fate: the unfairness of it, the lack of compassion shown by management, the embarrassment of losing their computer access and cleaning out their space. My job is to coax them away from their shock and anger to the task of evaluating their skills. This helps to restore their confidence and gets them to focus on the future rather than the past, something I would learn to do as well in the months to follow. We spent the afternoon discussing job-related accomplishments that they could include in their resume. They were starting to feel good about themselves. I could see it in their eyes, in the way they smiled and joked with one another. Assigning completion of their resume as homework, I ended the seminar around 4:00 p.m. and was back at the hospital within half an hour.

Barry, Andy and Ellen were in the critical care waiting room which, at that time of day, was crowded. Ellen was sleeping, her head resting on Barry's shoulder, the glowing red of her hair a contrast to the blue of his denim jacket. She wore a colorful vest that we had bought for her at the old market in Charleston a month before. I was so happy and relieved to see them. I knew that their presence meant a lot to Jay as well. He was sleeping and plans still called for him to be moved to the larger hospital that evening. Andy agreed to go with me to Highmount to check Jay in and see him once he was settled. Ellen and Barry went to get dinner. The wait for the next step seemed endless. Why does time pass so slowly in waiting rooms? Why do we spend so much of our lives waiting? My father was an endlessly patient man. He waited for bank tellers and doctors with equal equanimity. He had a kind word for those whose inefficiencies resulted in endless delays. He thanked the hapless store clerk who had not yet learned her job, smiled at the motor vehicle inspector after sitting in line for an hour and warmly greeted the corporate functionary who put him constantly on hold. Unfortunately I did not inherit his sunny disposition.

Andy and I waited in the same room where I had been the night before. The walls were beige, an improvement over the green from downstairs. The chairs were all upholstered in salmon colored vinyl. A television set, mounted high above our heads showed first the evening news, then a quiz show, then a sitcom. Gradually the room emptied out until we were the only occupants. In degrees of comfort, tonight's wait was infinitely better than that of the previous night. Jay was no longer fighting for his life and my family was with me. I am by nature a worrier. On Sunday night, alone, not knowing if my husband would live, I was in a state of extreme stress, not able to concentrate on even the most innocuous magazine article. I paced the floor, walked the halls and visited bathrooms with greater frequency than seemed possible. By Monday night I had calmed down. I read the newspaper while Andy napped. Eventually, around 8:00 p.m., Jay was discharged from Saint Agatha's and on his second ambulance trip in two days.

Highmount Memorial, no longer merely a hospital but part of a "health system", is in a larger town, the county seat, less than 10 miles from Saint Agatha's. From a small regional hospital, it has grown significantly over the years, adding programs and building new wings. We parked in a large indoor garage and walked to the hospital entrance. An electric Menorah at least five feet tall stood in the first floor lobby, which was dark and empty at this time of night. Chanukah, the Jewish Festival of Lights, was unusually early that year, beginning just a few days after Thanksgiving rather than coinciding with Christmas as it usually does. Since Jewish holidays are observed according to a lunar rather than solar calendar, they occur at different times each year in relation to the Western calendar. Jews celebrate the holiday by sharing gifts and lighting candles in a nine-branch candelabra or Menorah. Menorahs used to be small enough to fit on a table or mantelpiece and were lit only at home or in the synagogue but in these days of political correctness, they share public space with Santas and Christmas trees. In the deserted hospital vestibule, this Menorah seemed forlorn, a reminder of happier celebrations and holiday activities.

Ellen and Barry had invited us to celebrate Chanukah and Thanksgiving with them in Maryland two weeks earlier. As the newest member of the staff, Ellen had to work on Thanksgiving Day so our big meal was planned for Friday. On Thursday, Jay, Barry, Andy and I went to Washington to be tourists for the day. We ate lunch in a small cafe at the National Gallery of Art, our nuclear family together as we had not been on Thanksgiving for a few years. We each had a turkey platter with all the trimmings served by a congenial waitress. We joked about Thanksgiving dinners of the past in equally unlikely places. The year the boys and I had dinner on a flight to Florida when my mother lay dying in a hospice. The time I visited Andy in London where he worked for a semester while in college, when we ate at the home of a college classmate of mine. We had a table-breaking traditional American dinner with a large turkey, not easy to find in London in November, homemade corn pudding, stuffing, mashed potatoes and desserts unknown to colonial Massachusetts. The year that Barry and Andy, sharing a small apartment in Arlington, Virginia prepared a full dinner for us. Barry had asked the heaviest woman at work for her sweet potato recipe. It was all butter and worth the calories. Following our Washington Thanksgiving lunch, Andy had to leave to return to Virginia. He would not be able to join in our Thanksgiving dinner the next day. Although far from lavish, we enjoyed our brief meal together. How could we have known it would be our last?
Ellen served her first Thanksgiving dinner the following day. She had worked hard to prepare the turkey, stuffing, salad, spinach, sweet potatoes and dessert. It was all delicious. Barry was so proud. We exchanged Chanukah gifts and took pictures that were still in my camera. We were an ordinary family celebrating the holidays. Nothing remarkable about us. Multiply us by the millions across the country who ate similar

Thanksgiving dinners albeit on Thursday. But Friday was fine for us. Separated as we were in distance, we were happy to be together. Now unexpectedly, we were together again - our lives focused on the beat within one person's chest.

The Admissions Department, right off the lobby, was eerily quiet. The large waiting area was empty, like a train station hours after the last night train has pulled out. A lone worker sat behind a counter at one of the stations. She greeted us and asked for the usual information, which she mechanically typed into her computer. As I had done the day before at Saint Agatha's, I gave her Jay's health insurance card, which I had found in his wallet. The information included, of course, the name of the insurer, the policy number as well as his social security number. I didn't know at the time that the social security number on the card was incorrect. He had evidently notified the company but never corrected the card itself. This created serious consequences later on. Andy and I again waited until Jay was finally settled into a room and we were allowed to see him. He was on the second floor of the Colonial Wing. The main floor corridor leading to the elevator had pictures of Monticello and Mount Vernon. The decor of Jay's room was meant to look more like a Best Western Motel than a hospital, with furniture of pale wood rather than gray gunmetal. There was a cabinet to hold a patient's few possessions and wooden chairs with red vinyl seats. The extra bed was empty. The day had been long and tiring for all of us so, seeing Jay settled, Andy and I soon left for home, about fifteen minutes away, up the interstate.

The days of that week fell into a routine. We were lulled into a false optimism believing that, despite the anguish we felt, everything would turn out all right. We went about our tasks as if what we were doing was normal. But there was nothing normal about it. We were clinging by our fingernails, trying to climb back into a life that was rapidly falling away. Ellen returned to Maryland. Having been at her job for only a few months, she could not take more time off. I completed the three-day workshop that had started on Monday and planned to return to do another with a new group the following week. When I left work on Wednesday, my boss asked if I felt comfortable working the next week. I assured him that I did. Jay would be in the hospital until the following Tuesday. Barry, whose schedule was the most flexible, agreed to stay with us after Jay came home so I would be free to work for three days. The job was close and I could be home by 4:30 in the evening.

Barry and Andy spent the days at the hospital and I know they cheered Jay by being there. They discussed teams and players, baseball statistics, football trades, and basketball greats. They followed the college and professional teams - watched lacrosse and soccer and track. When the boys were young, they and their father spent hours playing basketball in the backyard. They teased Jay about his old fashioned two-handed set shot, but he often won. There were arguments and even disagreements but they loved, admired and respected each other and that made their relationship special.

Ted, Jay's hospital roommate arrived the next day. He was a friendly man of about 50 with previous heart problems who was scheduled to undergo angioplasty the next day. His wife came each morning before work to bring him breakfast and after work to discuss their real estate business. She was beautiful — with perfect blond- streaked hair and stylish clothing, the kind of woman who makes me feel instantly inferior and dowdy. She wore tweed suits and leather shoes even when the weather was bad. She never spoke to me which did not upset me since people who make me feel inferior rarely inspire me to conversation. Ted liked to joke. He said that Jay's illness was God's punishment for being a lawyer. He sent Barry and Andy to the gift shop to buy him candy bars because he hated hospital food.

One afternoon when I arrived for my visit, Barry, with a giggle, directed me to look at the bulletin board in the corridor. An article was posted: "Sex After a Heart Attack." "Read it, Mom," he said. It was not the type of advice I usually received from my sons. They probably had been laughing about it all day and couldn't wait for me to get there so they could point it out. "A heart attack does not mean the end of sexual activity," the article explained along with some instructions in outline form. I promised to keep the advice in mind wondering if the sex life we had known would ever return.

Jay's angiogram was completed on Tuesday showing a blockage of the left main coronary artery. Dr. Siegel sat with Jay and me to discuss the results. He recommended angioplasty to clear the clogged artery. He called it a "procedure" not an operation. The death rate, he said, is one to four percent, figures I have heard for everything from a wisdom tooth extraction to a hysterectomy. The procedure is performed thousands of times a day throughout the world. We both asked many questions. How long does the procedure take? What is the recovery process?

Angioplasty normally takes less than two hours. Jay would stay in the hospital for another three or four days after the angioplasty followed by a rigorous rehabilitation program based at Saint Agatha's.

"What will happen if Jay does not have the procedure?" I asked. "That is a very good question," answered Dr. Siegel. "People ask many questions but no one has asked me that before." I found this odd since it seemed a fairly routine question. He said that Jay's blockage was severe and might not respond to medication.

I called Jay's brother who had earlier conferred with Dr. Siegel. Larry agreed that angioplasty was the correct course of action. I also consulted my internist Dr. Morgan whose office had referred us to Dr. Siegel when Jay was in the emergency room. Arthur Morgan was a long-time family friend as well as my doctor and I trusted his opinion. I told him that Jay was scheduled for angioplasty and asked whether he thought Dr. Siegel was qualified to do the job. "Don't worry about these young guys," Arthur assured me. "His training is current and the medical group he is with would not have hired him unless he had excellent recommendations. He's the kind of person I would want to operate on me."

Hindsight is so powerful. Was Dr. Siegel the best? I knew he wasn't. Why did we, Jay included, not seek excellence? Would the results have been different? We will never know. Angioplasty was planned for Friday morning. Jay's roommate Ted underwent his angioplasty on Wednesday. "Tell your husband it's a piece of cake," he said with a big grin as he was brought back to the room. By Thursday, Jay was well enough to walk down the hall and spend some time on the phone with clients. Four days had passed since he smoked his last cigarette. I made a comment about his quitting "cold turkey" but something about the look he gave me made me question my judgment.

"You are going to quit," I half said, half asked. His response stunned me.

"The doctors say the greatest danger is scar tissue, not smoking." I could feel my blood pressure rising.

"After all you have been through and all the anguish you have caused your family, you are actually considering smoking again," I shouted. We glared at one another. I wanted to put on my coat, pick up my purse and storm out, but a silent force prevented me from doing so. I sat on the edge of the bed and slowly calmed down. Our conversation returned to small talk. We did not mention smoking again. Before leaving, I told him that Barry and Andy would be there early the next morning and that I planned to come and spend the day with him after he returned from surgery. I kissed him goodbye and left. It seemed like such an ordinary goodbye. It was the last time we ever saw one another.

"Breakfast At Tiffany's," one of my favorite old movies, was on TV that night. After such a stressful week, I looked forward to watching this bittersweet movie about young people in New York in the 1960's. Beautiful Audrey Hepburn as the whimsical Holly Golightly, dressed in a wardrobe far too chic for the poor working girl she portrays, and her co-star George Peppard, have a series of adventures around the big city. In a quiet moment on a warm summer evening Holly, perched on a fire escape, sings in a sweet lilting voice:

"Two drifters off to see the world, there's such a lot of world to see

We're after the same rainbow's end, waitin' round the bend

My huckleberry friend, Moon River and me."

Jay and I first saw the movie when we were newly married and everything seemed possible. We lived in a small apartment. He was at the beginning of his career but I knew he would be successful and I would share in the glow of that success. We were off to see the world, with good educations and youthful optimism. Watching it alone at home that night as a woman rapidly approaching senior citizenship with a seriously ill husband, I wondered if somehow we had passed the rainbow's end without noticing, or maybe it was still to come. Surely there was more world to see and I hoped there would be time to do it together.

The phone rang about 9:30. It was Jay. He wanted to remind me to bring his bedroom slippers and electric razor to the hospital the next day. He didn't say so but I think he was nervous about the surgery and wanted to talk. We spoke for a few minutes about ordinary things. The recycling had to go out the next day. Among household jobs, our division of labor assigned the garbage to him. He told me where to put the boxes, bottles and cans. I told him to get a good night's sleep, and I would see him in the morning. We said goodnight. On the TV, Audrey Hepburn and George Peppard were standing in the rain with her wet cat, enjoying a drenching reconciliation. If only real life problems could be solved as sweetly.

Barry and Andy left for the hospital early on Friday. Andy had packed his suitcase, ready to take a 10:15 bus from the hospital into New York where he could change for one to Maryland where he had left his car. The previous day, the nurse told me that the angioplasty was scheduled for 7 a.m. and that I would not be able to see Jay prior to the surgery. I was working at home on three articles for a New Jersey newspaper. The deadline was the following week and, due to Jay's illness, I was behind. I had been lulled into a false security by the doctor who saw no cause for concern. If I thought there was any danger, anything beyond the "routine procedure" I expected to take place, I would have gone with my sons. Instead, I chose to stay at home to work, planning to leave the house around 9:00. Barry said he would call as soon as Jay returned from surgery so I became concerned when I hadn't heard anything by 9:30. I called Jay's room and Barry answered. He said Jay was still in surgery. When they inquired, they were told that he had not gone down as early as planned.

I sat at my desk in an upstairs corner room overlooking the front of the house, where I now sit writing this. I cannot tell you what I wore last week but I know that on that morning I wore a blue sweat suit that Barry and Andy gave me the year before. I planned to change before leaving for the hospital. About an hour later, I saw Jay's car coming up the driveway. Barry and Andy got out looking grim. They were usually joking but neither said a word as they headed toward the house. I wondered why they were home. And then I knew. They had come to tell me terrible news.

All We Need of Hell

Barry and Andy came into the house through the front door as they had hundreds of times before. Coming home from school, coming back from the playground or coming in from the front yard. We have a back door used only by workers who park their trucks back there. The family always found it too much trouble to walk all the way around when a quicker route was so easily available. As I made my way to the top of the stairs, Barry called up to me. "Mom, Dad passed away this morning during the operation." He blurted the words out before I could reach him, as if they had been waiting to fly out of his mouth because he could hold on to them no longer. I ran down the stairs. We stood in the front hall. I started to cry and Barry hugged me. No one spoke. "Come sit down," Barry said as he led the way into the living room where we sat, side by side, on the sofa.

I sat calmly trying to absorb what they were about to say. They told me what had happened. After waiting for a long time in Jay's room, they were called to a waiting area near the Operating Room. There they were met by Dr. Siegel who said he had inserted the catheter twice and everything was fine. Jay was awake and joking with the team of doctors who were assisting. On the third insertion, Jay's heart went into arrhythmia and stopped beating. They inserted a pacemaker but it was not effective. They did everything they could. He was sorry. Barry said that one of the nurses had suggested an autopsy. I would have to call the hospital to order it. "What good would it do?" I asked. "It wouldn't bring him back." A clearer thinking person would have requested it. Now, with a calmer mind I cannot imagine why I did not. The decision haunts me, but it is something I have to live with.

Barry handed me a clear plastic envelope that looked like a sandwich bag. Inside were Jay's watch, glasses and wedding ring. For something as personal as the items a man had with him at his death, I would have expected a little box or perhaps a cloth bag with a drawstring. But we are a plastic society and hospitals must watch their economies. If people come home from war in plastic bags, I could not expect a more genteel container for a watch and ring.

The ring was a plain gold band. When we were married, I had it inscribed on the inside, SIK to JMM, 5/29/60 so Jay would not forget our anniversary. To my knowledge, it left his finger only once. We were packing to move from our third apartment to our first house when he noticed the ring was gone. We searched through mounds of crumpled newspaper in cartons of china and pots and useless wedding gifts that followed us from home to home — silver platters for formal banquets, soup tureens and salad bowls, steak knives and coffee grinders. Not enough quantity for a garage sale, too expensive to give away and, we might need them some day, might we not? Eventually we found the ring in one of the boxes and he wore it until a nurse removed it and placed it in the plastic sandwich bag that rested in my lap.

The ring now sits in a box with the small black lace headpiece that the funeral home provided with a pin to place on my head during the funeral. Someone asked why I didn't bury the ring with Jay. I thought that perhaps Andy would want it; that it might become a family heirloom. I was married with a gold ring that had been in my family for generations. It was too large for me to wear permanently so I left it at my mother's house where it was stolen during a robbery several years later. Maybe Jay's ring would start a new tradition. His 60th birthday and our 35th wedding anniversary were less than 6 months away and I had started to think about celebrations. Perhaps a big party or a trip to Hawaii. We talked about that as I sat fingering the ring. The outside of it was scratched from wear but the monogramming on the inside was like new. Again and again I ran my fingers over the etched writing as if I could somehow conjure up a better future for the ring and its owner.

I had bought the watch for Jay as a gift for his fiftieth birthday. Wanting another opinion before making the decision, I took Andy, a high school student, to the jeweler with me. Jay was a man for whom appearance was beside the point. He wore classic clothing that he thought never went out of style, not realizing that although his tie was the right width, his lapels were too big or raincoat too short. When watches became fashion statements, I bought him a good gold one. I know he would not have liked a Rolex, no matter how trendy. Watches and clocks seem almost alive, ticking along as they do, deciding when they want to speed up, slow down or just stop. When I was a child, we sang a song about a grandfather's clock:

My grandfather's clock was too big for the shelf
So it stood many years on the floor.
It was taller by half than the old man himself
Though it weighed not a pennyweight more.
It was bought on the morn of the day that he was born
And was always his pleasure and pride
But it stopped short, never to go again
When the old man died.

Unlike the grandfather's clock, Jay's watch ticked for several years after his heart did, keeping perfect time in the drawer where I stored it. I gave the eyeglasses to the Lion's Club, which collects them for the needy.

We sat on the sofa for a long time. The room was cold. We seldom used the living room so I kept the heat to a minimum. When Andy took piano lessons as a child, he wore a hat when he went into the living room to practice. Jay called the room a museum. He said we should hang a red velvet rope across the entrance as a reminder to the family and others that it was off limits. Other rooms were less formal and more welcoming to men and boys who wanted to put their feet up on the furniture and eat a sandwich while watching TV. I liked the living room. On a sunny afternoon, I sat there in a corner wing chair and read the paper with my feet up on a footrest I had found in an antique shop. The room represented my need for order, a place that would stay neat, no coats draped over the arm of a chair or muddy footprints on the carpet. To me it represented "gracious living", a term we used at Mount Holyoke College in the 1950's to define the meals when we had to wear skirts to the dining room. On these twice-weekly occasions we found clean starched linen napkins in specially built cubby holes labeled with our names in alphabetical order. Following the meal the house mother served tea or coffee in the living room and we stretched out on the floor to play bridge. My living room, an ample room with a pretty view, had been the scene of parties, meetings and gatherings of all sorts. With a fire in the fireplace and a platter of hors d'oeuvres on the coffee table, it could be warm and welcoming. Now it seemed a forlorn place that would never again hear a laugh or a tune. The December sun that shone so generously through the broad windows lit the floor at our feet but brought no warmth.

I don't know how long we sat on the sofa but finally I got up. "I have to do tasks," I announced, reverting to my "take charge" mode, as if my husband's untimely death were only an inconvenience, a minor interruption to my otherwise orderly day. I knew that being busy would make me feel better. I had to gain control of my new life so I could understand it. Also, it was Friday afternoon and we had to plan the funeral. We decided to call relatives after the funeral arrangements were made since all were out of town and would have to make travel plans. Like the young woman I had seen in the hospital waiting room, I picked up the telephone directory and turned to the Yellow Pages to search for Funeral Directors. My local directory listed only one Jewish facility. I called it. The kindly man who answered and learned that my husband had died that morning asked where the burial would be. I had no answer. Cemetery plots were one type of real estate that Jay and I had never considered buying. His parents and other members of his family are buried in Trenton, New Jersey where he grew up. When I once inquired, he told me no more plots were available there.

I occasionally visit cemeteries, especially the older ones. I read the inscriptions on the stones, to see how long people lived and how their families chose to remember them. Epitaphs have disappeared. We are now remembered only by name, the numbers that proscribed our lives and, perhaps, our roles: wife, mother, daughter. How sweet to be commemorated like Lucy Ann Tucker, wife of Judge Nathaniel Beverley Tucker, who, according to his tombstone, was "Descended from Virginia's best blood." Mrs. Tucker, buried in Bruton Parish churchyard, Williamsburg, Virginia was described on her monument as, "admired, respected, and beloved. She lived an ornament of the society in which she moved. The Kind neighbour and friend, the charm of her household, the faithful wife, the devoted mother, the pure christian. In her life and character were happily blended gentleness and firmness, affability and dignity. She died lamented as living she was beloved, by all classes of the community."

In some places, whole families—mothers, babies, grandfathers are buried near one another, many stones bearing the same family names. But families are scattered now and the concept of a multi-generational family plot seems antique. American families, often far-flung in life, remain so in death.

In Meriden, Connecticut, my home town, the Jewish cemetery sits on a lovely hilltop. I always thought that would be my final resting place and my husband's too. My parents owned several plots there but after 40 years in New England, they pulled up stakes for Florida declaring they never wanted to see snow again, and that included not being buried under it. Having severed their ties with the north, they sold the cemetery plots and made their own pre-funeral arrangements with a mortuary near their new home. They chose the spot where they now rest under a solitary tree in a vast new cemetery near the Sawgrass Expressway, not far from one of the world's largest outlet malls. Unlike the Connecticut hillside, the land is flat and sandy, the sky open and sunny. Friends made late in life lay nearby, not kin but the next closest thing in a society like the Florida soil, where roots are shallow.

With Jay's sudden death, I quickly had to find a new family burial ground with room for him and eventually, me. The funeral director on the phone suggested a cemetery that I had passed many times without actually noticing it, the way a day has no meaning until it suddenly becomes a birthday or anniversary. The funeral director gave me the name and home telephone number of the cemetery's representative, a man named Louis. I was surprised to find him at home on a Friday afternoon. When he answered the phone I could hear an infant wailing in the background. Louis seemed somewhat flustered by my call, as if I was taking him away from something more important, which perhaps I was. He asked how many graves I would be needing. I wasn't prepared for the question but told him I definitely needed at least one. Actually two since I assumed that I, too, would be buried in that spot. He informed me that the space available was in a section that did not permit standing stones, only markers flat to the ground. He quoted prices and rules - prepayment was required for purchasing the plots and for perpetual care.

The baby continued to cry. I tried to sound calm and businesslike while Louis seemed in a hurry to end the call. I felt guilty for calling him at a bad time for him. Wasn't it supposed to be the other way around? I sat at the kitchen table and looked out the window. The sun barely cleared the tops of the tall oaks. Children walked home from school. My reality was still my former life. Phone in hand, I might have been sitting at the table to order dessert from the bakery or to inquire about whether the dry cleaning was ready to be picked up. Choosing my husband's gravesite seemed to fall into the category of those other routine telephone calls. I tried to focus on the cemetery. The location was good and I knew I could visit often. I was not in a mood for comparison shopping. I agreed to the terms, and since Louis would not be available the following morning, I made arrangements to meet the caretaker at the cemetery to choose the grave sites. Louis told me that if I had any change in plans, I should call the caretaker on his truck phone, and he gave me the number which I scribbled somewhere near the phone.

I called two additional funeral homes. Their rates, facilities, locations and programs varied. I didn't know how to make a decision. "Look at the obituaries in the paper and see who handles the most funerals," Andy suggested, always logical. Memorial Chapels had conducted the most Jewish funerals during the previous week. They had conducted my father's funeral two years before. My dad suffered from Alzheimer's disease. When he could no longer live on his own in Florida, we had moved him to New Jersey to live near us. At his death, we returned his body to Florida for burial, with Memorial Chapels handling all the arrangements. Memorial had provided good service at that time. Although their facility was far from our home and the cemetery, it would be convenient to many of the people who would attend the funeral. We decided to use Memorial.

Jewish law requires that burial take place as soon as possible. We scheduled Jay's funeral for 11 a.m. on Sunday— just about the time he would normally be returning from the supermarket. I arranged a meeting at the funeral home for Saturday morning following my visit to the cemetery. Barry offered to make the phone calls. He took my address book and called relatives, friends, neighbors and some of Jay's clients. Very few even knew he had been ill. "But I just saw him last week," they said, or "We were supposed to get together on Tuesday." "I meant to call when I heard he was sick but I didn't get a chance." A life disappears among the details of daily living.

By dinner time, most of the phone calls were made. Ellen would drive up from Maryland that night and Jay's brother would fly in from Denver the next day. Barry offered to pick him up at the airport in the afternoon. Although we weren't hungry, we knew we had to eat so Barry ordered takeout Chinese food. How quickly he had assumed a take-charge role. Barry and Andy ate lo mein while my dinner was wonton soup which has always been a comfort food for me - a steaming little meal in a bowl, the meat nestled in soft dough like a baby in a receiving blanket, the soup hot and filling. We soon finished eating and Barry began vacuuming the living room.

"You don't have to vacuum," I told him. "I'll do it tomorrow."

"I have to do tasks," he replied, mimicking me while he went on with his cleaning.

Our town consists mostly of big old houses built as part of a summer community during the 1920's. Our house is a brown wood shingle colonial style less than 30 years old but designed to look as if it had withstood many winters on Cape Cod. A few days before Jay's attack, we had started work on a new bathroom off the master bedroom. This was "a gut" as they say in the trade. The previous bathroom was torn out in addition to a closet to make room for the shiny new room to come. Because the master bedroom was covered with construction dust, and served as a staging area for the builders, Jay and I had moved into the guest room. Andy reclaimed his old room while Barry and Ellen used another bedroom with a double bed in it. That night, however, due to a construction problem, the electrician had cut off the electric heat in Ellen and Barry's room. Having to choose between a cold room and a dusty one, they chose the dust of the master bedroom.

Exhausted by the strain of the day, I took a sleeping pill and went to bed. It was December 9. I had begun the day as a wife and ended it, a widow. The next morning I woke up crying. It was quite early but I started to get ready for my 9 o'clock appointment at the cemetery. My clothes were in my closet in the master bedroom now occupied by Barry and Ellen. Reluctant to disturb them I quietly knocked on the door and Barry told me to come in.

They were still in bed but not sleeping. Ellen's red hair was bright against the white pillow. "How're you doing, Mom?" Barry asked.

"I'm all right," I replied as I rummaged through the dresser in the half light, looking for underwear and a turtleneck shirt. I found a blue blazer and tweed pants in the dusty closet. I thought I would start to wear black the next day for the funeral.

Returning to the guestroom, I was dressing when I heard loud, unusual guttural noises.

"Is that you, Andy?" I called to him in the next room.

"No, it must be Barry," came the reply.

I ran to the master bedroom. Andy was right behind me. Barry was on the floor face down at the side of the bed. He seemed to be having convulsions. Ellen was on her knees next to him trying to see what was wrong. "Call emergency," she screamed while she and Andy turned him over and moved him to the foot of the bed where there was more room.

I dialed the number and, for the second time in eight days, begged them to come as soon as possible. Ellen and Andy were on the floor with Barry who seemed to have stopped breathing. He had gotten up that morning, dressed, and had leaned over to tie his shoes when he fell off the bed. Ellen thought he had bent over to pick something up until the noises started.

The ambulance seemed to take forever. I called again. They had gone to the wrong street. Finally they arrived. Several emergency technicians raced up the stairs and began to work on Barry. All volunteers, they worked with a quiet and determined efficiency. "I don't want to lose this one," I heard one of them saying.

"He's only 30," Ellen pleaded, as if that alone could somehow save him. I went downstairs and called the cardiology practice that had treated Jay to ask them to send a doctor to the hospital right away. "Dr. Siegel is on call," a woman's voice responded.

"Please send someone else," I shouted into the phone. I never wanted to see Dr. Siegel again. I am sure the woman from the answering service was surprised by my outburst, but she said she would convey the message.

I waited downstairs, numb, unable to think, unable to absorb what was happening in the room above me. After some time, they brought Barry down on the stretcher. Beneath the blanket that was covering him I could not see his face, but I could see that his feet were blue. Barry was born with one crooked foot. When he was an infant, both of his feet pointed in the same direction, one in, the other out. The pediatrician recommended a tiny orthopedic shoe that I bought in a specialty shoe store. The shoe pointed the foot in the right direction and Barry wore it day and night for a few months until the foot turned outward of its own accord. One of the feet I looked at now, large and discolored, was the same to wear that tiny shoe. It was the last part of Barry that I ever saw.

Andy and I were dressed for our meeting at the cemetery, but Ellen was wearing only her nightgown and a pair of sweatpants she had hastily pulled on. She wanted to ride in the ambulance along with Barry. I handed her my long winter coat which she threw over her shoulders before running out the door to climb into the ambulance. For the second time in a week, the ambulance pulled out of the driveway, bearing fragile life to an uncertain future. The last thing I did before leaving the house was to call the mobile phone number of the man who was meeting us at the cemetery to cancel our visit. The call would not go through— a recording informing me that the phone was turned off.

I rode to Saint Agatha's hospital in a police car with siren blaring, making small talk with the young officer who was driving. I told him my husband had died the day before. "Yes, Ma'am, I know that," he said. In this small town the police know everything. Andy followed the police in our car. Ellen was waiting at the hospital entrance where Andy and I joined her. The attendants were just wheeling the stretcher with Barry on it into the Emergency Room. "Hurry, he's coded," Ellen told them, her nursing background instinctively coming through. We were greeted by a hospital representative, a tall, attractive, dark-haired woman in her early thirties. For a minute she and Ellen stared at each other.

"Ellen?" the woman asked.

"Barbara?" Ellen responded.

In an uncanny coincidence of time and place, Ellen and Barbara had been high school classmates in New York. Under normal circumstances they would have been thrilled to see each other, to trade the stories of their lives. Instead there were brief greetings and Barbara ushered us into a small, empty private room.

"This is different," I thought ominously. On my many trips to St. Agatha's emergency room, I had always waited in a big room with several other people, including patients and those who had brought them there. The room we were in had too much furniture for its size— a sofa with seating for two, more commonly called a love seat although that name seemed somewhat out of place for the setting, a few arm chairs, a table with more chairs, a telephone and a large wall clock. The furniture was upholstered in salmon-colored vinyl. All the wood was pale, a leftover 1970's look. When the hospital eventually decides to replace the pieces, they will turn up in Salvation Army and more expensive second hand shops as retro.

We waited for what seemed like a long time. I called the cemetery again and heard the same recording. At one point Barbara came in. "They're doing everything they can," she said, "but it doesn't look good." We sat with silence thick about us. I had waited in emergency waiting rooms before when my sons had injured themselves— sitting nervously while a bone was set or a chin stitched. This time, I did not allow myself to think that the outcome could be tragic. I was frightened but not as frantic as perhaps I should have been. Things had always turned out right before as we left with the cast or the bandages. Already shocked by my husband's death, I was simply waiting for Barry to be fixed up on this occasion. Surely he would walk out smiling, saying he was fine as he apologized for giving us such a scare. The room seemed to get smaller. Finally, Barbara returned, this time accompanied by a priest. "We're sorry," they said in small voices.

My life closed around me. I put my head down on the table and sobbed uncontrollably. Ellen, sitting next to me, cried too. Andy made a kind of groaning noise that came from deep in his throat and then said nothing. He paced the floor behind us. They asked us if we wanted to go in to see Barry. Ellen went, but I could not bear to do so. I wanted to remember Barry as the lively, vibrant person he was. I wanted to remember him as a happy two-year-old running around a pool club telling everyone his name, as a basketball player dribbling down the court before taking the jump shot, as a college student who knew everyone on campus, as a new husband in a black tuxedo dancing with his beautiful, red-haired wife. I know I could not have endured living with a picture in my mind of my son lying dead on a hospital table.

Although we were still in our twenties when Barry was born, Jay and I were among the last of our married friends to have children. Being the practical one, I wanted to work to accumulate some savings before embarking on motherhood. In contrast to women now who work until the week they deliver, pregnancy was not encouraged by employers in the 1960's. Employment interviewers routinely asked married women when they planned to have children and did not hire those who admitted they might "someday" want to start a family. Companies required women to resign when they reached the seventh month of their pregnancy and pregnancy leaves were rare. Childbirth at that time signaled the end to a woman's professional career, or at least interrupted it for many years.

When we reached our late twenties we knew it was time to start a family since most couples we knew *stopped* having children when they reached thirty. Barry was born on the due date, January 19, 1964. Jay was so excited to have a son. He played with him as though he had found a marvelous new toy that only he knew how to use. He examined the child's every component, as if he came with a warranty and every working part had to be checked out. He found the tiniest blemishes on Barry's skin and noticed the crooked foot that needed the little shoe to straighten it out. I was with the baby all day, but I had not noticed it. Barry spoke at an early age. A day short of his second birthday, as we sat in the waiting room for an appointment with my doctor, Barry pointed to a man who was smoking. "That man is eating a cigarette," he said as the man withdrew the cigarette from his mouth. Surprised at his speech, a woman sitting next to me asked Barry's age. "He'll be two tomorrow," I told her, assuming that his speech was the norm for two-year-olds. "I never heard such a young child speak like that," she said. I later learned that early speech is no more a sign of superior intelligence than early walking, but I was glowing with pride at the time.

He was a young child during the worst of the Vietnam War. The theme for his third birthday party was clowns. I went for the whole Hallmark deal - clown invitations, napkins, tablecloth, little paper holders for candy, hats, all in red and yellow. Long before Martha Stewart, I created a clown cake from a design in a woman's magazine. I baked the cake in several pieces and assembled it all on a platter for the three-year-olds — a round pink face with M&M eyes, gum drop lips, and a pointy yellow hat with a small cupcake for the tassel. I also assembled the Hallmark paper candy holders. Being January, the yearly special of Bob Hope's visit to the troops in Vietnam was on television. As I put together the little boxes, slot A into slot B, I watched pictures of young men in wheel chairs, in hospitals covered with bandages, and heard tributes to those who had died. Their mothers, too, had made sweet parties for them when they were three. The tears rolled down my face. I looked at my little boy sleeping so peacefully beneath his Snoopy quilt. "How can I protect him?" I wondered, already knowing the answer. "You can't."

For a long time we called him Butchie. When he was 10, he decided the name was babyish and from then on he insisted that we call him Barry. My occasional slip brought a strong reprimand: "My name is Barry." Eventually I caught on. Every night after dinner, Jay played with him, either in the basement when the nights were cold and dark, or in the park on long summer evenings. Jay taught him to play baseball and basketball. Barry loved to play on teams. He was on one losing Little League team after another but losses didn't seem to sadden him. He was a happy child, in his gray uniform and high red socks. I taught him to ski when he was five. He was a good skier until he gave it up when his eighth grade basketball coach forbid any of his players to ski during basketball season. Basketball became Barry's life. He spent hours shooting baskets in the yard and at the playground down the street. Bounce, bounce, bounce, I can still hear the ball as he walked along the street on the way to the playground, the ball hitting the pavement in rhythm with his gait. I can see him through the kitchen window, his pace purposeful, the bounces timed. Every day after school, bounce, bounce, bounce, Barry and his friends, choosing sides, shooting around, developing their skills. They learned to play together as skinny eighth graders and went on to become a varsity team. The boys in the playground now were not born when Barry and his teammates were high school stars, looked up to by younger boys for a year or two until a whole new group of stars came along. I occasionally hear the bounce, bounce, bounce as a young player walks to the playground but most of them ride bikes now and the ball is in the backpack.

Barry was a good student and a popular member of his high school class. He went through the rebellious, trouble-making years. He challenged himself and us. His ninth grade math teacher called us to school because he wasn't paying attention in class. Poor Barry, sitting there with three stern adults discussing his behavior. He hung his head and looked at the floor. The teacher talked, we talked and Barry promised to do better. As we left the building, Jay and I looked at each other and laughed. "I wouldn't pay attention in her class either," we agreed. She was that boring, but we never told Barry.

He and Mark, who spoke at his funeral, were best friends, together all the time. They learned to drive, went to parties and proms, took trips, studied for exams, applied to college and left us wondering how it all could have happened so fast. For the first year of college, Barry was in the pre-medical curriculum. He found it difficult and so time-consuming that he had no time left for fun. He considered transferring to a less competitive university. "Change your major, not your college," we advised. He could take the few remaining requirements later if he still wanted to go to medical school. He changed his major to psychology and found a new balance. He played basketball on the junior varsity team and was social director of his fraternity. He always seemed to be running around with a clipboard, signing people up for things. He needed volunteers to help with a fund-raiser. He needed people to clean up after a party. He worked nights at a restaurant making pizza, standing in the window flipping the dough before the topping went on. His graduation day was hot and muggy. The graduates wore shorts under their robes. A string quartet played Handel's Water Music, more appropriate for the weather than Pomp and Circumstance. As Barry reached the podium to shake hands with the President and receive his diploma, he reached under his robe and pulled out a sign. I poked Jay. I was prepared for something embarrassing, some type of protest. He held up the sign written in bold block letters: THANKS, MOM AND DAD. He reversed it. The other side said $45,000. (This was 1986). The whole place roared. The graduates stamped and cheered. We were so proud.

After college Barry and Mark shared a third floor walkup apartment in a Hoboken, New Jersey row house. Small single family houses built in the nineteenth century for workers at the end of the railroad line had been divided up, floor by floor to house young college graduates on their way up. It was a modest apartment but they loved it. They were grown up, living on their own, working in New York. A rite of passage. One summer, along with several others, they rented a tiny beachfront house at the New Jersey shore. The place was so small and their guests so numerous that some slept under the kitchen table.

Eventually they met their future wives. When Ellen walked into the classroom where Barry was taking a graduate psychology course, I am sure it was love at first sight. Ellen is tall, slim, and athletic. Her thick, wavy red hair sets her apart in any crowd. Bright, ambitious and witty, she brought a new dimension into our male-oriented family. Their wedding was an amalgam of Irish and Jewish, a priest and a rabbi, the hora and the jig. They were married for seventeen happy months, the overture to an unfinished symphony that ended abruptly at a hospital in New Jersey.

Ellen returned from the emergency room. I admired her strength in being able to spend a few last moments with her husband. How great the shock was for her and yet she had the courage to bid him that final, private goodbye. She and I sat at the small table and wept. Andy continued to pace. We were not alone for long. One of the first to arrive was Dr. Lee. He was the chief cardiologist in the group where Dr Siegel practiced and had come in response to my earlier call to his office. He asked if we wanted an autopsy which I quickly agreed to, forgetting that Ellen was the next of kin and it was her decision. At that point, the cause of Barry's death was not apparent— it could have been a heart attack or an embolism. Ellen, of course, requested the autopsy.

A hospital representative told us we could use the phone to call anyone we wanted. Andy called a neighbor, the father of Barry's friend Mark. Barry and Mark had been best friends since ninth grade. They had shared an apartment after college, been ushers in each other's weddings and, although parted by jobs and studies, remained close. Mark lived in the Midwest, but he and Barry were planning to get together in New Jersey during the Christmas holidays, a few weeks away. Andy also called David Prager, Jay's best friend and long-time client who just the night before, upon learning of Jay's death, had called to tell me he would do anything I needed to help. I didn't think I would need him so soon. Mark's father, Harold, soon arrived. He had misinterpreted Andy's call thinking it pertained to Jay's death. He stood still, his mouth open when he learned that Barry too was dead. With the introduction of each new person came the same disbelief. How could such a thing have happened? Men of Jay's age die of heart attacks with unfortunate frequency. But Barry was an apparently healthy 30-year-old who didn't smoke, was an outstanding athlete and almost as health conscious as his uncle in Denver. We were all in disbelief.

News of the double tragedy had spread through the hospital. A few doctors I knew personally came to express their sympathy. Among them was Norman Morgan, my internist, who had vouched for the abilities of young Dr. Siegel. He sat next to me on the small sofa and put an arm around my shoulder to comfort me. He is a big man and his bear-like size made me feel warmer as I shivered from shock in the well-heated room. He talked to Ellen and promised to get speedy results from Barry's autopsy. When I left our small waiting room to go to the bathroom, nurses and doctors in the Emergency Room were talking about a father and son who had died a day apart— not realizing as I passed them that I was the wife and mother.

Ellen, red-eyed yet composed and poised, kept repeating the morning's story to each new person who arrived. Barry woke up and seemed fine. They had talked, he got dressed and then just disappeared off the side of the bed. As a nurse who had spent a great deal of her professional life in hospitals ministering to others, she now ironically was a victim that no one could help. Suddenly, within a few hours, isolated from family and friends, she had to cope with a woman's worst nightmare. Not that she was a stranger to illness and death within her own family. Her father, a retired New York City policeman in his mid-sixties, had died of cancer two years before. Sitting there in her nightgown and her mother-in-law's coat, she must have been the saddest person on earth.

David Prager arrived with his wife Suzanne and son Chuck, who was close to Barry's age. With each new arrival we repeated the story — what had happened to Jay, what had happened to Barry. Eventually the conversation evolved to "tasks". Phone calls, funeral arrangements, someone to pick Larry up at the airport— all of these things had to be done. Amid unbelievable grief, the mechanics of mourning had to begin. Ellen, Andy and I agreed that there would be one funeral. Jay's funeral scheduled for Sunday, the next day, would be moved forward and he and Barry would be buried together on Monday.

"I already arranged one funeral," I said to David. "I cannot do another." He offered to call the funeral home to inform them of Barry's death and make the new arrangements. I forgot completely about the cemetery. Suzanne and Harold agreed to help with phone calls to family, neighbors and friends. Chuck would pick up Larry whose flight was due to arrive within a few hours. "How will I recognize him?" he wanted to know. "You'll know," we said. "He looks like a Schocket, except that he has a big mustache and reddish hair." Chuck was worried about how he would tell Larry— a complete stranger, about Barry's death. His fears turned out to be unfounded. During a layover in Saint Louis, Larry had called home and learned the news from his daughter, whom Harold had already called.

We left the hospital in tight little groups, the Pragers going home with us so we did not have to be alone. When we returned home, there was a curt message from Louis, the cemetery administrator, asking why I had not shown up that morning and wanting to know how I expected to have a funeral the next day if I had not yet chosen a plot. He left his number and David offered to handle it. Ellen called her family who live a few hours away. They are close and supportive. Shocked, they offered to come right away. Suzanne Prager, a warm, friendly woman, volunteered to make calls from our house. She called the same people

Barry had called the night before to tell them of his father's death. Barry's notes were neatly added to the margins of my address book, indicating changed phone numbers and messages left on machines. Formerly a realtor, Suzanne confided that she had made many phone calls but never had to do anything like this. How grateful I was to her. I know I could not have made those calls and the duty would have gone to Andy who was in his own state of grief and not yet ready to take on the heavy burden that had so quickly fallen on him as the only remaining male of the family.

I sat and watched Suzanne making the phone calls. I could not absorb what had happened. How would I learn to grasp the enormity of it? How would I survive? What would become of me? I looked out the same window I had looked out the week before when Jay was being lifted into the ambulance. I knew then my life would be forever changed but who, in her grimmest nightmare could envision something like this? The heading of the obituary that appeared in the paper two days later said "Jay, Barry Schocket, father and son." Father and son shared an obituary, as if each didn't deserve his own. Or perhaps it was the reverse. An editor wanted a headline to make the point that this was not a single but a double tragedy. Someone who writes obituaries deals with death daily. A fatal heart attack of a 59-year-old man is newsworthy only to those who know him. A sudden death of a 30-year-old might attract a little more attention, especially if the person is famous. But a father and son death is notable. Maybe that is what the obituary was trying to say.

Ellen, Suzanne and I sat in the family room, usually a warm, friendly place with an old brick fireplace and books lining the walls. Christmas cards that had arrived early were set on the oak mantelpiece. Suzanne finished her phone calls. Silence hung in the air. Some people are uncomfortable with silence and need words to fill the gap. Knowing that Ellen was a nurse, Suzanne began telling her how she had changed her mother's surgical dressings after an operation. Ellen nodded. I stared out the window. I knew that there were tasks, but I was powerless to do them. People would be arriving at my home. I had to greet them, find a chair for them to sit on, offer them food. Paralyzed, I did nothing. Andy was by himself in the kitchen. Although I did not see him then, I can picture him now sitting at the table staring out the window but seeing nothing. Since he was a small child, he has always retreated to his room when he was troubled. Like his father, he did not share his feelings easily. He would have been even more miserable in a room with three women. We all sat in our places, as if we were characters in a play, waiting for someone else to come on stage to move the plot along. Eventually they came, and our new lives went into motion.

ርჳၔၔჳၔჳၔჳၔჳၔ   **3**   ჳၔჳၔჳၔჳၔჳၔ

Parting

We did not wait long. The word that went out on that long, grim Saturday flew from house to house and town to town before circling back with swift response. Neighbors came, as people do, to view the site of a tragedy— to look at the burned-out church, the flooded house, the tree that fell through a roof. People want to see and hear so they can comprehend the enormity of it. We slow down to stare at the traffic accident. We call it rubbernecking, gaper's block, or curiosity. Some just want to take a look, some want to help. Those who arrived at our house found nothing unusual to see. Downstairs everything appeared to be in order. The two lives that departed had left so quickly there remained no trace of their pain or suffering. Their neatly displayed pictures showed smiling boys and men in various stages of life looking fit and healthy. In one picture, Barry about 13, and Jay are linked arm-in-arm, wearing identical striped shirts. The stripes are horizontal, seeming to continue from one to the other, the way cartoonists make the same stripes work for two characters. Upstairs, where Barry's attack had come, medical paraphernalia was scattered about, left by the emergency technicians. Pieces of gauze and discarded paper wrappings were on the dresser and some plastic tubing was on the floor along with a saw-horse and drop cloths left by the construction workers.

The first to arrive were Jean and Betty, both Mount Holyoke College graduates who had been my neighbors for eighteen years. I met Jean through committee work when we were both active in the New Jersey alumnae club although I lived about 15 miles away in a larger town. When I first went to a meeting at her house I fell in love with the town. It is country without being rural, dotted with lakes and waterways, old houses and tall trees.

"This is a lovely place to live," I told Jean not imagining that I could live here too.

"Why don't you move here?" she asked.

"There are no Jews here," I replied. At one time, the town was "restricted," no Jews or dogs allowed, said the signs that fronted on the highway. Friends of ours named Levy had looked for a house here several years before and were taken by a realtor to a neighboring town. But that had changed by the mid-seventies, Jean assured me, and while not exactly welcomed at first, Jews were slowly beginning to move in. Jean has always been a maverick, not afraid to be different, an advocate for all that is fair and good. Despite her family's impeccable ancestry, she would champion for the groups that were left out. Not out of a sense of noblesse oblige but because she believed in what she was doing. She invited me to lunch and introduced me to a realtor. Later, I brought Jay to have a look around. We drove down the broad avenue that is the town's main street and through the narrower, winding streets.

"It's seedy," he pointed out, noting the absence of manicured lawns and presence of overgrown brush.

"You'll get used to it," I assured him. We eventually bought a house across the street from Jean. She promised me that we would be happy living here and we were.

She and Betty sat on the living room sofa where Barry, Andy and I had sat the day before, only hours after Jay's death. The sofa had never served such a sad function. With its down pillows and straight lines, it was the first major piece of furniture that Jay and I bought when we furnished our first apartment. New upholstery has updated its look and I suspect that when it no longer has a place in my life, it will recycle its way into another home and family which will find it equally serviceable. My friends were full of questions—how, why, when? Ellen, Andy and I could only answer the how and when. We will never know why.

"What can we do?" they asked. They offered to order, pick up and set out all the food for the guests who would return to the house after the funeral on Monday. They recruited a few others and among them they settled it all. I gave them minimal instructions about number of people and where the food would be served but basically I knew that with the arrangements in their hands, I did not have to give it another thought.

Sally, who lives down the street, and our family have had a long relationship, especially through sports. Barry played varsity basketball with one of her sons and we spent many Friday nights in high school gyms around the county cheering for our team. Sally and I played tennis with and against each other for years. She wanted to know what she could do. Barry had vacuumed the night before but I had left the rest of the cleaning for Saturday. I am not sure how I summoned the nerve to ask but I was not my normal self. Words came out of my mouth that seemed not to be mine. " The downstairs rooms need dusting," I told her. Without a blink, Sally agreed to come and do some house cleaning the following morning when we would be out making funeral and burial arrangements.

Jay's close friend Joe and his wife Diane arrived next. Jay went to Joe whenever he needed a tool or an extra hand. With the cunning of a Tom Sawyer, and the rhetoric of a lawyer, he could usually get Joe to do the job. Not that Joe, sharp as he is, was unaware of Jay's intent, but being a good friend and neighbor of superior mechanical skill, he did most jobs willingly and well. Joe continued in that role for a long time, always ready to lend a piece of garden equipment, hang a hook or give advice. Since I have been alone, Diane and Joe have invited me to countless dinners, provided transportation when I needed it and brought food when I've been sick.

By late afternoon, Ellen's family arrived - her mother and sister, brother and sister-in-law. Like all the others, they could not believe that Barry was dead. Ellen's mother thought she had heard the message wrong on her answering machine. The message must have referred to Jay's death, not Barry's. They are a close family, and had welcomed Barry into their midst. He enjoyed the holidays and vacations that he spent with them, going out on their boat, playing with Ellen's lively young niece and nephew. Ellen cried again when they came, but I could see that she welcomed the comfort and support that they brought.

Chuck delivered Larry from the airport. From the family resemblance, everyone knew immediately who he was. Friends arrived with a full course dinner for at least 10 - pasta in a huge aluminum tin, salad and rolls. The neighbors left, and the family sat around the kitchen table. Someone set out dishes and forks, water and soft drinks. Ellen's brother Wayne, a big, hearty man, filled his plate. The rest of us nibbled. No one talked. Finally we cleared the table and put away all the food. Clustered in the warm, bright kitchen, we had not noticed that outside it had turned dark. The open view from the kitchen window was now only blackness. I thought Ellen would stay with us but she decided to leave with her family and meet us at the cemetery the next morning. She went to the cold, dusty room that she and Barry had shared and packed up her few things. I cannot blame her for not wanting to spend the night in the room she had shared with her husband only the night before. She had arrived from Maryland with clothes for Barry to wear to his father's funeral. She packed them up taking them with her so she could press the shirt and brush the suit. They were the clothes that Barry would be buried in.

After everyone left, Larry, Andy and I chose the burial clothes for Jay. We picked a dark gray suit, a white shirt and navy blue tie with red trim. We might have been packing his suitcase for a business trip. We doubted that socks were needed but included them too, just in case. We put all the clothing into a shopping bag and left it near the door that leads to the garage. We did all this automatically, without a trace of obvious grief. We had not yet begun to understand the darkness that engulfed us. Before going to bed, I took one of the Valiums that Barry had picked up for me at the drugstore the day before. I knew that sleep would not be easy. I wondered if I would ever live again as a normal person. Would I laugh and sing, enjoy a good meal or a funny movie? Would I ever climb out from under this tremendous weight of grief that had settled upon me, like a thick blanket of ash from a suddenly erupted volcano? A few years after the eruption of the volcano on Mount Saint Helens in Washington, I saw a picture of tiny green saplings growing up through the ash on the blackened mountainside. I did not know what would grow out of the ashes of my life, and how long would it take. I told myself that the next day was my future. Thinking beyond that was irrelevant.

The following morning by 9:00 we were all at the cemetery, Ellen with her mother and sister, David, Larry, Andy, Louis, the cemetery administrator and I. The cold was biting as the wind whipped past our ears and the damp from the frozen ground crept up into our shoes. The section of the cemetery where space was available was long and flat, about as wide as a football field and almost twice as long. The grass was yellow and brittle, its color and texture like an old woman's hair that has been dyed too many times. With Louis in the lead, we walked around looking at possible sites, as if we were deciding where to plant a new garden. The new section had few graves, most of them clustered in an area that faced the street, near the entrance gates. With Barry's death, we suddenly needed five plots since Ellen and Andy chose to be buried there as well.

With ample sites to choose from, we considered sunny locations, those closer to trees or nearer to a road. Stressing the importance of burial in his family, Louis told me his grandfather had given his grandmother a cemetery plot as an engagement gift. I didn't know whether this comment was a business statement or meant to be humorous. I didn't answer. Suddenly he asked if anyone in our group was not Jewish. I was surprised by the question. If I had been more knowledgeable of Jewish law and understood the reason for the question, I would have lied. Unsuspecting, I told him that Ellen is not Jewish. "The only section where non-Jews can be buried is over there." Louis pointed to an unattractive strip of land divided from the rest of the cemetery by a road.

"That is unacceptable," I answered. "We want five plots together in an area that is pretty. That spot is not suitable," I continued, frustration creeping into my voice. "Ellen is part of our family. Her last name is the same as ours and no one will know what her religion is."

Louis was insistent. "We are very strict about this," he said. "We cannot have non-Jews in this part of the cemetery. The Board will never approve it."

"How will they know?" I asked.

"It will be on the records," he responded. We had not yet completed any paperwork up to that point.

"It will only be on the records if you put it there,' I told him. "You can choose to ignore it. You are the only one who knows."

A wealth of Jewish law and custom pertaining to death and burial goes back to the Bible's first Jews— Abraham purchased a burial plot for his wife Sarah in the land of Canaan. The rules are intricate concerning who may be buried in Jewish cemeteries and the placement and order of the graves. In some, men and women lie in separate sections. The laws govern suicides, enemies, criminals, Jews who have denounced their faith and those of other religions. Jewish custom prohibits the burial of non-Jews in a Jewish cemetery. When I asked a rabbi the reason for such a law, he said that a cemetery is hallowed Jewish ground and not appropriate for non-Jews. For much of their history, Jews lived apart from their Arab and Christian neighbors, sometimes in their own villages, sometimes behind a wall in a larger city. They rarely intermarried. Applied to modern America where almost half the Jews marry non-Jews, or to Israel, where recent immigrants bring a heritage not sanctioned by Israeli law, this custom can have unfortunate consequences. When a 14-year-old Russian immigrant was killed tragically in a bombing in Israel, he was denied burial in a Jewish cemetery because his mother was not Jewish. A high government official who searched for a humane solution, said he had encountered "thick-headedness and obstructionism" within every camp. I felt that we encountered a similar reaction in New Jersey.

Recognizing the realities of American life, the governing board of this particular cemetery made an accommodation by setting aside a place where Jews and non-Jews can rest side by side. The land they chose is inside the cemetery gates, (not permitted by the strictest of Jewish laws) but set apart, less select. It is unclear to me whether this separate section is hallowed or unhallowed. If I chose to be buried there with my Jewish husband, sons and Christian daughter-in-law would we be in sacred Jewish land or just near sacred Jewish land? Is this compromise hypocritical or simply conciliatory? I have not learned the answer to these questions, and probably never will. Many laws sanctioned by the world's religions are as timely to our lives as they were thousands of years ago. Some lose their thrust in the realities of life in the twenty-first century. How do we keep those that continue to have a meaning we can embrace and remove those created for another time? Compared to the enormity of suffering that Jews have endured, and the bloodshed that continues over turf in Israel, denying a Christian woman the right to be buried next to her husband and his relatives seems petty. I wonder how Jews and their neighbors can find a solution to sharing land in Israel if they cannot achieve that goal in a cemetery the size of a football field in a quiet corner of New Jersey.

Putting aside the non-Jewish issue for the moment, we looked at available plots and found five that were nicely located near a planting of small evergreens but Louis would not consider the location. Only he was suitably dressed for the extreme cold. We should have worn down jackets, woolen scarves, hats and thick-soled shoes but, not realizing the difficulties we would encounter at the cemetery, we had all dressed for our meeting at the funeral home. Our woolen coats and the clothes we wore under them offered little resistance to the cold. We blew on our fingers, stamped our feet and watched our words come out in puffs of frosty steam. Sensing the impasse, David suggested that we continue discussions in his car. Ellen, Louis and I quickly agreed. David started the engine and turned on the heat. The windows soon became foggy enclosing the four of us in our own space, apart from the other cars and graveyard beyond. David and Louis sat in front, Ellen and I in back. Her eyes were red from crying and she was holding a blank check in her hand, waiting to buy a cemetery plot in a place where she was not welcome. I asked Ellen if she was sure that this was what she wanted to do. I thought that, as a young woman, she would find a new life and eventually remarry but that was not her plan. Ellen was strong and steadfast. As she was Barry's partner in life, she wanted to share his resting place in death.

While Ellen continued to plead for her six feet of earth I tried to learn from Louis what his chief objection was and if there was a way we could address it.

"It is Jewish law," he said again. Time was passing and we were not making any progress.

"We have to settle this," I said. We were already late for our appointment at the funeral home. Suddenly, with a tone of defeat in his voice, Louis relented. Perhaps he too had a schedule to meet and wanted to rid himself of these bothersome people.

"We do not allow crosses on the grave markers," he informed us. If that was the crucial issue he should have mentioned it earlier. Ellen could be buried next to her husband if she agreed not to put a cross on her stone. I was so relieved with the decision that the absurdity of the verbal agreement did not hit me at the time, but Ellen readily agreed. The papers we signed contained no mention of religion or crosses. I hoped that Louis did not have another secret set of papers that contained the missing information. Having paid for our graves, we were about to leave for the funeral home when I realized that I had forgotten to bring Jay's burial clothes. Andy and Larry went home in my car to get them and I went ahead to the funeral home with David. Ellen, her mother and sister followed behind.

Memorial Chapels is in an area that was once densely populated with Jews who had left the neighboring big city for a taste of suburbia. A Jewish-style delicatessen across the street does a brisk business on Sunday morning but I suspect that the local customers are now a much more varied group since the Jews have moved on, farther out into the newer suburbs. We are, after all, descended from nomadic tribes. Moving is in our blood. Ellen, David and I met with a funeral director named Mr. Katz. When Ellen removed her coat, I saw that she was dressed all in black. I was not and I felt guilty, as if I wasn't showing enough sorrow. I thought wearing black started with the funeral and continued for a month or so. I resolved to wear black as soon as I returned home.

Mr. Katz explained the procedures. He combined kindness with business objectivity, as one would expect from someone in his profession. His voice was firm and even. He might as well have been selling insurance, which in a way, he was. I wondered if he had ever met simultaneously with two widows before. If he harbored any curiosity about the unusual circumstances of father and son deaths, he did not express it. He requested information for the death certificates. Name, address, age, social security number, occupation, parents' names. For the newspapers, he needed names of survivors, colleges and universities, military service, and charities we would like to designate for donations. I gave the information pertaining to Jay and Ellen spoke for Barry.

Except for military and charities, the information was straightforward. Since Army reservists are not considered Veterans, I did not mention Jay's military duty and it did not appear in his obituary. I think Jay would be angry at me for that because he was proud to have served. I hadn't thought about charitable donations until that point. Ellen requested that donations for Barry go to the graduate psychology program at the university where he was a student. I wanted more time to think about a charity for Jay, but Mr. Katz told me I had to make a decision immediately since the funeral home had to notify the newspapers. Someone suggested a charity and I agreed. It is a very worthy beneficiary but Jay would not have chosen it. A better solution might have been a memorial fund in Jay's name so that later Andy and I could choose a charity that would honor Jay's memory in a way that would have the most meaning for him. We discussed the Social Security benefits to which we were entitled and ordered death certificates from the County Hall of Records.

The last decision was the choice of coffins. Mr. Katz led us to a large room filled with different types of caskets, from plain pine box to elaborate fine wood. There were all grades of liners and hardware. Faced with such a display of options, many quite expensive, I can understand why people choose cremation. This was never a consideration for us. Orthodox Jewish law prohibits cremation. Although I am not Orthodox, I believe strongly in the sanctity of the body. Burning my husband's remains was not something I could do and I was glad that Ellen agreed to bury rather than cremate Barry. We chose dignified matching caskets of light wood lined in pale blue satin. I went through the motions of funeral and burial protocol, but the enormity of the tragedy had still not sunk in. As though these were normal business arrangements, we compared prices for caskets, discussed schedules and pallbearers, decided which newspapers would carry the obituaries. That these decisions regarded the funeral of my husband and son was still far beyond my emotional comprehension. But before I could grieve, these were the tasks I had to do.

Andy and Larry arrived with Jay's burial clothes. "Your cleaning lady was there when we got to your house," Larry informed me. I started to laugh.

"That wasn't my cleaning lady, it was Sally, my neighbor," I responded and we all laughed. Not at Sally's generosity but at Larry who would never suspect that a neighbor would volunteer for such a task. With funeral and burial arrangements complete, we returned home to greet out-of-town relatives and friends who had come to pay condolence calls. Having a house full of people helped to distract us from thoughts of the terrible day that lay ahead.

The following morning, the day of the funeral, the phone rang at 7. It was George, a friend of Jay's who had seen the obituaries in the morning paper. "I hope I didn't wake you," he said softly, trying to sound polite. "I waited until 7." George is a very early riser and often on weekends when the sun was barely up he called Jay to confirm a tennis date scheduled for hours later or to ask if it was raining where we lived— although we lived only a hundred yards from where he lived. Now he was calling because he wanted to know how Jay and Barry had died. Similar calls followed, including people who wanted more information about the funeral, the time and place of which were in the papers. That was when I realized that I had to find someone to watch the house while we were gone. I have heard stories of thieves who read wedding and funeral announcements so they can rob the house while the family is gone. Again, I turned to Sally for help in finding someone. She called a few neighbors and recruited people who could come in shifts so that the house would not be left as easy prey to burglars.

Then I had to dress for the funeral. I don't know why I even cared about my appearance. Vanity must be deeply ingrained. According to Biblical custom, Jews rend or tear their garments as a sign of grief. Cutting or tearing a garment allows the mourner to express anger and anguish in a manner sanctioned by religious custom. In this country, with the exception of the Orthodox, the observance is symbolic, with the Rabbi cutting a black ribbon pinned to the mourner's clothing. In Israel, Jews actually cut their clothes. When my brother, who lives in Israel, arrived for my father's funeral in Florida two years earlier, he wore an old jacket expecting it to be cut. He was surprised to see that we wore dress clothing. Knowing that my clothes would not be cut on this occasion, I dressed in a black suit, leaving an attractive pin on the lapel from the last time I wore the outfit—ironically to a wedding the previous fall. I fixed my hair and put on makeup, as if doing this could somehow create a normalcy on the most abnormal day of my life.

At the funeral home, we waited in a large reception room where people could speak with us before the funeral. I was amazed at the number of people who had learned of the deaths by reading the obituaries that morning, changed their plans for the day and came to the funeral in the afternoon. For almost an hour people poured in. Barry and Ellen's high school and college friends came from all over the country. Barry's university classmates and professors who, the year before had come to his wedding, were here for his funeral. Jay's clients and people he had worked with closed their offices to attend. Many of my current professional colleagues but also some I hadn't seen for years came, some arriving with co-workers who had offered to accompany them. Friends, relatives, people from our small town, people who had moved away long ago. A few Mount Holyoke alumnae had called dozens of women and many of them came, including my closest friends from college and many others who were only acquaintances. A high school friend of Andy's, living in Boston, flew down a few hours after Andy called him on Sunday, and was at the funeral with his mother the next day. So many people whose paths had crossed ours at some point in our lives took the time and traveled great distances to be there with us. I was surprised and helped enormously by this overwhelming outpouring of support.

When the funeral was about to begin, we were escorted into a large chapel. There were the two caskets. My legs felt weak and I held on to Andy for support. Seeing the two coffins in that room was almost unbearable, knowing they held men who just days before were very much part of the living, active world. The coffins brought home the enormity of the tragedy. Before this, it was talk. I had not seen either of them dead, only listened to the words. The wooden boxes were the reality. They held father and son who were gone and would soon be delivered to the earth. The room filled up with people and doors were opened to a side chapel to accommodate even more.

We were not members of a synagogue so David asked his rabbi to conduct the service. The rabbi came to our house on Sunday afternoon and spoke with us about Barry and Jay prior to preparing their eulogies. He led a beautiful service and spoke eloquently about each man. It was difficult to believe that he had never met either of them. Following the rabbi's talk, Barry's friend Mark spoke of their seventeen-year friendship, how they met as two new kids in town, grew up together, and shared an apartment for two years after college. He described Barry as his soulmate, the best friend a guy could ever have. David talked about Jay who was his lawyer, business advisor and best friend. He talked about the closeness of our families over the years.

Andy then walked to the pulpit and spoke at length without notes about his father and brother. His speech was both sad and humorous as he described his memories of growing up with Jay and Barry. He described Jay as a cave with a small opening that gives little hint of the vast heights and depths that lay inside. He joked about Jay's golfing ability and his sense of humor. He described the year that he and Barry shared an apartment in Arlington, Virginia. They had agreed to share expenses and Andy took on the telephone bill without realizing that Barry and Ellen, who then lived in New York, spent hours each week on the phone. I don't know from where in the depths of his being he gathered the strength to speak so eloquently. All three men who spoke showed great presence in addressing a few hundred people that afternoon. I could hear sobs throughout the audience but they were soft and private. Unlike more demonstrative cultures where emotion is open and acceptable, we American Jews take the British approach to grief, solid and stoic. We do not wail and although women may cry openly, men seldom do. I would like to have torn my clothing, I would like to have cried aloud and shouted that life was not fair but I did none of these things. I stood silently while tears rolled steadily down my cheeks and onto my black suit. Eventually all the handkerchiefs I brought were wet. I rolled them into a tight ball and stuffed them into my purse.

Twelve pallbearers were summoned to carry the coffins to the waiting hearses. Barry's friends who, at his wedding, had lifted him in a chair above their shoulders and joyously danced around the room, raised his silent body and with eyes lowered bore him from the room. Jay's pallbearers, an older group of cousins and friends, followed with his casket. Silently, wiping their eyes, people walked toward the doors. As I put my coat on in the outer vestibule a couple approached me. It was Ted, Jay's roommate at Highmount Memorial Hospital, and his attractive wife. He looked fine in a camel's hair coat and she, as usual, was perfect. They saw the obituary in the paper and came to the funeral. "I feel so bad," she confided, "I never even spoke to you in the hospital." I was very moved that they had come. They were, after all, complete strangers, and he had only recently left the hospital himself. They were among the many strangers who would show amazing kindness in the days to come.

Andy, Larry and I were ushered into the rear of a large black limousine, Ellen and her family into another. We waited for a long time while people went to their cars and lined up for the ride to the cemetery. I know that occasionally catastrophes result in several members of a family dying at the same time but I have never seen a funeral procession with two hearses. Just as seeing the two coffins in one room was devastating, driving behind the two black hearses was equally painful. More than twenty cars joined the procession to the cemetery. As we drove from the interstate to local roads, I wondered whether drivers who pulled to the side of the road to let us pass were curious about what event had led to their witnessing a double funeral.

When we reached the cemetery, the sky was the color of pewter and the numbing cold continued. The coffins were taken from the hearses and placed above the open graves. We left the warmth of our cars and stood in a semi-circle around the rabbi. During the service, I started shaking so vehemently from chill and grief that Larry put his arm around me to hold me up. The rabbi conducted the brief service. After we chanted the prayers, the cemetery workers lowered the coffins into the graves waiting side by side like twin beds. It is Jewish custom for mourners to shovel dirt onto the coffin. The shovel is not passed from hand to hand but is lifted by each individual, to bid his own personal farewell. The weight of the shovel and the sound of the dirt hitting the coffin are said to be therapeutic— that finally there can be no fantasy that perhaps this is all a bad dream. The mourners must face the reality of the death as the first step toward their own recovery. We invited anyone present who wished to participate in this ceremony to come forward. The line was long as relatives, friends, neighbors, our co-workers, Barry's classmates and Jay's clients lifted the shovel and tossed the gray, winter soil onto the wood where it made a dry, thumping sound that echoed up through the cavity.

Finally, amid new tears, we chanted the burial *kaddish*, the traditional prayer of mourning. Then, the service completed, the other mourners formed two rows through which Ellen, Larry, Andy and I proceeded to our cars. As we did so, the clouds parted and the late-day wintry sun, low in the sky, shone in our faces. I raised my eyes, which had been looking down at the dead grass as I walked, and looked straight up into the sun. I believed the sun shining at that moment was a sign from my husband and son that I would find the courage to go on.

A Time to Mourn

W e invited those who had accompanied us to the cemetery to join us at home after the service, handing out directions hastily done up on the computer that morning. Cars lined our narrow street on both sides. People whom I had never seen before (I assumed they were Barry's friends), my co-workers and classmates and some of Jay's clients, wandered about the house, peering at the family pictures and snapshots on the walls, shelves and tables illustrating a typical family history of happy occasions: weddings, babies, parties, travel, graduations. No one brings a camera to funerals. We do not want to remind ourselves of our sad events. Beth, a childhood friend of Ellen's now living in California, had flown in for the funeral just as she had for their wedding. I didn't think I would see her again so soon. She was the life of the party at the rehearsal dinner that we held at our house the evening before the big day. It was a frightfully hot day, and the air-conditioner wheezed from the humidity, but we did our best trying to ignore the heat. Beth, Ellen and her sister Joyce reminisced about their school days, making us all laugh. The next day, dancing at the wedding, Beth looked like a star from Riverdance.

My neighbors and friends had ordered ample food which they set out on platters on the dining room table. When the local delicatessen that provided the food learned the reason for the large order on a Monday afternoon, they included additional food at no charge. Bottles of soda and juice were lined up on the sideboard and a large pot of coffee was already brewing. The women had brought piles of paper plates, napkins and cups. The silverware was mine. It had acquired the patina of use from 34 years of dinners, parties, meetings and ladies' luncheons. It will outlive me despite being cleaned in the dishwasher against standard advice.

Every so often, even on this saddest of occasions, my mind would slip and I would think what a nice opportunity I had to entertain people I hadn't seen in a long time, and how good it was for them to visit. It was as if I was a guest at my own party. I have read since then that when someone experiences great tragedy, it is not uncommon for the mind to build a shell to protect the individual from enduring a sorrow too great to bear. I believe I was in that state for a long time. I was emotionally unable to deal with the loss I had sustained, and the inability to recognize this occasionally resulted in inappropriate behavior.

I spoke with all the guests and thanked them for coming. Many had long trips to make and, always the hostess, I wanted to be sure that they were well fed. Someone offered me some food but I was not interested. "You must eat," my friends advised. "You will need your strength." The plates were shiny yellow plastic, the type that food slides right off if you tip them even slightly. I took a plate and filled it with macaroni salad as if I was at a picnic. The salad was tasteless. I was sorry to be serving tasteless food to my guests. I considered apologizing. I should warn them to watch out for the macaroni salad. But when I looked around, people seemed to be enjoying their food. It was late afternoon and many had not eaten lunch. They were talking and smiling. They didn't look unhappy. Perhaps it's all right, I thought. A young couple brought a child of about two. When he became impatient and started running around the house, his father took him upstairs. The bedrooms were messy from the construction and sudden influx of overnight guests. I hoped the child's father wouldn't notice the clutter and that the little boy wouldn't get into too much trouble.

Slowly the guests finished their lunch, said their goodbyes, wished us well, offered to pray for us and went on their way. The self-appointed food committee cleaned the kitchen, and packed away the extra food. They agreed among themselves to send a delegate to the house every day for the coming week to help with chores when visitors came. They left the house all in order with little evidence of the fifty people who had come that day to say goodbye to Jay and Barry. Finally only Andy, Larry and I were left. The quiet was welcome after the constant contact with people during the past three days. Was it only three days? It seemed impossible that only four days ago my life was whole, that I was part of a family, now half gone. I couldn't imagine how my life would progress, except that I knew I would be sad and lonely. The challenges I would have to face were hazy at that point but I had no doubt they would be daunting. I wondered how Andy would cope with his losses. We had been so busy with the tasks of mourning that we had not yet begun to mourn. There would be plenty of days ahead for that.

Larry said little about his brother. Six years apart in age, they were not close as children and even less so as adults. Larry didn't know much about Jay, living as they did half a continent apart, and this was hardly the time to ask. It was as though none of us was connected to the other in any way. We were solitary boats that had lost their moorings and gone adrift. We didn't talk about how we felt, or even about our lost loved ones. We talked about what still had to be done to clean up the house. Back to some normality no matter how bizarre. One last thing I always do after a crowd has left is count the silverware. Not because I suspect guests of thievery but because utensils accidentally get thrown out. I have rummaged through bags of garbage after a party or meeting to retrieve one fork or teaspoon. This occasion was no exception - five pieces of silver were missing. Andy, Larry and I donned rubber gloves and searched through all the trash until we found them. Our therapy was to complete the job at hand. This was a team project that ended successfully.

According to Jewish custom, mourners observe a one-week period when they remain at home, do not perform any type of work and receive visits from those who wish to express their condolences. Jews refer to this custom as "sitting *shiva*," *sheva* being the Hebrew word for seven. (A Christian woman I once worked with, not realizing I was Jewish, told me that for a week after a death, Jews "sit and shiver.") There are customs associated with this period that are observed in various degrees, depending on the family's religious orientation. An Orthodox family would observe them faithfully, a Reform less so or not at all. One such custom requires that the mourners sit on stools, low chairs or cushions. This derives from Biblical times when mourners literally sat on the earth, relating their physical status to their mental status of feeling low. Another custom requires the removal or covering of all mirrors during the *shiva* period. The meaning for this is obscure and some Reform rabbis consider it a superstition. I was unaware, or had forgotten the rule about the stools so we never considered that one, and I chose not to cover the mirrors.

Andy drove Larry to the airport the following morning. His friend, Eric, who had flown down from Boston for the funeral went along for the ride so Andy would not have to drive back by himself. Later that day Eric returned to the airport for his own flight. This was one of the hundreds of kindnesses that were extended to us during the days and weeks to come. That same morning at 10 o'clock, the doorbell rang. A woman stood on the porch holding a tray of cookies.

"You don't know me," she said, "but I heard about your tragedy and I wanted to do something."

Shortly afterward, another stranger arrived. She explained that she had moved from town several years before and now lived about 15 miles away. Her children attended high school with Barry and she wanted to pay her respects. They were the first of the more than seventy people who came to the house that week. Many Mount Holyoke alumnae who were not able to attend the funeral, and some who did attend, returned with their husbands. Teachers from our town's three schools came after school. Most had taught Barry and Andy but some who did not came as well. Two car loads of people I had worked with at one consulting firm arrived. The men wore Santa Claus ties and the women were all in red, green and silver bells for their office Christmas party later that afternoon.

The week was a strange combination of special and ordinary. Construction continued on the upstairs bathroom. Workers trudged up and down the stairs, and the sound of hammers and saws was the background for our conversation. The workmen, who were always considerate and polite, were the first to send flowers which were sitting on the front table when we arrived home from the funeral. Gifts arrived in great quantity, sometimes two fruit baskets at a time. Since Andy and I were the only ones living at home, the gifts we most appreciated were the meals. A neighbor brought a large platter of chicken in a delicious wine sauce. A woman I used to ski with brought a container of homemade pasta and sauce that went from her freezer to ours, ready to be used at a later time. Ellen's mother, a widow who understood the timing of grief, brought us Nova Scotia salmon that lasted for several months in sealed packages. She knew it was a food that Barry liked and hoped we would too. An outplacement client who had recently started a new job with a soup company brought dozens of containers of soup that Andy and I relished on those cold winter nights.

We received many financial donations. Some were to the charities we requested and many more were to charities favored by the givers. We were grateful for all of them. A neighbor who is a New York lawyer sent a beautifully lyrical cassette tape of professional quality of himself playing the guitar. A dear friend in Austria sent a box of Viennese chocolates. A professional association I belong to sent a Christmas cactus in full bloom. Letters and cards came in such great numbers that the mailman must have needed an extra container. He sent his own card, with cancelled stamp, as well. Starting from the first week, and for months afterward, we received hundreds of notes of sympathy. Like the strangers who came to the house and funeral, some were from people unknown to any of us. A Yale graduate (Jay's alma mater), read the newspaper obituary and sent a card with a note saying that the death of one member of the Yale community diminished all members. A woman who lived across the street from the cemetery sent a letter saying she knew Jay and Barry would rest there in peace. There were beautiful letters from Barry's high school friends, and cards from people I had not seen in more than 20 years. Men whom I had worked with sent thoughtful, handwritten letters. People sent beautiful poems which brought tears. Even more surprising to me, every card had a note. Not one person, no matter how tenuous the connection, simply bought a card and signed a name.

After news of the deaths appeared in the Mount Holyoke alumnae magazine, I received letters from Florida to Alaska. At a university where I had worked several years before, an e-mail announcement resulted in a flood of cards and letters from former co-workers. A man called from Oklahoma. We had been neighbors in New Jersey more than 30 years before. He had heard from a mutual friend in Florida. Such response overwhelmed me. I didn't expect it. But how would I know what to expect? This is not the type of tragedy one thinks about or plans for. I have saved all the mail and still occasionally read it. As a miser might open a box of treasure and recount his gold, savoring the feel of it, I open the box of letters reading a few at a time, remembering some that I forgot and reading others as if for the first time. Years later, I draw comfort and support from them.

Ellen came to spend every afternoon with us during our week of *shiva.* According to Jewish custom, the bereaved sit, pray and do little but receive guests for a week while others attend to their chores. When the week is over, they may leave home but do not return to work for a month. They say the *kaddish* prayer for the dead for a year. In this manner, mourners are eased back into society and a normal life. In late twentieth century America, such customs are followed by only a small percentage of the most observant Jews. We had no extended family to run errands for us or clean up after guests. Neighbors would have shopped for us if we had asked but we didn't see the need. Andy did the errands and I prepared the food, did the laundry and cleaned the house. We assumed a routine that would have seemed normal if ours was a normal household.

On Friday night that first week we attended Sabbath services at a synagogue in a neighboring town. Our group included Ellen, her sister and mother as well as four college friends of Andy's who had arrived from Virginia the day before. (With the resourcefulness of graduate students they had found a place to stay in town and announced that they were there to support and cheer him up.) We must have seemed an odd group arriving at the synagogue unfamiliar and unannounced. Although the rabbi did not know us, he made us feel welcome and extended his sympathy. He asked our names and the names of those who died. Andy and I were the only ones who were Jewish but that didn't matter. When the rabbi announced the deaths of Jay and Barry, all of us stood as mourners to recite the *kaddish.*

After the first week, visits stopped and the phone rang less frequently but mail continued at its previous pace. Andy and I started the sad job of sorting out Jay's belongings. As anyone knows who has undertaken this unhappy chore, cleaning out the possessions of a person who has died is a task that tears at the heart. Unfortunately, I have done it too many times—for both parents, a cousin who died of cancer at 41 and two single aunts of my husband. So many memories are imbedded in such pedestrian things—a hairbrush with hair still in it, a calendar with handwritten dates that will never be kept, a worn-out baseball mitt, souvenirs from trips, matches invoking memories of elegant dinners in exotic places and terrific pizza at a place just off the interstate in Connecticut, items of clothing that should have been thrown out long ago and some that were never worn, stored away in a drawer with their price tags still on them.

When Jay and I looked for our first house, we saw one being sold by a widow whose husband had died the year before. Everything was just as her husband had left it. His suits and shoes were in the closet. His pajamas and underwear were probably still in the dresser drawers. I was a young woman at the time, still in my twenties. I felt sorry for the woman clinging to her husband's possessions and I wondered why she had kept them for so long. Now, I can understand why but I also know that letting go is part of the grieving process. I wanted Jay's clothes to be useful. It was winter and they could keep someone warm. Starting the task while Andy was there to share the decisions helped.   We found a collection of major league baseballs, some autographed by famous players, some where the ink was too faded to recognize the signature and several with names that have been lost to obscurity. Jay must have spent considerable time in his youth shagging fly balls in Philadelphia or New York, another part of his past I would like to know more about but never will. There were suits and sports clothes, some fashionable, some sadly passé. With ample closet space, Jay had little incentive to part with old clothes. He insisted that if you save things long enough, the style will return. "Yes," I would respond, "that is true but they never return in exactly the same way. And when they do return, you should buy new ones not wear the actual clothes that are older than the designers who are now recreating the style." Occasionally I invaded his closets and packed up bags of clothes for the thrift shop—1970's print shirts with broad collars, bell-bottomed jeans, jackets with wide lapels. I knew that in New York this clothing was on sale in retro shops frequented by a new generation of the hip and trendy, but as far as Jay was concerned, it went out with sideburns and no longer belonged in his closet. As Andy and I sorted the clothing, he tried on a few of the jackets. He is taller, but not as broad as his father was and he looked a little like a child wearing grownup clothing, as though his shoulders were not yet big enough to bear the load he now had to assume. He kept a few shirts and sweaters that fit and we gave the rest to charity.

The saddest items to deal with were the most personal. Diplomas, yearbooks, large group pictures—Bunk 5, Camp Dunmore, 1947, typed references from high school teachers, a recommendation to the Bar Association of New York. There, in a manila envelope was a yellowed newspaper article—my engagement picture from the Trenton Times. I don't know if Jay ever looked at it after putting it into that envelope but he never threw it out. With the closets empty of clothing, there was plenty of room for such memorabilia. We put it all into boxes, postponing the decision to a time when it would be less painful.

Cleaning out a closet can become a therapeutic activity. I always ask my workshop participants how they have spent their time since losing their jobs. The women cleaned out their closets, the men built something. The responses are consistent. These are hands-on jobs that we can control. We finish our work and see an accomplishment. Some of our confidence is restored. After I cleaned out Jay's closets, I started to clean my own - and the garage and the cellar. I remembered my friend Jill's experience. She and her husband sold their house which had been on the market for many months, on the condition that the buyers could take possession in three weeks. She had 21 days to rid herself of a lifetime of belongings that were not needed in her new home. She worked from 5 in the morning until bedtime, furiously cleaning out.

Although I had no immediate plans to move, I knew eventually I would leave this big house and I would need plenty of time to dispose of possessions that would not go with me. I would have to dispose of a past that will be defined by memories, not things. I would also have to rid myself of things I was saving for a future that no longer exists. In the months to come, I carted load after load to the county dump —moldy furniture and broken toys, old light fixtures, worn-out linens, aged electrical appliances, boxes of games with parts missing, chipped bowls and heavy, scratched luggage. I filled my car's trunk with donations to rummage sales and bargain shops. But like my husband, who saved his high school varsity jacket, I have kept the parts of my past that tell who I once was— an out-of- style suit bought in Paris, elegant shoes that always looked better than they felt, a prom dress, and a college gym suit. I have promised to send the seemingly worthless boxes of scrap books and diaries to the archives of Mount Holyoke College which seeks to preserve for future generations of students a glimpse into the lives of women at mid-twentieth century: dance cards with little pencils attached, formal invitations to fraternity parties during Spring Weekend at all-male colleges, class notes neatly printed with a fountain pen and term papers typed on a manual Royal portable.

Andy went to Maryland with Ellen to help her clean out Barry's things. What a sad job that was. Ellen had decided to give up her job and the apartment so everything had to be dismantled and packed up. Andy took some of the clothing. As a gift, Ellen gave him the beautiful leather jacket she had bought for Barry as a birthday gift the year before. Andy wore that jacket for years until the lining was in shreds. I know it meant more to him than just an expensive jacket. It was a tangible link to his brother and he didn't have many.

After cleaning out the closets, we decided it was time to start writing thank you notes to all who had been so kind to us. The funeral home provided printed thank you cards but I wanted something more personal. I designed a 4" x 5" card for Andy to create on the computer. It said, *In Memory of Jay and Barry Schocket* across the top, and had our names— Sandra, Andrew and Ellen on the bottom. The rest was blank for a message. Andy delivered a camera-ready copy to the printer who was able to produce 400 cards, quickly and inexpensively, although it was his busy season. Instead of Christmas cards, we used the cards as announcements to people on our Christmas lists who had not heard the news. To everyone else we wrote notes of appreciation.

Our goal was to thank every person who had supported us during this sad time— those who came to the funeral, visited the house, called, sent gifts, cards or letters. For a while, we kept up with the thank-you's, each of us writing several a day. By the end of December there was still a huge pile but we had an added incentive. On January 1, postage would increase from 29 to 32 cents. On December 31, Andy and I sat at the kitchen table. We gathered all the letters and cards still to be acknowledged and divided them up. We each started writing furiously, as if we were entering a contest with letters that had to be postmarked by midnight. Eventually we tired of this forced activity and left the remaining thank-you's for the next year, postal increase or not. I put all the notes into a pile and Andy took them to the post office. The money we saved was insignificant but having a deadline helped to get the job moving. That was how we spent the last day of the year in which our loved ones left us. They would not accompany us into the new year. There was nothing to celebrate. The following week brought work and new chores so we never reached our goal of thanking everyone, but we tried.

Part II

So Hopeless to Conceive

You Can't Measure Grief

When we buried the two men in our lives – husband and son, father and brother, Andy and I became unwilling members of a group that defines itself by what it has lost. We joined a category of bereaved who have suffered "multiple loss." This term was new to me when I found it on the Internet describing one of the many specialized bereavement groups whose members post messages and communicate with one another on-line. I sought a definition of "multiple loss" so I could seek out others whose experience was similar to mine. I questioned psychologists, searched the literature and spoke with many people who told me they had experienced "multiple loss," but found little agreement regarding a time frame that connected the losses, or who should be included among the "multiple." By living long enough, we all experience many losses. We lose parents and grandparents, spouses, siblings, friends, children and pets. Although the deaths may have been separated by months or even years, some people continue to mourn all their losses, piling one on top of another until they see them as a whole rather than as isolated events.

I concluded that it is the perception of the losses that connects them, rather than the time frame. I communicated with many people on the Internet who described their losses. Placing herself into the multiple loss category, Mary told of losses that spanned 20 years, including both her parents and the relatives who raised her. Kathy included her grandfather who died 15 years before several additional family members and friends whose deaths were more recent. Tracy mourned her dog among her many losses: "Until last week, when I put my dog to sleep, it had been nine months since the last person died and of course a dog isn't supposed to be that big of a deal. People don't realize how four deaths in a year and a half can aggravate an already bad situation." My friend Julie, on the other hand, who lost her mother, younger brother and daughter within three years does not include herself in this group. "Sad things happen to people and mine occurred within a short period of time," she says. "We all lose our parents eventually. I don't think a three-year period makes me a victim of multiple loss."

Failing to find agreement on the parameters of multiple loss, I tried to find a hierarchy of misery related to loss. Knowing how others with similar losses had reacted would provide a barometer for my own thoughts and feelings. I sought specific research studies that would tell me if the loss of a spouse is worse than the loss of a sibling but less painful than the loss of a child. I wanted to put my grief into a framework, like a chest of drawers where I could open the "spouse-loss" drawer, take out that specific brand of grief for a while, place it back in and search through the "child" drawer for some help in that department. A "loss-of-a parent" drawer would be helpful too. I found a study (Julia Leahy, 1992-3), indicating that, after two years, women who lost children were significantly more depressed than women who lost spouses. But the study did not include women who had lost both a child and a spouse. Other studies contradicted these findings. Death of a spouse ranks highest on a commonly used scale of stress factors. Mountains of literature exist about the loss of a child. Experts say there is no greater loss. Books with such titles as *The Worst Loss* and *The Ultimate Loss* support this theory. So did the questionnaire for my 25th college reunion. In response to the question: "What do you fear most?" most of my classmates wrote "losing a child", followed by loss of a spouse and serious illness. Losing a spouse, a parent, a sibling, a close friend is greatly feared; losing a child is unthinkable. Whether the "child" is three, thirty or fifty, nothing in life prepares one for a loss that denies the laws of nature which say parents die first.

Just as no death is like any other, Barry's death did not change my world in the same way as Jay's. Jay's death propelled me into unsought roles. The soft side of me hardened, like the calluses that used to form on my tennis hand each spring so I wouldn't get blisters by July. The roles eventually became routine. Although living without my husband continues to diminish my life, I have found systems and methods that allow life to continue, that enable me to go on without wallowing in perpetual self-pity. In some ways, I have become a stronger and better person. But I have not yet found the path that leads to acceptance of Barry's loss. The pain of giving birth to him was transitory, but the pain of living without him will never fade. His death has put me into a place where no flowers grow, although I have tried to plant them, where music doesn't play, although I raise my voice in song. No calluses protect me here. Losing a child puts one into a world apart.

I felt uncomfortable grieving more for my son than my husband so I asked women who had lost several family members how they had fared. Julie wrote, "There were many changes in my life when my parents died and when my younger brother died, but when my daughter died there was a change in ME." Two years after losing her husband and daughter in an automobile accident, Amanda said: "My husband seemed to be the easiest one to tackle. I am just now dealing with the loss of my daughter." Wendy lost her husband and two sons. As she summed up her situation: "I guess when all is said and done, it was the deaths of my two beautiful sons that took so much away from me. My life has never been the same since I lost them, and no matter how I try, I just can't seem to get it back." Erica sent me an e-mail: "I know for me to lose a child is the worse thing ever. Losing a husband was bad but to lose a child to me was so much worse." This is how Sigmund Freud expressed his anguish over the death of his daughter Sophie, "Although we know that after such a loss the acute state of mourning will subside, we also know we shall remain inconsolable and will never find a substitute. No matter what may fill the gap, even if it filled completely, it nevertheless remains something else." (Volkan, 1993)

Unlike small children whose every need depends on their parents or teenagers whose noisy presence dominates a house, Barry was not part of my daily life when he died. Married and living a few hundred miles away, he could not even claim his old bedroom when he came to visit because Andy had usurped it years earlier. During the week that Barry stayed with us while Jay was in the hospital, I asked him to clean out his belongings that were still in his old desk and in the attic—his college textbooks and papers, possessions from his teenage years and old clothes. He put them all into the trash hauler that the construction workers had brought to take away debris from the old bathroom. How could I know when I asked him to remove his old possessions that nothing new would ever replace them? No new snapshots would sit framed on my dresser or hang on the wall. No cards or letters would ever arrive bearing his home address. When he threw everything away, it was as if he took a big eraser and wiped out a portion of his life. He left behind his high school diploma, sports awards and trophies and a big empty space where his laugh used to be.

For a time after his death, it seemed as if Barry was just away. I was used to that because I did not see him that often. But as the time got longer and longer, I began to miss him more and more. He was my psychological consultant. Whenever I had an outplacement client who seemed to have mental health problems, I consulted Barry, who helped to clarify issues for me and suggest courses of action. I missed his phone calls and the visits when he and Ellen came for holidays or weekends. Barry and I did not share many interests. As an adult, he refused to ski or travel with me and teased his younger brother for doing so. He would not go to art museums until Ellen took him to the National Gallery in Washington. There he found art he could enjoy: vast pictures of the Rocky Mountains or the Missouri River painted by American artists before photography. "Have you ever heard of Bierstadt?" he asked excitedly over the phone. He came to computers later than I did and when he used one in college, someone was always available to give advice. While living in Hoboken, he typed his master's thesis at home on the Macintosh computer that Andy and I had bought a few years earlier. He once called me at work because he had made a file too large and the computer could not save it. I told him what to do step-by-step so he wouldn't lose the work he had completed. While we were on the phone, Mark dropped in. He wanted to know what "help desk" Barry was speaking to. Barry told him. Mark's mouth dropped open. "You call your <u>mother</u> for advice on how to use the computer?" he asked, astonished. But Mark's teasing didn't bother Barry. He was comfortable with his own skills and knowledge and not afraid to seek help when he needed it.

Barry was quick to discuss his problems and thoughts. When he was at college he always called when he had a sore throat or sprained ankle. "Take aspirin, drink lots of water and go to the infirmary if it doesn't go away," I recommended, as if that were something he didn't already know. He continued to call when he was sick even as an adult until he met Ellen, a nurse, who was more than qualified to help him with his illnesses. He chose jobs that served the poor, the stricken and those who needed an advocate. He worked with mentally disturbed children in a New Jersey hospital and in a methadone clinic in downtown Washington, DC. He volunteered as a "hugger" for Special Olympics, greeting participants with a big hug when they finished their event. When he died, he was about to complete a doctoral degree in Clinical Psychology. He had studied for so long and was so close to his goal. With his empathy, kindness and desire to help others, I know he would have changed the lives of those who needed his help.

Early on, I was not aware of the subtleties of grieving. My pain was such that I did not make distinctions. Doing so would be like deciding which hurt is worse—a toothache or a sprained ankle when both seem equally intolerable. Each loss requires different psychological adjustments depending on one's age, needs and relationship with the person who died. Loss of a spouse leaves one lonely, without loving companionship, with children to raise and bills to pay. Loss of a child slams shut a door into the future, wiping out hopes and dreams, and painting the past in a hue forever tinged with sadness. Loss of a sibling removes a lifetime companion who shares a common biological heritage and a common past. The bond between child and parent is so strong that loss of a parent may affect a child or young adult for the rest of her life. Older adults can also experience profound and unexpected sorrow at a parent's death which eliminates the buffer between them and their own inevitable demise. Shortly after Jay and Barry died, a woman in her fifties told me she was "in the same boat" as I was because her father had died recently. The man was elderly so I didn't see the parallel but she did and her grief was as deep as mine. Another woman went on and on about the death of her 89-year-old mother, one year earlier. Finally she said, "But why am I telling you this, you know how it is." I responded, "No, I know how it is for me. I can only guess how it is for you."

I had a long conversation with a woman whose husband died of cancer. We discussed whether it is better to know and face the death for a long period as she did or to suffer the sudden shock as I did. While her husband was well enough, he took his grown children on a trip knowing it would be their last one together. They now cherish their combined memories of that trip. Her husband was able to prepare her for the business and financial decisions he knew she would have to make. She thought her path was easier than mine. I don't know how I would have coped with knowing ahead of time about the tragedy about to befall my family.

I think the pain of knowing I would lose two loved ones before the end of the year would have been excruciating. I am glad that they did not know, but that is my projection. They may have had unfinished needs and unspoken words that would have been important for them to convey to us who remained. Psychiatrists say that victims of sudden loss have a more complicated healing process. I am not so sure. Awaiting an anticipated death is like sliding slowly down a long hill into an abyss with no way out; for survivors, an unanticipated death is like jumping off a cliff. In either case, you end up in the same place.

When my husband and son died, I did not differentiate my feelings about their deaths. One was as terrible as the other. I wrapped both of them in the same bundle of grief. They shared a funeral, an obituary and lie next to one another in the cemetery. My initial reactions to both deaths were the same: shock, denial, guilt and pain, strong physical pain. My chest, arms, legs, gums, feet—everything hurt. I recalled something that my friend Julie had told me several years before. For months after her daughter Susan died in an automobile accident she awoke during the night feeling as if knives were stabbing her. When my doctor, a family friend, came to the house to pay a condolence call, I told him that I hurt all over. I thought he might diagnose some strange, stress-related illness but he just looked at me and replied softly, "That's understandable."

As time passed, like twins beginning to establish their own identity, the deaths began to separate. Although they shared an empty place in my heart, I missed them differently and I mourned them differently. Jay's death left me drained of strength from the sheer weight of its burden, Barry's asked for no space at all. Jay's thrust me into a place where I had to do everything, Barry's put me where I could do nothing. Slowly, as my mourning for Barry took on its own meaning, I realized that I had not had time and space to mourn him sufficiently when he died. My coping skills were too overburdened. My psyche, to aid my survival, suppressed some of the grief until I was ready to bear it. Gradually, an enormous, numbing sorrow began to emerge. Not the early sharp pain but a gnawing discomfort. It was then that I became aware that the process for mourning each of them would be separate and distinct just as my relationship with each was unique.

The chronicle of deaths in my family began on December 10, 1990, when my mother died of cancer in a hospice in Florida. Four years later, on December 10, my son, her grandson, died of a heart attack at a hospital in New Jersey. These two dates, like bookends, enclose four years when funeral followed funeral— my father, my 21-year-old nephew who took his own life, my husband and son. Until my mother died when I was 54, I had two living parents, which was unusual for my age. I had lost grandparents, much-loved aunts and uncles, both in-laws and a 41-year-old cousin. I missed and grieved for these people. I still do, and I grieved for my mother, but she had suffered so greatly for a long time that I had accepted her loss long before she died.

When my mother was dying in Florida, Barry, Andy and I flew down to see her on Thanksgiving day. Although she was heavily sedated with morphine, she awoke from her sleep and recognized us. "It's a miracle, my family has come," she said, looking from one to the next. That recognition was the greatest gift she could have given me. Leaving the hospice the next day, I knew I would never see her again and she died soon after. I felt sad but not angry or guilty because I knew I had done my best for her during her long illness. I wish she had lived longer. I wish she had lived to see her grandsons graduate from college. I wish she had lived to fulfill her wish to dance at their weddings. My mother loved to dance. She taught me to do the Charleston when I was 12 and the rumba at 16. There are so many questions I wished I had asked her. Several years after her death, I drove through a small New Hampshire town where we spent summers when I was a child. My mother had hay fever and each year she packed us up as she joined other hay fever sufferers in this mountain town which still boasts an absence of ragweed. We rode for hours on a train and got off at a place with the strange-sounding name of White River Junction. There someone came to fetch us in a station wagon for the long, dusty ride to the big old boarding house where we would stay.

The town hadn't changed much in the 50 years since I had last been there. I drove up and down the streets looking for the large wooden house with a big front porch. There were several candidates but I couldn't identify one with any certainty. I left disappointed. The following summer I went back again and found a woman whose family had lived there for generations. "Mrs. Roy took in boarders," she told me. "You probably stayed there." I looked for Mrs. Roy's house but the woman's description of it and my memory didn't match. My mother would have known for sure. This may seem like a superficial reason for missing a mother, but as with all loss, it is sometimes the small thing whose absence is most noted when it is gone. We suddenly awake to find portions of our past erased with no way of retrieving a name, a place, a saying, a memory. So much is left undone and so much unsaid.

My father died eighteen months later and his death saddened me greatly. I spoke at his funeral because I wanted to say things about him that only a member of our family could express, especially about his love and devotion for my mother. They met when she was a pretty, blue-eyed teenager and he worked in a town nearby. They went to Havana on their honeymoon. During 60 years of marriage, they rarely quarreled. After she developed cancer and became an invalid, he cared for her for seven years without a complaint. He learned to cook and do other domestic chores that had never concerned him when she was able to do them. He gave up his beloved card games if she was in pain and needed someone to stay with her. Second only to his love for her and his family was his passion for baseball. Among my earliest childhood memories are hot summer afternoons when baseball on the radio was the background music of our lives. "It's a lo-o-ong fly ball to center field," I heard the announcer drone long before I had the slightest idea of what a baseball field looked like. In the years before television, my father listened to two games simultaneously and could tell you every detail of each game – the lineups, batting averages, pitching records, who was on base and who was on deck. In those days, most fathers didn't take their daughters to ball fields but he took me to Boston's Fenway Park to see Ted Williams and the Polo Grounds in New York to see Willie Mays. He never cared much for the Yankees and was disappointed when I fell in love with a fair-haired teenager named Mickey Mantle who came to play in Yankee Stadium. My father never took me to Yankee Stadium but I went on my own when I was old enough. Without his training, I never would have gone at all.

My father and my Uncle Joe opened a small automotive parts store in Meriden, Connecticut in 1935. The town was not devastated by the depression. Its factories remained open and many men had jobs. They also had cars. Since they couldn't afford to buy new ones, they bought tires, fan belts, batteries and dozens of smaller items that kept their cars running. Factory workers were my father's customers. The International Silver plant sat in the middle of town along the train tracks. Huge white letters painted on the side of a building announced to all railroad passengers that they were approaching Meriden, home of the International

Silver Co. The plant's buildings stretched for blocks. More silverware was manufactured here than anyplace in the world. After the Second World War, my father's store sold home appliances and then television sets to returning veterans. Despite working long hours six days a week, my father enjoyed his work because he loved people. Selling things to them was a way to help them. He loved to talk about his family and sports with his customers. It all came together when he could tell his stories and make a sale as well. Business was good until the early 60's when discounters opened up on the highways and the International Silver Co. left town.

Dad was a champion gin rummy player who won many tournaments and quite a bit of money. He once cleaned out some card sharks on a cruise ship who thought he would be easy prey. His mild manner and conservative clothing gave no hint of his steel-trap technique once the cards were dealt. He remembered every card that was in play and, trying to teach me the game, would criticize me if I gave him the card that he needed to win. "I already picked up one king, why did you give me another king?" he would scold as once again he laid down his hand with gin. He did the same thing with his grandchildren. I guess he wanted all of us to be the sharp player that he was but we knew that, barring incredible luck, the only way we could beat him was if he chose to lose. His kindness was legendary especially when he retired and moved to Florida with ample time to do favors for his friends and neighbors. Even with his mind clouded by Alzheimer's disease and in a nursing home, he maintained his sweet disposition, greeting me with a big smile when he saw me from across the room. He wasn't always certain if I was his daughter, wife or mother but he knew I belonged to him and that was enough.

The guilt, remorse and sorrow that started on the day my father died grew to encompass my husband and son and lasts to this day. Nevertheless, if you had asked me before everyone died how I thought I would react to all these deaths I would have given the same answer then that I give you now. I would grieve for them and miss them all, but nothing would compare with losing my son. My friend Lynn, whose only child Lisa died at 11 in a fire, told me how her life changed because she was no longer a mother. She had been very involved with Lisa's activities, her Girl Scouts, her lessons. Like losing a limb, that part of her life was suddenly severed. She continued to volunteer at her daughter's school for a few years after the tragedy, and still teaches Sunday school at her church. She kept in touch with Lisa's classmates and was invited to their high school graduation ceremony.

"Was that painful?" I asked.

"No, it represented closure," she responded. Until that time, she always knew what school Lisa would be in, who her friends would be and what activities would have consumed her young life. When she saw her daughter's classmates dispersing, Lynn could only guess what the future might have held for Lisa.

My first experience with death occurred early in my childhood. When I was eight years old, Marlene, a pretty girlfriend of mine, died of complications from measles. One week she was in school, the next she was dead. Her mother worked in a children's clothing store downtown and I always felt guilty when I saw her in that store because I was alive and Marlene wasn't. As the years passed, I wondered if Marlene's mother thought of her when I tried on clothes, picturing what her daughter would have been doing and wearing at my age. I wondered if it hurt her to see me. I never mentioned Marlene when I shopped in the store although I wish now that I had. I wish I had told her Mom that I missed her. I occasionally see Barry's friends, now in their mid-thirties, established in their careers, mothers and fathers of babies and school-age children. I know what they are thinking when they see me because I am thinking the same thing. Their silence says "I was Barry's friend and you are his mother. I wish he was here with his baby as I am with mine. I wish I could say this to you but I don't know how." They are wondering if it hurts me to see them. Yes, dear friends, sometimes it does. I am happy for their health and success, but they will forever be a reminder of my loss. A few of Barry's friends have stayed in touch with Andy, welcoming him to their homes, introducing him to their babies. One man has stayed especially close, a surrogate older brother, an understudy who is not quite the lead but is trying hard to fill the part.

"Happy families are all alike; every unhappy family is unhappy in its own way." Tolstoy's opening line of *Anna Karenina* would apply as well to mourners. Although we may have lost several dear ones, each loss affects us in a different and sometimes, unpredictable way. Women who lost their mother when they were children or teenagers say that was the defining event of their lives. No matter how long they live, or what other relationships they form, the loss of their mother will always affect them. No one will ever fill the void created by their mother's absence. I wanted to learn more about different types of loss. In addition to reading several books, I turned to the Internet for first-hand information. I posted a message on bereavement bulletin boards asking readers to contact me regarding their experience with multiple loss. Responses flooded in; many broke my heart. Several women described the anguish and sense of abandonment they felt when their mother died. A few called their mother their best friend. One said she still weeps on the anniversary of her mother's death more than twenty years ago.

My mother lived until I was well past middle age so I have no personal experience of a mother dying young, but I was a close observer to such loss. Two close friends lost their mothers to cancer during their senior year in high school. Vicki was a high school friend, a pretty, vivacious girl. We rode around in her car, which had no radio and no air-conditioning, with all the windows open, singing at the top of our lungs – she the soprano, I the alto—so we could hear ourselves above the noise of the traffic. We were in many of the same classes and were both cheerleaders. Sitting together on long bus rides to out-of-town games in remote parts of Connecticut, we talked about boyfriends and any girlfriends out of earshot. I knew her mother had been in and out of the hospital, but I never knew she was dying of cancer.

A friend called early one morning to say Vicki's mother had died. My mother told me to pay a condolence call so after school I baked some chocolate chip cookies, put them into a blue tin that was made to look like Wedgwood china, and took them to Vicki's house. She lived in a pretty Cape Cod house on the other side of town. When I arrived she had just returned home from the funeral home and her eyes were red from crying. It was the first condolence call I had ever made and I wasn't sure what to say. We sat in her living room and talked quietly about school but we never talked about Vicki's mother. Occasionally, a single tear rolled down her cheek and settled on her blouse. Vicki was an only child and her mother's loss left her especially vulnerable. A few months later, she came to school with a black eye, saying she had bumped into a doorknob but I think her father had hit her. After high school when we both went off to college, we saw one another during vacations and summers. Vicki got married at 21 to a man she met at college. She asked me to be her maid of honor which flattered me because she had become close to a few of her sorority sisters. She said she wanted me because I was kind to her when her mother died. Her father had remarried by this time and Vicki didn't like her stepmother. I think I represented a link to her mother and the home she had lost. Vicki's husband was in the military so they traveled and we lost touch. I later learned that she, too, had died of cancer in her thirties.

On the day that I started college, I was as excited and nervous as any new freshman could be. My room was on the fourth floor of one of the few dorms with an elevator. My parents and I rode up, each with our arms full of clothing, followed by a student from nearby Amherst College, hired to work for the day, who carried two of my suitcases. When we arrived at my room, my roommate Carol, her father and sister Linda were sitting on her bed. Carol jumped up and hugged me. Then the three of them sat in a row on Carol's bed and watched as I unloaded my clothes. Carol's mother had died in the spring, as Carol and Linda were finishing their final exams. They looked so forlorn. When we left the room, my mother said it was the saddest thing she had ever seen, the three of them sitting there on that bed on the first day of college. I don't think I was as kind to Carol or as supportive as I could have been during the time we lived together. I was dealing with homesickness, adjusting to the routine of college, trying to turn myself from a flighty cheerleader into a serious student and not always doing a good job at it. I was probably too self-absorbed to understand that Carol was going through the same adjustment problems that I was in addition to missing and mourning for her mother. Her problems were far greater than mine but I was too immature to recognize that at the time. At the end of our freshman year she chose to room with someone else but we have remained dear lifelong friends.

Just as several women described their mother as their best friend, young men look to their fathers for the leadership and companionship that will shape their manhood. My sons were especially close to their father. He played with them, helped them with their homework and took care of them when I worked nights or was out of town. Together they went to football, soccer, baseball and basketball games. Although most boys reach an age where they think they know more than their fathers, Barry and Andy seemed to be the exception. They always respected Jay's intelligence and expertise even as they ignored his advice. As adults they watched TV together, discussed sports constantly and were always joking with one another. He taught them how to become the men they were. Raising sons is a difficult job for two parents. I can only imagine how arduous it is for women doing it alone. My friend May, whose husband died when she was 45, leaving her with two young sons, said they always sought out the companionship of older men as they themselves grew older, looking for the father they so badly missed. After Jay and Barry died, Andy became friendly with Don, a man he met at his part-time job. Don was a retiree in his fifties who had moved to Virginia and taken up a second career. I think Don's quiet manner and concern helped Andy through some lonely times.

I asked Andy how he related differently to the deaths of his father and brother. He replied that he thought more about Barry than he thought about Jay. Reading between the lines, I think he missed Barry more than he missed Jay although he probably had difficulty saying those words. When I asked what he missed most about his brother, his answer surprised me because I thought he would say he missed the companionship. He said he missed a shared language and symbols. He missed someone who would know instantly what he meant when he referred to a place or incident. "Remember the time Mom fell into the water when she was showing us how to step from rock to rock to get across the stream?"

From earliest childhood, Andy worshipped his older brother. As a baby, he would stay contentedly in his carriage or playpen for hours if Barry was in the room. When Barry was in kindergarten, Andy and I went to watch the children's Halloween parade. Andy, 17 months old at the time, sat patiently on my lap waiting for the parade to begin. As soon as he saw Barry walk in wearing his costume, Andy's whole face lit up. "Bah" he exclaimed, pointing to Barry as he quickly squirmed off my lap to walk next to his brother in the parade. Barry was embarrassed, not wanting his baby brother beside him when he was feeling quite grown-up himself but Andy wanted so much to tag along that the teacher let him stay. Twenty-two years later, Andy left a pleasant and roomy house that he shared with other young men in a Washington suburb to rent a small and somewhat seedy apartment with Barry who had moved to Washington to attend graduate school. Growing up, they fought territorial wars in the back seat of the car and kicked one another when forced to share a bed on vacations. But their skirmishes never diminished Andy's love and admiration for his older brother. When I occasionally see two young brothers holding hands, the younger looking up adoringly at the older, my heart is filled with such sadness remembering what was.

Whether we lose a parent, child, sibling, spouse, dear relative or close friend, each successive death reduces by one the resources available to us. At Jay and Barry's funeral, Julie said to me, "Either one of them would have helped you so much with the death of the other." They would have helped in very different ways. Jay would have been as devastated by Barry's death as I was but he would have been stoically silent. He would rarely have mentioned Barry's name. If I had asked him how he was feeling, he would have answered, "You know how I feel." I would have become enraged. "No I don't know how you feel. Tell me how you feel. What do you miss about him? When do you think about him? When something happens that reminds you of Barry, talk about it." I know that he never would have shared his thoughts because I had learned through all the years of marriage that Jay did not discuss feelings. I suppose he had them deep inside someplace but they were not available to me so I stopped looking for them. Instead I accepted his strengths. His support was physical, emotional and financial. He would have helped me with Barry's death by just being there, by putting an arm around me when I cried even though he could not cry too. He would have gone to the cemetery with me and stood apart staring at the gravestone while I puttered with the grass and the dirt. He would have listened. I counted on his support "in sickness and in health, in happiness and sorrow, till death do us part." When death did us part, that support was gone. There was no replacement.

Barry would have brought a note of cheer to my life after Jay died. He was a ready source of advice and a good son. He would have called often. "How are you doing, Mom?" he would have asked just as he did during the last minutes of his life. He would have felt an obligation to look out for his widowed mother and he would have kept that obligation. In their different ways, both men offered unconditional love and I couldn't do much better than that.

Independence

"Life goes on." "You have to move forward." "Don't do anything for a year." These were some of the platitudes I heard from kind and well-meaning people around me trying to help me to get on with a life that had changed so abruptly. In our culture, mourning does not occur in a vacuum or a place apart. For the first week, I was sheltered, pitied and catered to. Then, like a bird pushed out of the nest by its mother, I was on my own. While emotionally I was trying to absorb the loss of my loved ones, I could not postpone the unaccustomed tasks related to their deaths. Making funeral arrangements was just the beginning. I suddenly controlled my finances, my house, my income, my future. I had to incorporate all of this into my new life as an unmarried woman. I always saw myself as an independent person, a free spirit. While preparing myself for my ultimate goal, to become a wife, I engaged in many endeavors that taught me how to fend for myself as a single woman. I traveled alone, managed money, supported myself in a strange city and thrived on challenge. Looking at my past through the prism of my current status, I see aspects of my behavior that foreshadowed the ability I now need to survive.

After college graduation, I went to Europe by myself for three months, which was daring at the time, although I didn't realize it then. Transatlantic phone calls required making an advance reservation and were so expensive they were for emergencies only. I never called home during the time I was away. Credit cards were non-existent. The money I left home with had to last. I knew there would be no bailouts. For six weeks, I went to summer school in Austria. The rest of the time I traveled, without advance reservations, sometimes alone, occasionally with Americans I met along the way. I budgeted my travelers checks, managed the currencies and languages of the eight countries I visited, stayed in tiny garret rooms in Paris and London, and a converted palazzo in Rome. Most trans-Atlantic travel was by ship then but I arrived in Amsterdam on a chartered flight for students, a huge propeller plane that stopped to refuel in Goose Bay, Labrador on the way over and Gander, Newfoundland on the way back, or perhaps it was the reverse. I knew no one on the plane when I arrived at what was then Idlewild Airport, now JFK in New York. Most of the students were engineers, all male, going to Scandinavia on an exchange program to work for the summer.

I was one of six women going to a variety of places. In Amsterdam, I spent a few days with people I met on the plane before our paths diverged. One of the other women and I met up again, by agreement, on the French Riviera where we spent a few days before traveling together to Italy. An American we met in Belgium had told us that the American Embassy in Rome threw a great party on the Fourth of July, by invitation only. A few weeks ahead we each wrote to the embassy requesting an invitation to be sent to the American Express office in Rome. To my amazement, a beautifully engraved invitation awaited each of us when we arrived in Rome. From the bottom of my suitcase, I found a fresh white blouse that I paired with a skirt and brand new Italian sandals I had purchased the day before. The reception was held outdoors on the spacious grounds of the villa where the embassy was located. A band played American music. Grilled hamburgers and hot dogs were a treat after a month of inexpensive European food. The Americans gathered were the greatest number of my countrymen I had seen or would see in one place for three months.

I had many such experiences traveling independently. I slept overnight on wooden slat seats in a third class train carriage in Italy with a pair of honeymooners, danced the waltz with a prince in Vienna, was serenaded by a gondolier in Venice and loved every minute of it. Few Americans visited Europe then. We were welcomed wherever we went, even by the French. We kept meeting one another by chance as we showed up in the popular places at some point in our journey. I don't recall ever being nervous or afraid on that trip. It was all a big adventure for a girl from a factory town in Connecticut. In later years, when I have felt apprehensive about flying alone into a new city, I think of the 22-year-old who got off a train in Paris, found a comfortable hotel room on the Left Bank for $2.00 a night and strolled down the Champs Elysee as if she was in heaven, which she was.

Returning home after my stay in Europe, I spent two years as a single woman in New York negotiating the life of the big city. Needing to find a job quickly, I went to all the large insurance companies because they offered the best prospects for a well-paying job. The first insurance company gave me a test that included English and math. The English was no problem but I had difficulty with some of the math questions. I memorized the questions I missed and my boyfriend, who was brilliant in math, told me how to do them. The next company I applied to gave *the same test.* By the time I got to the third company, I was a mathematician, at least on that test. Within two weeks, an insurance company offered me a job as an underwriting clerk in the group underwriting department.

The job was all math. I worked in a very large room filled with gray metal desks, each with a Monroe calculator the size of a microwave oven. All day long, I punched numbers into the calculator using a large spread sheet, a real paper spread sheet, as I figured health insurance renewal rates for client companies in the Midwest. I multiplied numbers and inserted them into little cells on the spreadsheet. They had to balance, top to bottom and left to right. The function, if it is done at all now, would probably take 10 minutes on a computer for each case. For the longer cases, or if I made an error, it sometimes took days. I earned $70 a week plus a free lunch, which was excellent pay. I shared a spacious apartment with two other girls, one of them, my college friend Julie.

On a fall Saturday, a crisp sunny day that no city in the world does better than New York, I went to one of the best department stores to buy a dress with money I had saved. The dress I chose, a New York black wool dress, straight from shoulder to hemline, had a round neckline and no collar. It was so stylish, and so different from my tired college wardrobe that I couldn't bear to take it off. I asked the saleslady to cut off the tags and I wore it out of the store, carrying my old clothes in the store's shopping bag. I felt so sophisticated walking down Fifth Avenue in my black dress swinging the prestigious shopping bag although it only contained old clothes. I wore the dress a few weeks later on my first date with the man who would become my husband.

After about a month at my underwriting job, I knew that I could not do it for more than a year because I found it so boring. I was in a tight spot about that year commitment. When my prospective boss interviewed me for the job he said he was reluctant to hire me because the girls didn't stay. They got married, or pregnant if they were already married and they left. He didn't want to train me only to have me leave. I promised him I would not get married or pregnant for a year while secretly knowing that if Mr. Right came along, I'd get married in a week. My answer about the pregnancy part was 100 percent truthful.

My co-workers, all young and male, had been there for two or three years which seemed an eternity to be doing a job that could be challenging but did not offer the type of challenge that I wanted in a job. To amuse themselves, and me, the guys played games with the calculators, which I guess was the equivalent of playing computer games now. By pressing a particular sequence of keys, they could get the machines to make noises that sounded like a march or a cha cha cha. If they had known what a waltz rhythm was, they probably would have done that too. They were in the company's actuarial training program and all were taking a series of extremely difficult examinations. Each time they passed an exam their pay increased and they were closer to becoming an actuary which is one of the best positions in an insurance company. They spent a lot of office time studying for the exams and then worked overtime getting paid extra for the work they should have been doing while they were studying. I had no actuarial aspirations, thus severely limiting my advancement prospects in that department. I pictured myself old at thirty, my eyesight gone from having placed one number too many into cells on the spreadsheet, my finger tips callused from years of pounding the calculator. Out of the blue came my deliverance.

A job that I had applied for before taking the underwriting job became available. Another insurance company, the world's largest, offered me a job in its Employment Bureau. It paid $80 a week plus lunch, a princely sum in those days, and I had my own office, actually a good-sized cubical, with a window that looked out on the Empire State Building. All I had to do was interview people all day for a variety of jobs, from elevator operators and cafeteria workers to management trainees. I couldn't believe that someone would pay me to do such an enjoyable job. During Easter vacation, what seemed like the entire graduating class from a local girls' high school came to apply for secretarial and clerical jobs. They were bright, clean, polite and energetic. We worked until 7 p.m. to interview all of them and hired most. My favorites, however, were the part-time generals. These were not military positions but part-time jobs for general clerical workers. They worked 27 1/2 hours a week with 35 minutes for lunch. The hours were perfect for women with children in school. Whole mah jongg groups came from the Bronx and Brooklyn to apply. If they met the company standards and I liked them, I hired them. If I found them lacking, I turned them down, but not before asking a lot of questions that would land me in court today.

Most of my Mount Holyoke classmates married shortly after graduation and worked for a few years before settling into parenthood and domesticity. It was the anticipated outcome of our education. Some of us who waited a little longer thrived on the independence we acquired at a women's college where no one questioned the feasibility of our dreams even if few of us pursued them. We worked to put our husbands through graduate school. When their professional lives began, ours ended. When I stepped out of my wedding gown and into the clothes of a wife, I surrendered large chunks of my autonomy to my husband. It was easy to do. He had the training, the expertise and the interest. Eventually I cared for two boys, pursued a career, managed a household, and engaged in sports and hobbies, all of which made me feel as if I was leading a life of independence and responsibility. Until my husband died, I didn't realize how much I needed and depended upon him. His death taught me that my perceived self-reliance was based on educated risk and a strong safety net. I knew that Jay, and also my sons as they reached adulthood, would be there if I tumbled.

Jay had been a constant source of advice for the 35 years I had known him. As a lawyer, he knew how to make informed decisions. He was more knowledgeable about business than I was and more level headed. He knew how to distinguish the useful information from the irrelevant, the meat from the hype. My decisions usually come from intuition, a gut feeling that something is right for me. Even when I stubbornly insisted on an answer or solution, I always asked him the question first. I needed his input, whether I decided to do as he recommended or do it my way as I often did. And I could not blame him, as I also did, if my way was wrong. He made decisions, I made arrangements. I loved him because he was stronger and wiser. When he died I had to learn to find my strength, to make my decisions and if something went wrong to assume responsibility for the mistake. That was the difficult part. I alone was in control.

The challenge I faced as a widow was far greater than anything I had done before, harder than going off to college by myself, harder than going to New York alone, harder than caring for a crying new baby. Those were the challenges of youth, when parents were a telephone call away and optimism was high. The challenges of mid-life and old age seemed heavier and lonelier, an unanticipated burden when the people I needed to guide me were gone. It is a difficult time of life to assume a new job and I had to begin the job of being a widow. Because it was a job I never applied for I wasn't sure how I was going to handle this new assignment. Imagine the want-ad.

Job: WIDOW

Responsibilities: Total and all consuming. Considerable overtime.

Experience: None

Qualifications: Courage, strength, flexibility, intelligence, sense of humor, coping skills and so on and so on and so forth.

In workshops for those who have lost jobs, I ask the participants to list what they will miss when they are not working. The lists invariably include the companionship of co-workers, having a schedule and a place to go every day, regular salary and benefits, a computer, fax machine, copier and sometimes a car, an identity, confidence and self-esteem. If I were to make a personal list related to the loss of my husband, I would include many of the same items.

In the weeks and months following Jay's death I had to find ways to address each of these losses. My home life had lost its structure. Ironically I had acquired the freedoms I missed when I was married. I could read in bed at two in the morning or play the same passage on the piano over and over, which drove Jay crazy. The only restrictions and demands on my time were those that I imposed. If I so chose, I could eat Cheerios for dinner every evening and let the dirty laundry pile up until nothing clean was left in my closet. Although Jay and I did not share household chores equally, and I thought he did much too little, adding his "little" to my responsibilities created a heavy load. After he died, I had no time left to relax, to put my feet up and read a book or take a quick walk in the neighborhood. I had all the freedom I wanted but lacked the time in which to enjoy it.

I thought about the advice I give to my classes. I urge them to accept change. I challenge them to make their lives better. I promise them that their confidence will return and self-esteem will follow. I assure them that they will find another job, maybe even a better one. They stare at me blankly, not always convinced. I can understand why. Applied to myself, my advice sounds shallow, an echo of all the self-help recommendations that flood the media. But I know some of them work because I have tried them. Do first things first, keep the end in sight, don't worry about the little things, believe in yourself.

When I set out to take charge of my life I knew that I would have to work hard, and that I would have to overcome doubt and insecurity. I didn't anticipate that the necessary steps would be easy but I also didn't think that I would fail. Somehow, I would move on. Perhaps I was naive in not anticipating how many obstacles there would be but I had no choice—no one was suddenly going to drop from the sky to solve my problems. I wrote "to do" lists on sheets of paper and crossed off the jobs as they were completed. Then someone gave me a washable board, 8" x 11", with its own felt-tipped pen and magnets that attach it to my refrigerator. I have written dozens of to-do lists on that board, and each time I feel a sense of accomplishment when I wipe off all the crossed out items and start again with a clean slate. My first list looked something like this:

- get will from safety deposit box
- probate the will
- collect life insurance
- change ownership of bank accounts, IRA's and stocks
- pay Jay's credit card bills
- change his car registration to my name
- cancel his car insurance
- get new health insurance
- transfer his frequent flyer mileage to my account
- collect widow's Social Security payment
- pay income taxes
- file Federal and estate tax return
- write new will

Most of the tasks were administrative. The difficult ones would have been simpler if Jay and I had discussed his business affairs. I wish I had asked more questions. His heart attack should have been a warning to me. When he was in the hospital I could have inquired about the will and taxes as well as other assets he owned. Feeling assured of his recovery, I never considered doing so. Such questions were for a far -off future when we could sit in a rowboat discussing investments, as attractive gray-haired couples do in commercials for brokerage firms advertising retirement plans. Despite the doctor's assurance that he had recovered and would be able to return to an active life, we should have recognized his illness as a signal for me to become better informed about his financial affairs. But we didn't want to talk about it. We were not unique. A woman, whose husband suffered from a long and terminal illness, told me he was in complete denial until the day he died. He refused to discuss his financial affairs with his wife and never rewrote his 20-year-old will, which had become seriously out-of-date following the death of their son eight years earlier. With his papers in disarray, his widow found the paperwork overwhelming. Even when women know their husbands are dying, both parties often pretend that somehow he will get well. Magically he will rise up out of the bed and be restored to health. To discuss death, to ask for his help in handling his affairs, is acknowledging the inevitable. I would later regret my reluctance to bring up the subject. I wish I had said, "You have the expertise, please help me with this now before it is too late." My life was filled with would's, could's and should's after Jay died. It didn't have to be that way.

After the official week of mourning was over, the transition was swift. The phone rang less frequently. Guests no longer came to the door. I realized that I had to begin the steps that would legitimize my life as a widow. The first move was to obtain Jay's will from the safety deposit box where he kept his papers. As I drove to the bank, I wondered what to say about the co-renter of the box, who was my deceased husband. In some states, and I believed mine was one of them, both renters of the box must be alive for either renter to gain access. As long as I have been renting safety deposit boxes, I have always checked yes on the form asking if all renters of the box are living. If I checked yes on this occasion, the bank clerk would politely ask me to wait while she informs her boss that Jay Schocket's obituary was in last week's paper. Would they notify the police? If I inform them of Jay's death, they could seal the box and require me to get a court order to open it. Being led away in handcuffs by a sympathetic but unsmiling young patrolman did not seem like a good option right then so I decided to take my chances with the truth.

"My husband has died and I need access to our box," I said with feigned confidence when the bank employee handed me the card. I asked her how to sign it.

"That rule no longer applies," she said. She expressed her sympathy, took my key and gave me the box. I heaved a huge sigh of relief – one hurdle passed. We had safety deposit boxes at two different banks. Jay primarily used this one. I had rarely visited it. It was filled with various documents which I removed and spread out on the table in the small generic room that banks provide for this purpose. (Some of these closet size rooms have a small picture on the wall or silk flowers in a vase from Taiwan. Some provide scissors on a chain but this was bare bones.)

At first, I casually leafed through the papers, not specifically seeking the will, just looking, item by item, at the box's contents: savings bonds my children had received when they were born, certificates for stocks that Jay had inherited from his mother, his birth certificate. I was surprised to find our marriage certificate, which I thought had been lost. Finally, I was at the bottom of the pile and realized I had not seen the will. Surely it's here, I told myself. Like a squirrel digging for buried acorns, I frantically dug through the papers. I looked again and again. I examined each document, each piece of paper — irrationally, since a will is a large and easily recognized document.

I stared at the box and peered into its empty recesses. The will was not there. He had told me there was a will but it was not there. Slowly, I returned the contents to the box and left the bank. I tried the box at the other bank, although I knew the will wasn't there. I used that box all the time and I would have noticed Jay's will. A widow told me that one of the first things she realized after her husband died was that there were questions that only he could answer. She looked in vain for the keys to her husband's boat. With no one to ask, their whereabouts remain an unsolved mystery. I knew there was a will somewhere, but where?

Jay's office was another possibility. Most people file a will with the lawyer who drafted it. Since Jay wrote his own will, I hoped he had kept a copy at his office. I called to say I would be in to clean out his papers. Jay worked not far from home in a small office building in a quaint town, a stop along New Jersey's inland waterway, a canal built early in the 19th century to transport iron ore from the interior of the state to its harbor seaports. Replaced by the railroad, the canal was filled in and is known now only by assorted signs that mark its passing. When I arrived at the office, the job was done. Jay's personal papers and belongings were packed in a few boxes and one of the men helped me carry them to the car.

The secretaries sat at their desks, uncomfortable, not knowing what to say. It was a small staff and we occasionally saw each other at dinners or parties. They said they hoped I would keep in touch. We always say that. When someone moves thousands of miles away, I urge her to call or write. I tell her I'll definitely come to see her when I am in — _____ (fill in the blank). I know I will never see her again but saying goodbye is painful.

With each parting, we are giving up a little part of ourselves and our past. I remember a friendship quilt I once saw in a museum. Such quilts, assembled from squares stitched by friends and family, were created for special occasions, usually a wedding or a new home. The squares included pictures or writing, and sometimes, signatures to remind the recipient of the loving person whose needle, thread and nimble fingers contributed to the quilt. The quilt I saw was a gift to a young woman in the nineteenth century who was leaving her east coast home to move west with her husband. One of her friends wrote that although they never again "on this earth would meet" she hoped they would see one another in heaven. In these days of instant communication and rapid travel, we maintain the illusion that future contact will occur. The women who stitched the quilt acknowledged and accepted the finality of partings. Their friend was lost to them for their lifetime. My grandparents left Russia knowing they would never see their parents or their village again. A letter was the most they could hope for. They believed in heaven; we have jet planes, telephones and e-mail. I never saw or spoke with the secretaries again.

I hastily drove home, opened the car trunk and without taking the boxes out, rifled through the papers like someone in a spy movie who has broken into the office where the secret files are kept and has twenty seconds to find and photograph all the material. I opened any envelope large enough to contain a will, looked in all the file folders, rummaged through the loose material. There were years' worth of papers but the will was not among them. Angrily blaming the boxes and their contents for being useless, I stored them in the garage and waited for months before returning to any of them. I looked throughout the house. Jay kept papers everywhere—in closets, on shelves, in shoeboxes in the attic, in his desk, even in cartons in the garage. I never found his will. Maybe he had one and destroyed it, maybe he never had one and only told me he did, and maybe he had one that I will find some day when I am looking for something else. I decided I had to move on without it.

In the meantime, trouble came from another source. Highmount Memorial Hospital called to say that Jay's Social Security number as I gave it to them was incorrect. A quick look at his papers revealed that the number on his medical insurance card was wrong and he had not bothered to correct it. I was angry at him for this because it was the number I had given to both hospitals as well as the funeral home. The wrong number was on the death certificates and I had already mailed out several. I called the County Hall of Records expecting a major bureaucratic snarl involved in changing the certificates. I was pleasantly surprised to learn that I could take Jay's Social Security card, which I had found while searching for the will, to the county office. New certificates would be issued immediately for a nominal fee.

All of this adversity sounds as if I was encountering more difficulties than anyone should have to bear. Actually these were administrative tasks that had to be done and I saw them as such. In my view of life, they did not weigh heavy on the scale of things to be upset about. Little could be worse than what I had already endured. Lynn told me that a few months after her tragic fire and loss of her daughter, she drove over a curb. Two of her tires immediately became flat. Normally, she would have been upset about the tires. In the scope of her suffering, such an occurrence seemed insignificant. Like Lynn, my determination to get past life's smaller roadblocks actually kept me going. I developed a sense of priorities about what was essential, what was important and what wasn't worth worrying about.

Administering Jay's estate would have been easier with a will but I viewed its absence as just one more administrative hurdle. I called a lawyer, a family friend, to ask him what my next step should be. He said I had to go to the Office of the County Surrogate and offered to accompany me. He promised to make an appointment and call me back. Next I called my friend Carol, who practices law in New York, specializing in the planning and administration of estates. She was my freshman college roommate whose mother had died shortly before we met, two eighteen-year-olds with little in common, except that we were both Jewish, which was how Mount Holyoke paired people at the time. While I am tall and reserved, Carol is small and outgoing. I admire her energy. She is like a hummingbird always in motion. When we met, I was an athletic country girl who arrived at college, to Carol's amazement, with three pairs of sneakers, red, white and blue, left over from my cheerleading days. Most girls, as we were called then, owned one pair of white canvas Keds. When we had to choose our required gym courses, I always picked swimming or tennis. Carol chose "Dance and Movement." She learned to sit and walk straight, which I suspect she already knew, as well as the proper way for a lady to get into and out of a car. Carol was a cosmopolitan New Yorker who took me to Radio City to see the Christmas show during winter vacation.

Our interests eventually converged. I am not sure what I have contributed to our long friendship but Carol has been a strong source of support for me on many occasions. Since Jay died, she has guided me every legal step of the way and I rarely make any legal decision without consulting her. She told me that laws for dying "intestate" (without a will) are different in each state so she could not advise me on how New Jersey would handle the estate. She suggested that I call the County Surrogate, who administers such matters, to ask if I would need a lawyer. The person who answered the phone at the Surrogate's office scheduled an appointment for me and said I could come without a lawyer if I chose. The lawyer who promised to accompany me never called back so I went alone. I was required to bring a list of all assets that were listed solely in my husband's name. Although most of our assets were jointly held, Jay was the sole owner of several stocks, a car and a small bank account.

The Sunday following Jay and Barry's deaths, Carol came to my house by bus, bringing a New York coffee cake which she knows I love and the previous day's business pages from the New York Times. "Hold on to this, you will need it to establish the value of Jay's stocks," she advised. The value of an estate is the value on the day of death so the stock listings were important. Jay, like many small investors, held on to his stock certificates rather than register them with a broker. It was my responsibility to determine their worth. Most people do not think about saving a newspaper when someone dies but having it can save a lot of time later on.

I typed a list of Jay's stocks and the value of each on the day he died. I went to the library, looked up the value of his year-old car, and took the list, along with a death certificate to the Surrogate's Office. The office is in a complex of county courthouse buildings that sits on a hill not far from the hospital where Jay died. The oldest building has served the county's needs since before the Civil War and is familiar to people who have served on a jury, applied for a passport or registered to vote. The Surrogate's Office was on the third floor of a new building across from the county jail. I registered at a counter and was directed to the waiting room. It was a pretty, sunny room with prints on the wall showing the town in earlier days. Unpaved roads surrounded the town green, ladies carrying parasols strolled to shops, new citizens holding tiny American flags proudly posed on the courthouse steps. In the crowded waiting room, people sat in clusters of two or three—each group including a lawyer who could be easily identified as the only one in a business suit. A few clients had manila folders. One group included a baby in a stroller. I was the only one who came alone.

A probate clerk, a pleasant young woman in a green sweatsuit called my name and ushered me into a room big enough for only a desk and two chairs. We spoke about the purpose of my visit and she gave me forms to complete. When I returned the forms to her I noticed her long, red, perfectly manicured fingernails, each with a diagonal stripe across the top. She took all the paperwork and disappeared for fifteen minutes leaving me to regret that I had not brought something to read. The room was windowless and the gray walls were bare. With a bed instead of a table, the space could have been a jail cell. The longer I waited, the more nervous I became.

When the clerk finally returned she told me I would have to meet with the Surrogate. I was suddenly a teenager summoned to the principal's office. When I was in high school, my friend Lenore's mother drove us to school every morning. Meriden, at that time, was a factory town bisected by the railroad which ran north-south, New York to Springfield, Massachusetts. There were no tunnels or overpasses. To get from one side of town to the other, we were at the mercy of the railroad. You may wonder what all this had to do with being called to the principal's office. I lived on the west side of town. The high school was on the east. When a train came through, the gates went down and traffic stopped. Cars lined up for blocks on either side of the crossing. Everyone knew the schedules. Passenger trains were short, six or eight cars at the most, causing only a brief delay but a 100-car freight train guaranteed lateness. If we didn't get across the tracks before the 8 a.m. freight, we could not get to school by 8:15. Getting caught by the evening train meant missing the bus to an out-of-town basketball game.

Lenore was so fussy about her clothes that she ironed them before school every morning. Her perfectly starched and unwrinkled white blouses caused both of us to be late at least once a week, but I was the one that the dean scolded. I anticipated the call as I sheepishly slipped behind my homeroom desk hoping the teacher wouldn't notice. Miss Boyle, called a dean although she was an assistant principal of a public high school, was a tough disciplinarian. As she reprimanded me, I hung my head or stared at the wall behind her, afraid to look at her stern face. "If you continue this lateness, you will never get into college," she scolded. "Yes, Miss Boyle, I won't be late again." Blaming it on Lenore would have been useless. Miss Boyle would have told me to walk to school as she did when she was a girl before cars were invented. Winter mornings were harsh in central Connecticut, the distance was well over a mile, and I had no intention of walking. Miss Boyle was an agreeable person when she wasn't in her disciplinarian role. She tutored me in Latin for the SAT's and my score was high enough to convince college admissions officers of my worthiness, despite my chronic lateness and the dean's dire warnings.

The railroad still divides Meriden but the trains are few and the factories are gone. An elevated superhighway built in the 1970's cuts through the town from east to west at treetop level. Driving on the highway, high above town, I feel like Wendy, flying with Peter Pan over rooftops that towered above me when I was a child walking to school on the streets below.

These were my thoughts as the County clerk escorted me to a bright office with white walls and dark colonial-style furniture. The Surrogate rose, shook hands and greeted me warmly. As an elected official, he had a politician's demeanor. His broad smile, eye contact, and good handshake were asking for my vote but his friendliness reassured me. He was efficient and respectful. After looking at the forms I had completed and the list of assets, he explained the New Jersey laws regarding dying intestate. The Surrogate said he felt I would administer the estate honestly and fairly, and issued "Letters of Administration" a form that came in the mail a few days later, bearing a shiny gold seal. The Surrogate's Office pleasantly dispelled my expectations of government bureaucracy and inefficiency. The frustration of negotiating the government maze would come later from the Federal agencies that I would have to deal with. At least the county experience was a good start.

Sitting at Jay's desk, I turned my attention to the two life insurance policies that he owned. After the experience with the will, I was afraid that they might not be in order. The smaller of the policies was with a New York insurance company that I contacted directly and received a check within the week. I called the independent agent who had sold Jay the larger of the two policies. He had heard of Jay's death and seemed to anticipate my call. I wondered why he hadn't called me. He instantly quoted the amount I would receive and promised to contact the insurer. Obtaining the money was not the simple procedure it should have been. I had to complete many forms and make several phone calls to acquire what was owed me.

Since most insurance companies are also in the investment business, a company representative asked whether I wanted to receive the money in a lump sum or have it invested by the company and paid to me according to a schedule. With the second option, I would never see the money and would have little control over how it was invested. I chose to receive the full amount. I wanted to see my name on the check, to hold it in my hand, my dead husband's gift to me. When it finally arrived I wept. Jay's insurance, in addition to my job and savings, would provide me with financial security but at such a cost. He had faithfully paid his premiums so that I could be free of financial worries. Like the will, I thought insurance was something I would need in a future that was still hazy. We would talk about it sooner or later, when we were old—that frontier that continues to push farther away the more we age. When Jay was alive, I never thanked him for assuring my financial future. Now I will never be able to.

With the insurance in hand, my financial affairs seemed to be progressing. I cannot overstate the relief I felt knowing that, with careful planning and some hard work, I could count on a secure future. My years of employment had provided me with a marketable skill and a bank account that enabled me to be self-sufficient. I was still a long way, however, from having my business affairs all in order. The next challenge soon appeared. Searching among Jay's papers a few months after his death, I found vouchers for estimated income tax, both state and Federal that were due <u>the previous month</u>. This was something I knew nothing about. I thought taxes were due in April and that I had at least another month to start thinking about them. Whether he prepared them himself or paid someone else to do it, Jay had always handled the taxes. It was his area of expertise and one that I cared to learn little about. Each year I collected all the information pertinent to my income, expenses and charitable giving, handed it all to him and signed the returns when they were completed, which, when Jay did the job, was usually the day they had to be mailed. I knew I would have to find an accountant but I hadn't counted on finding one so soon.

Since we were both self-employed and did not have taxes withheld by our employers, it seemed we were required to pay estimated taxes on a quarterly basis. I had no idea of how much to pay and the deadline had already passed. It was like a dream where I am in college and have to take a final exam but have never attended the class. I am walking down long halls in strange classroom buildings, not knowing if I am on the correct floor, looking for a classroom where I will have to answer questions about math or English when I have never seen the problems or read the book. I have learned that this recurring dream is common among adults. Many of us are still failing the examinations of our youth.

The tax problem was not a dream I could awaken from but I pushed it off, deciding to ignore it. A few weeks went by. The husband of a friend I was visiting told me he had paid a big fine for a delay in making Social Security payments for a household worker. "Don't fool around," he warned. "You'd better send in a payment." Suddenly, making this payment seemed urgent. I panicked, deciding it had to go out immediately, in that day's mail, but I didn't know how much to send and I couldn't reach Carol. If I had looked at Jay's check book I could have sent in the same amount he had paid the previous September. I could have asked someone for advice. This is hindsight talking. With a pathetic faith in Uncle Sam, I figured I would receive a refund if I paid too much and would probably not end up in jail if I underestimated. I had already avoided prison when I gained access to the safety deposit box. I could do it again. I wrote a $1000 check to the Internal Revenue Service for the Federal tax, mailed it to the address on the voucher and put the state voucher, unpaid, back into the drawer.

Then I started to look for an accountant. Someone recommended Jack Ward who another widow had used and liked. When I called to make an appointment, his secretary recognized my name. "I knew Jay," she said. She had previously worked for a lawyer who had business dealings with my husband. "How are you doing?" she asked in the same tone everyone used, as if speaking to an elderly invalid. I assured her that I was fine. She transferred the call to her boss. Jack told me to bring the tax returns from the previous year as well as all the supporting material for the current tax year— income statements from employers, interest and dividend statements, self-employment expenses, medical expenses, charitable donations. This was not difficult since it was the same information I had gathered yearly for Jay. The hard part was piecing together Jay's end, trying to figure out what bank accounts he had opened or closed, what stocks he may have sold. I did the best I could and took whatever I thought was relevant to my first meeting with Jack.

His office was on the second floor of a building in a group of look-alike structures that were part of an office complex. From the outside, the buildings looked like two-story garden apartments, as if the architect had used the plan before for housing but changed them slightly to turn them into offices. By the time I arrived in the evening, the secretary had left. From his office, just off the small waiting area, Jack heard me arrive and came to meet me. He was tall with blue eyes that seemed too pale for his dark brown hair. He escorted me into a large office with the usual framed diplomas and licenses, pictures of blonde children, bookcases stuffed with black binders of codes and regulations, a computer and a large desk piled with papers.

As with any first meeting, I tried to assess him and how our relationship might proceed. A quick calculation of his diploma dates showed him to be in his early forties. He was friendly and casual, leading me to believe we would get along. A different and darker side to his personality would later appear but that was still a few months away. I handed him the previous year's tax returns and all the information I had collected. I felt like a student handing in a term paper to be graded and watched anxiously as he looked at the material I gave him. Slowly, as I squirmed in the chair, he shuffled through the papers and made pencil check marks on the old return. I had never seen an accountant in action before. Is this what's known as ticking and tying? "Well, it's all here," he stated. It's all there? I was so relieved I wanted to jump up and dance but of course I didn't. Waltzing around an accountant's office to a tune only I could hear would not have been dignified. In fact, it would have been downright crazy. I sat in my chair, smiled and used my best business voice to say that I was glad to know that the papers were all in order.

I told him about the $1000 I had sent to the IRS for the estimated taxes. I had underestimated to some extent but the penalty would not be too hefty and would not involve prison. He answered my questions and I made a list of things to look for or find out so he could complete my tax returns that would be due in April. We briefly discussed my financial situation and I expressed the desire to work with a financial planner but was not yet ready to do so. Jack said 98% of financial planners are selling something and he recommended finding someone who would have no financial interest at stake in the advice he or she gave me. I promised to think about it. Jack completed my tax returns well before the April deadline. He gave me vouchers which indicated amounts due for the quarterly estimated tax to the Federal and state governments. No more guess work. I told him I would call later in the year when I was ready to develop a comprehensive plan for my financial future.

In addition to income tax, I would have to file Federal and state estate tax returns reporting Jay's assets. My friend Carol offered to prepare the Federal return for me. This process of evaluating and reporting an individual's assets is tedious and time consuming. I didn't realize until I saw the completed return what a magnanimous gesture this was for Carol to offer her services in this way. The Federal government was always good for a laugh. First I had to apply to the Internal Revenue Service for an EIN, Employer Identification Number. The government gave no explanation as to why a private estate must obtain an Employer Identification Number. I applied. The IRS sent the following reply: *Based on the information shown on your Form SS-4, you must file the following forms(s) by the date we show. Form 1041 04/15/95. If the due date (04/15/95) has passed, please complete the form and send it to us by **2-21-95**. If we don't receive the form by that date additional penalties and interest will be charged.*

Another asset that had to be valued was my house. To determine the value of Jay's half I had to have the house appraised. I called a professional appraiser to do the assessment. I hoped the appraisal would be high because when I sell the house I will have to pay capital gains tax on the difference between the value of the house when I inherited it and the selling price. I wanted that gap to be as narrow as possible. The appraiser did a very thorough job. He measured the rooms, noted every convenience, took pictures and then rated the house according to comparable houses that had recently been sold. He came up with an assessment that was much lower than I thought I could sell the house for. Our egos are so tied up in our homes.

I asked a friend who sells real estate what she thought. Not wanting to commit herself she admitted it sounded "a tad low." Disappointed, I called the appraiser.

"How can you compare my house to the one on Harbor Lane?" I argued. "My house has a beautiful view. It has charm. My street is nicer."

"We do not measure view or charm, Mrs. Schocket," he responded coldly. "We go by square footage, lot size, condition." He stood by his appraisal. I spoke with my accountant, who said that the IRS had accepted an appraisal by realtors who provided the service free of charge for one of his clients. I called a local real estate agency that was pleased to do the job. Two cheery ladies came to the house. They poked into closets, oohed and aahed over the new bathroom, loved the view from the living room window and came up with a considerably higher appraisal. Maybe that's why women succeed in residential real estate. In addition to measuring and counting, they see things that the men miss. Carol completed and filed the tax return and I moved on to new challenges in the process of staking my financial future.

As the months went by in that first "winter of my discontent", my emotions see-sawed from anger to sorrow, disbelief to resignation. When my husband and son left me, I was like a building whose foundation has begun to crumble. The building leans sideways, then without its foundation for support, suddenly collapses. When my life collapsed, I had to build a new foundation and then new supports to put my structure back together but I didn't know how to go about the building process. Having discussed the so-called "stages of grief" in outplacement classes, I knew that as a victim of loss I would experience emotions beyond my control. But until tragedy actually turned my life inside out, I did not understand how shock, anger, guilt, denial, bargaining and depression could become my constant companions, as familiar to me as my own two hands.

Stages

My experience with sudden and complicated loss was limited and unique. Yet I knew there were commonalities. Otherwise, why would mourners seek out one another for support? We spend hours on the Internet looking for another person thousands of miles of away who will respond, "Yes, that's exactly how I felt too." We read piles of books and seek out support groups to find a glimmer of assurance that we are not alone in our pain. To validate my own feelings and actions, I interviewed people I knew who had lost loved ones and I communicated on the Internet with many others.

I asked them to describe how they felt and what they did immediately following the deaths and as time passed. Several told me that they awoke from a fog after six months. The sudden change from being married to being single, from being a parent of two to being a parent of one or none, from being a sister to becoming an only child, was so wrenching that every fiber of their physical and mental being was affected. They said that time lost its meaning and nothing at all took on any urgency. "I felt as if I had stepped off the world for a while," commented my friend Lynn after her only child died. They spoke of their anger, guilt, sorrow, loss of confidence, confusion and depression. Bonnie, 30 years old, whom I met on the Internet, lost three brothers and a nephew within three years. She said that after the last death she cried constantly and did not move from the couch for almost two weeks. When the light bulb went out in her kitchen, she called a friend to change it for her. "Now that I think about it," she said, "I don't know why I even cared about the light at all." Unlike those who do nothing, I did too much. I was on automatic pilot, working, shopping, cooking, going about my life at a hectic pace as if nothing at all had happened. Yet inside I was suffering so severely I didn't know if I could live through another day.

Thinking I could handle it, I returned to work within a few weeks. I did a workshop for three women who had lost their office jobs at one of the big discount stores nearby. One of the women cried the whole first day. I kept thinking, "Lady, you don't know what trouble is," but of course I had to be upbeat and try to help her cope with *her* loss. I had difficulty concentrating and went home depressed. I knew then I should not have taken that assignment. A few weeks later, I went to a corporate site to do a workshop. A company that manufactured baby products— cups, teething rings, infant toys, was closing within a month and the workers were all about to lose their jobs. Only the office employees and the supervisors were entitled to outplacement counseling. The hourly workers, women who worked on the assembly line and men who drove the fork-lift trucks in the huge warehouse, were told that their jobs were over and sent to the nearest unemployment office.

We held the workshop in a small room used for meetings. There was no flip chart so we propped up an ancient blackboard against two chairs and I used that for my lists, charts and words of wisdom that they might want to write down. I enjoy working in plants. The people are not spoiled by corporate entitlements and are usually realistic about their prospects. This group was appreciative and didn't take their anger out on me, as some groups do. They made room for my lunch bag in their refrigerator and shared their coffee at the beginning of the day. It was a good place for me to be to ease my way back into the work force. In the same industrial park was a factory outlet of a well-known manufacturer of casual sport clothes. No one loves a bargain more than I do, so after work I headed straight for the outlet. Looking for the magic pill, I hoped that some new clothes would make me feel better. But once inside, I could not concentrate on anything. All the clothing looked alike. None had the slightest appeal. I wandered around staring at sweaters and pants and sweatsuits. I picked up a shirt to try it on and put it back on the shelf. I couldn't imagine what I would do with any of it. I was so defeated and dejected, I left the store and went home.

Dr. Elizabeth Kubler-Ross, an authority on death and bereavement, wrote that people who are about to die, as well those who survive the death of loved ones, experience similar psychological stages, which she identified as isolation, denial, anger, bargaining, depression and acceptance. (Kubler-Ross, 1969) Although the stages appear to be in a sequence, they may occur in a different order, all at the same time and some may not occur at all. Where grief is concerned there are no rules. Working through the stages toward acceptance is a process that some psychologists describe as grief work. Before my tragic losses, I told participants in my job search classes that, for many, job loss is devastating and those who are jobless experience many of the stages of grief. I compared job loss to divorce or a death in the family. I wanted people to know that what they were feeling was not unusual. I gave them advice about what to expect in each stage and how to overcome their grief. Was I mistaken.

I have lost jobs and been upset at the time. I suppose I felt some of the grief stages, especially anger, denial and depression, but losing a job is nothing like losing a person. It's not in the same realm of experience; it's in a completely different frame of reference. When I lost my husband and son, there was nothing on this earth that I could compare it to. My only comparison could come from others who had suffered similar loss. I wanted to know how they dealt with their anguish and sorrow. I needed verification for my pain and my behavior. "Emotional grief triggers incredible emotions and lacerates a survivor with such swift power that [it] paralyzes even the strongest, smartest, and most responsible individuals. Knowing the stages or phases of the emotion may help you to cope with the feelings and to understand that you are not going crazy," wrote Eva Shaw. (Shaw, 1994) Understanding the stages of grief helped me to give a name to some of what I was going through but it didn't always happen in the neat way that the theory describes. Knowing the name of the emotion I experienced was intellectually useful but it didn't help me to feel better, just as knowing one has a toothache doesn't cure the pain. Yes, I felt angry, guilty and depressed, but it took years to address those feelings and learn to live with them. In the meantime, while integrating the loss into my being, I had to find a way to continue my life.

I had not had time to absorb Jay's death, even to comprehend that he was gone, when Barry was stricken. As I waited in my comfortable family room filled with family pictures, books and souvenirs of long ago travels, while upstairs the emergency technicians tried to save him,

I was numb. I was no longer a person but more like a mechanical toy that keeps repeating the same the message. "This can't be happening," I assured myself over and over. Never for a minute did I think that he would die. I wouldn't allow myself to engage in such thought. Barry was not ill. He was a healthy, 30-year-old man. He must have fainted. He would be fine in a few minutes. My husband had died the day before. Surely, Barry would not die too. I was already experiencing denial which, along with shock, is one of the first reactions to news of tragedy. "No, that can't be true," is our response to words that we fear are correct but cannot bear to hear. At the hospital when I actually heard the words, "We're sorry" from the priest and the social worker, my grief was so profound I could do nothing but lay my head on the table where we sat, and sob. For the first few hours, even denial was not there to protect me. Like having surgery without anesthesia, only the pain came through.

According to one psychologist, denial is a mechanism that enables us to adjust to a level of pain and sorrow that we can endure. It is a shock absorber that filters the unbelievable truth, letting it sink in slowly, drop by drop. (Volkan, 1993) By denying the death, we cling, however feebly, to the comfort of a reality that has vanished. During the first few weeks following the deaths, although intellectually, I "knew" I would never see my husband and son again, emotionally I had not yet accepted that they were gone. I conducted my daily life in a routine manner, doing what was needed. I expected the door to open at 6 o'clock and Jay to walk in with his briefcase. I literally waited for the sound of his car in the driveway. I expected the phone to ring and hear Barry's voice saying "Hi, Mom."

My sons sounded very much alike on the phone. Based on the two words, "Hi, Mom" I couldn't tell them apart. This created a lot of joking at my expense because invariably I guessed wrong. "A monkey would guess right 50% of the time," Barry told me. "You ought to be able to do better than a monkey." Time after time, as I guessed wrong Barry would remind me, "The monkey, Mom, remember the monkey." Shortly before Barry died Andy was at our house for the weekend. When Barry happened to call and said "Hi, Mom," I immediately answered, "Hi, Barry." He was amazed that I got it right. I never told him the reason. For a while after Barry's death when I answered the phone and someone said, "Hi, Mom," my mind's initial reaction was still "Which one is it?" Eventually, my mind adjusted. When someone said "Hi, Mom" I knew who was calling.

It is not unusual for people to see individuals who look like their dead loved ones. I have heard of people following someone down a street somehow believing it is their dead husband or sister. Jay's looks were not common so I rarely see anyone who resembles him, but Barry was the opposite. Six feet tall, medium build, dark hair— even when he was alive I often saw men who looked like him, especially from the side or back. I still see people who look like him. I stare at them wondering how Barry would look now instead of frozen in time at age thirty. Usually I quickly shrug off the idea that the person I see is my son because I know very well that Barry is dead.

But one day, I saw a man step off a bus and embrace a woman who was waiting for him. He was at least 25 feet away and I could not see his face, but my mind snapped. I was sure it was Barry. He wore Barry's denim jacket. He had the same haircut. I stood and stared at the couple while thoughts raced through my head. If only I could see his face. Could he have been alive all this time and not been in touch with us? Why would he want to disappear, and how did he do it? Did he walk out of the hospital? This all happened within seconds as I stood frozen at the bus stop staring at two strangers. Then my mind skipped back to reality as I sadly turned and walked away. This experience was also a type of denial, where one part of my consciousness has accepted the death while another still refuses to believe its reality.

Another aspect of denial is postponement. When death is anticipated, as in the case of terminal illness, some of the denial takes place when the illness is diagnosed. Mourners have said that they experienced their greatest shock and grief when the doctor gave the diagnosis of terminal illness. Although the grief is no less severe when the loved one eventually dies, the family has had some time to absorb the impending loss. If the death is sudden, there is no such time for mental preparation. People, consciously or not, find ways to postpone their grief by engaging in routine behavior. My friend Julie scrubbed her kitchen floor after receiving news of her daughter's death. She knew friends would be coming to the house and having a clean kitchen was something she thought was important at the time. At my home following the funeral, I engaged in the behavior that was most familiar to me—the gracious hostess greeting guests, making sure they were well-fed, showing them my new bathroom under construction. "Sandra is taking it remarkably well," people commented. The truth was I wasn't taking it at all, because the shock was so new I had not yet begun to absorb it. I was in denial for a long time and I learned from others that I was not alone in this. Two years after the deaths of Bonnie's brothers and nephew, she still felt she was in denial. "Of course I always understand that they are dead, but it is too easy to put it out of your mind and think they are only on vacation," she confided. In a way, Jay's death was not entirely unanticipated. Not that I expected him to die suddenly at 59 but in the back of every married woman's mind is the little thought that someday she may be a widow. Even without the statistics that support us in this, we can look around and see the evidence, at Saturday matinees in the theaters, in senior citizens' housing and, saddest of all, in the nursing homes.

Widowhood did not surprise me in the way that losing Barry did. I missed Jay in every unaccustomed task that I had to do, on every walk that I took alone, at every holiday and every happy occasion that was rendered joyless by his absence. But I had no template for missing Barry. Since he no longer lived at home, I suppose I already missed him a certain amount. Mourning him became postponed until all the little ways that I missed him began to pile up. The phone calls, the weekend visits, the knowledge that sank in so slowly that he would never be a father, never live to see the new century, to enter the career that he had studied and worked so hard for. Postponement of grief came in many forms— the unexpected tears triggered by a song that made the hurt as real as it was years ago, the lump in the throat seeing happy families embrace in the airport. I have experienced most of the elements of grief related to Barry's death but only the sadness remains.

Denial eventually gave way to anger, rage, envy and resentment. After "This can't possibly be true," came "why them, and why me?" Although I knew the statistics, was aware that thousands die of heart attacks, and thousands of young people die annually, I felt isolated and violated that this had happened to me. Mourners become angry at the person who died, at others who are still alive, at doctors and hospital staff and at people who seem insensitive to their loss. In this I was no exception. I was angry at Jay for not taking better care of himself. Right after his heart attack, when his life was in danger, I wanted only for him to live. When he seemed well on his way to recovery, I became angry at him for putting me through so much stress. We all know the experience. We await anxiously the arrival of a loved one who is driving in a terrible storm. We pray for his safe arrival. When he does arrive, instead of being overjoyed and thankful, we are angry at him for not leaving earlier, for not calling, for being out in the storm to begin with. All the "should's" were allies in my anger. Jay should have taken better care of himself, gone for regular check-ups, quit smoking. After his death, I was angry when I couldn't find his will and I was angry at myself for not knowing where he kept it. I "should" have known that. I was angry when I had to sort through papers that he "should" have thrown out years before and I was angry when I wanted to clip the shrubbery and found that the clippers had not been sharpened in years.

Several women told me about their anger. Paula, a widow in her thirties, went to her husband's grave and yelled at him when things went wrong. Cynthia's mother died two months after her son. She wrote: "I am angry at her for leaving me at the worst time in my life. I never had time to grieve for my son, and then she ups and dies on me also." My greatest anger, justifiably or not, was aimed at the doctor who "killed" my husband. Dr. Siegel called on Friday afternoon, the day Jay died, but I refused to speak with him. He called again during the following week. This time I answered the phone. Other than hanging up on him, I had little choice but to take the call. He said how sorry he was, which was about the only thing he could say. "I understand," I responded coldly although obviously I did not understand at all. I was so filled with anger at him that I did not ask the questions that a more sensible person would have asked. "What happened? What went wrong? You told me there is a 1 - 4% fatality rate with this procedure. If 96% survive this surgery, why did my husband die?"

My anger at others was a typical reaction, but I could never find a way to be angry with Barry. His death was so unexplainable and he was so blameless in its cause that I could not attach a moment of anger to it. Instead I directed my anger toward others. Only a few months after Barry died, a friend described to me over the phone every detail of her son's upcoming wedding, to which I was not invited. She went on and on about where the cocktails would be served, how the wedding party would walk in, what the menu would be. I listened silently, but I wanted to shout, "My son was married less than two years ago. He too had a beautiful wedding and now he is dead. Can't you understand that what you are telling me is painful for me to hear?" How I resented her beautiful wedding and her babbling on about it. I listened politely and a month later I looked at the pictures. She didn't mean to hurt me. She simply didn't understand that sharing her joy was beyond my ability at that time.

Another friend called me describing in detail the trials of taking her 85-year-old mother to the eye doctor. She wanted my sympathy, but I had no patience for her complaint. I had gone through that for years with both parents and my later troubles rendered such events trivial. I reminded her she was lucky to have a mother to take to the doctor. She called me back an hour later apologizing for her lack of sensitivity. Actually it was I who should have apologized to her. Both of these women would do me a favor at a minute's notice and I should have been more tolerant of their conversation. In early December, shortly before Jay and Barry died, I sent out a few Christmas cards with notes saying the year had been uneventful. I mentioned this to someone later on. He joked, "That will teach you not to send out your cards so early." I nearly gasped at his tactless remark. Eventually, I learned to tolerate insensitive comments that were not intended to hurt.

Although psychiatrists tell us that anger is normal, there is a danger if it becomes prolonged. Anger at the dead as well as at those who say the wrong things may help at first, but I had to learn to overcome it. My anger at Jay occurred early on and has subsided over the years, or perhaps has become something else. My anger toward others has lessened because I know I cannot use it to become an eternal victim. My suffering does not give me the right to expect special treatment from others nor to be angry when they do not understand my need. I remind myself that friends as well as strangers owe me nothing. Kindness and understanding are a gift not my entitlement.

Bargaining is another phase of the mourning process. My mind, at first, denied the sad events that occurred. When denial no longer worked, I became angry at people and God. But anger was not a productive emotion. I had to find some other mechanism for removing myself from this painful situation. Maybe bargaining would help. We see a similar reaction in children or teenagers who are told they cannot do something. First they get angry, then they try to bargain by volunteering to do something around the house that they would never do under normal circumstances. When Andy was in graduate school he rented a house in the country and adopted a dog he called Hobbs. Andy loved Hobbs and the dog, who had never had a good home, returned the affection. The following year Andy moved to a house in town which did not allow pets. Andy begged Jay and me to take Hobbs, a sweet affectionate animal but rather large and unruly. Jay wouldn't admit that he was afraid of dogs, and I didn't want the responsibility, so adopting Hobbs was out of the question. Andy pleaded desperately, "I'll wash all the windows in your house," he promised. The answer was still no, but I couldn't blame Andy for trying to make a bargain. (Hobbs eventually found a good home.)

But who hasn't bargained when circumstances are bleak? I often try to bargain with God. "Please God, let my x-ray be normal and I will never ask for anything again." For a mourner, bargaining is only fantasy. We have no leverage. What would I give to have my husband and son again? We have all used the expression, "I would give my right arm" — "Yes, God I would give my right arm. But it's an all or nothing deal. For my right arm I want both of them, healthy and strong." A woman whose whole family was killed said she would live in the gutter, if only she could have them back. On my way to New York, I pass through a gritty area that was once residential but is now a mix of warehouses and freight yards. On a busy street directly under a six-lane highway overpass are five small wooden row houses. They front directly on to the street which has probably been widened to accommodate the trucks and buses that constantly thunder by. The houses are well-maintained. Cars are parked in front. The people who live in these houses go to work, celebrate life's joys, watch TV and probably complain about the same things that I do. When I pass by, I think about a sad song I used to hear on the radio as I commuted to work. A lonely man sings that he would give up his heart, his home and all he owns if he could just have the one he loves back again. Would I give up my beautiful home to live in a shack if Jay could live there with me, and Barry could call to say, "Hi, Mom?" Yes, God, I would. Send them back to me and the movers would be on the way.

A widow told me she wished she could have even her worst day back when her husband was alive. Maybe I'm selfish but if I ask for only one day, I want it to be my best. Not an average day, but an extraordinary day. I want my day to be July 4th, 1986 when New York celebrated the 100th anniversary of the Statue of Liberty. As part of Liberty Weekend, two million people were expected to visit the city for the celebration and to view the parade of Tall Ships as they sailed up the Hudson River. For the week preceding the holiday, all the media warned about not driving to the city where colossal traffic jams were predicted. I decided early on that, although I love celebrations and marvel at the Tall Ships, New York with its loud, pushy crowds and aggressive traffic would be a place to avoid on that day. I didn't want to go. To accommodate tourists arriving from throughout the world, the city had set up a campsite in a large city park near Shea Stadium. On the evening TV news on July 3rd, a reporter interviewed people from Nebraska, Florida and Pennsylvania camping out in New York City. Standing in front of their tents and R.V.s they told New York viewers how excited they were to be there and how much they were looking forward to the July 4th events. The weather forecast was for a perfect day—sunshine, low humidity, temperatures in the 80's.

The following morning I awoke to find the glorious day that was promised. Bright blue cloudless sky, just hot enough to be July 4th but not so hot that moving around sapped one's energy. I thought of the people who had traveled thousands of miles to come to New York and here we were, 40 miles away. How could we not go? Jay and Andy were in the kitchen eating breakfast. "Would you like to go to New York?" I asked. They readily agreed. I went upstairs to wake up Barry and was surprised that he wanted to come as well. He rarely accompanied us on family trips considering himself, at 22, too old and sophisticated for such outings. I put on blue shorts and a white shirt with red trim. If I was going to be a tourist I might as well look like one. Andy also dressed in flag colors but Jay and Barry were above all that. They wore clothes they would have worn on any other summer day.

Jay suggested that we drive to Newark and take the train. We drove on empty roads, parked near the train station and took a commuter train to the World Trade Center. The train was filled with holiday riders— families with baby carriages, folding chairs and enormous picnic chests, groups of young people, the men carrying beer in lunch coolers, the girls in colorful jewelry and short shorts. As we crossed the meadowlands, the buildings of lower Manhattan spread out before us like a stage set against the perfect sky. We emerged from the train to find the streets closed to traffic and the whole area strangely quiet. We walked along a deserted West Street following the Hudson River uptown and staked out our place from which to watch the ships. Off to our left across the water, looking no bigger than the replicas sold on the street stood The Lady herself, her newly refurbished golden torch glowing in the morning sun.

Battleships and aircraft carriers looked like bathtub toys bobbing out in the harbor. The predicted crowds began to arrive but there was room enough for all. By late morning the procession of ships began. First the fireboats from New York City, water spouting from their decks, the ugly ducklings preceding the swans to follow. And what a parade it was with ships from around the world. Tall-masted Scandinavian boats with sailors in glowing white uniforms standing, legs and arms spread apart, on the yardarms. There were double and triple-masted ships from England and Holland, Portugal, Italy and Indonesia— barks and brigantines, sloops and schooners. And darting about among the celebrity craft was a constant flow of private pleasure boats viewing it all from their own special vantage point.

In addition to the magnificent nautical pageant, we watched an ever-moving human parade of visitors strolling, walking, jogging and running in front of us. Some walked uptown to gain a better view, others headed downtown for the same reason. Toddlers held balloons tied to their wrists, teenagers ate cotton candy, young couples held hands, older people fanned themselves, strangers smiled as they greeted one another. With vendors hawking all manner of goods, lower Manhattan had become a giant street fair, Anytown, USA on the Fourth of July, the all- American holiday. Eventually we tired of the ships, relinquished our prized standing spots and found a small restaurant open for lunch. We got word that the downtown post office was open, hurried over and patiently waited in line for special issue postcards. We met people from England and Brooklyn, Maine and Minnesota. By late afternoon, we returned to our car, Andy wearing the green foam Lady of Liberty headdress he had bought from a street vendor. Yes, God, if it's not too much to ask, this is the day I want.

Another aspect of mourning, perhaps the most powerful, destructive and painful, is guilt. Almost everyone who has suffered the death of a loved one experiences some form of guilt. The guilt may be based on fact where someone has actually caused another's death but more commonly it stems from situations that were not controllable. We feel guilty about how we treated the person who died, about things we did or neglected to do and we feel guilt about our feelings and actions after they died. We may even see their deaths as punishment to us for wrongs or sins that we have committed. Our Western European culture, with its technological underpinnings, values the logical sequence. From religion to physics, if A is true then B must follow. We don't espouse the circular and the mystical. In looking for cause and effect, we may attempt to make connections where none exist. In our strong desire for everything to make sense, it is not difficult to feel guilty about events that are beyond the realm of explanation. Grasping for any truth, no matter how tenuous that might help me to understand my husband and son's deaths, my first inclination was to blame myself. I saw cause where there was only coincidence.

The morning that Jay died, just about the time that he was in surgery, I was at home cleaning up the breakfast dishes. A talk show was on the radio where listeners call in to speak with a psychologist. A woman called to say she was unhappy in her marriage but did not have the courage to leave her husband. She stayed with him because it was the easiest thing to do.

"Is having a man the most important thing to you, whether you are unhappy or not?" the psychologist asked.

"No it isn't," replied the caller.

"Then leave him," advised the psychologist.

"Thank you very much," the caller answered. She sounded relieved, as if she had the approval she needed to start packing her bags.

That's right, I echoed. That's what I should do too. Look at what he has put me through during this past week. When all of this is over and he has recovered, I am going to leave him. I said this out of distress and anger, not any real intention to leave. But what if somehow Jay knew I was planning to leave him and decided to leave me first? Unlikely. He certainly wouldn't choose death as his method of leaving. If he had wanted to leave, he could have packed a bag and cleared out at any time during our marriage. He even turned down sleeping pills in the hospital because he was afraid that if he took them, he might never wake up. I know there is no rational connection between his death and my anger at him but the knowledge does not prevent me from thinking about it. That's how guilt works.

So many of my Internet correspondents talked about their guilt: A woman felt guilty because her father and uncle's deaths coincided with the births of her children. "Stupid the ways the mind works," she said. "I figured I gave birth, He took loved ones." Another was helpless in preventing the suicide of a dear friend. She is consumed with guilt feeling she failed. A third did not invite friends to stay for dinner when they came to visit. Later that day they died in a fire. "If I had invited them to stay for dinner that night, they would be alive," she told me. "It's as though I haven't put a finish to this yet, and it happened over 20 years ago."

I felt guilty about the things I did and those I didn't do. As Andy, Barry and I sat on the living room sofa the morning of Jay's death, one of the things I said was, "I wish I had treated him better." He was dead only a few hours and guilt had already come to plague me. Like any long-term marriage, ours was not always smooth. I'm sure there were ways in which I could have made him happier, met his needs more, put his contentment ahead of mine. But that can be said of any relationship. I was also thinking about the radio show. As he lay dying in the operating room, I was not there. Furthermore, I was planning to leave because I was angry.

An unexpected death can trigger unresolved grief for a previous loss. I didn't understand then that some of the guilt I felt that morning was related to my father's death two years earlier. My father, who suffered from Alzheimer's Disease, contracted pneumonia in the nursing home where he lived in New Jersey. I begged the administrator to send him to Saint Agatha's, the hospital near my home but they sent him to a different hospital fifteen miles away. He had adjusted to life in the nursing home but in that hospital he seemed confused and hurt. His eyes had the look of a wounded deer. I knew he didn't understand why I had put him there. I visited every day spending as much time as I could with him. One Friday I took a day off from work so I could be with him. As I was about to set out for the hospital, the phone rang. It was my father's doctor. Dad had died that morning, alone in a strange hospital. I felt so guilty not being there with him. I also felt guilty because his illness may not have occurred if I had found a way to keep him at home rather than putting him into that nursing home. The guilt I bore from my father's death remained with me two years later when my husband died, also without warning, in a hospital and I was not there. Suddenly the deaths seemed linked. By staying away, I had failed my father and my husband. I was not there when they needed me and they each died alone.

There were other things that I neglected to do. Maybe Jay would have seen a doctor sooner if I had called and made the appointment. More important he might have lived if I had insisted on hiring the best doctor available after his attack. With Barry's death, the guilt was less tangible. Maybe I could have prevented his death by preventing Jay's. Barry's condition, according to research, was not hereditary, but could I have done something during pregnancy to harm his fetal heart? I asked a doctor about this. "Don't blame yourself," he told me. Blaming myself would create the type of cause-and-effect situation that helps us to make sense of the world although not a bit of evidence exists that would put me at fault.

My mother believed in a vengeful God who punishes us for our sins. She taught me to believe that we must pay for the good things in life and suffer for the harm we have done. My mother might have said I deserved what I got - as you sow, so shall you reap. Hearing her voice telling me so, I believed that these deaths were punishment for all I have done wrong in my life. But even if God was punishing me for my sins, why did Barry and Jay have to give their lives for such a punishment to be exacted? And surely Andy and Ellen have done nothing to deserve such tragedy. What terrible sins could they have committed that caused their loved ones were taken away? As Jay often responded when I asked questions that had no answer, "You tell me."

I felt guilty mourning one loss more than another. Going up and down like a see-saw, one always seemed more prominent than the other in my thoughts. If Barry had been my only loss, I would have been inconsolable. Yet coming a day after my husband's death, I had neither the space nor capacity to mourn them equally. I suffered from what psychologists call "bereavement overload." Because Jay's death required more of me, my mourning for Barry was delayed. This created more guilt because I did not have the strength, was not up to the job of giving Barry the full measure of mourning he deserved at the time he died.

Barry's death required no special behavior of me while I was overwhelmed by the work of the widow. Ellen performed the sad chores related to Barry's death. I was only a bystander. I had to create for myself a way that would enable me to grieve for him, to talk about him, to learn to live in a world that lacked him. But these behaviors, more subtle than the widow's, took longer to learn. I'm still struggling to integrate my role as bereaved parent into my being. I'm uncomfortable with the language. I know how to say "I'm a widow" because my marital status explains who I am but I hesitate to tell the tangled story of my "children." Although I want all the world to know how handsome Barry was, how beautiful in spirit, how kind in deed, I, a speaker and writer, lack the verbiage to convey this. I feel only guilt in my sad silence when I tell a stranger I have only one son and end there, erasing Barry from my life. I feel so guilty when someone refers to Barry's college and, like any other proud parent, I do not say "My son graduated from there." I know the next question will be, "What is he doing now?" So the layers of remorse and guilt accumulate - my father, husband and son, and the nagging guilt that cannot be assuaged eventually turns to sorrow and depression, one of the most pervasive aspects of mourning.

Depression is not a stage but a persistent condition to be fought and conquered daily, weekly, yearly. An unwelcome companion, it disappears for a time only to return when even a happy event becomes a bittersweet reminder of those who are not there to celebrate. I recognized the symptoms because, as a counselor, I knew them by heart: sadness and lack of purpose, fatigue, inability to concentrate, loss of confidence , indecision and poor sleep habits. All of those demons plagued me. Never a decisive person, I sometimes became paralyzed with indecision after Jay and Barry died. Suddenly the most common choices became weighty: roll or bagel, car or bus, sweater or jacket. I spent mornings staring at a closet filled with garments only to change my clothing three times before leaving the house. I changed my mind as frequently. If these picayune decisions were hard, imagine my difficulty in making larger ones, whether to sell a car, choose a vacation trip, or leave a job. Making sound decisions requires a confidence in one's own judgment, but defeated by tragedy I found my self-confidence in short supply. Choosing the wrong alternative could lead to further unhappiness which I already possessed in over-abundance.

I often awoke at 3 a.m., wide-eyed with no prospect for returning to sleep. Ellen suggested warm milk. I crept downstairs, the stone floor of the front hall cold to my feet and poured the milk into a small glass. If using a pot had been necessary, I probably would have stayed in bed, but the microwave made the job quick and simple. I sipped the warm milk in the chilly kitchen, my eyes squinting in the unaccustomed light and made my way back to bed to search for sleep. A friend who was a child in Berlin during World War II recommended processed cheese, a remedy Berliners used to comfort frightened children following air raids. I read whole books during the night then tried not to yawn, or worse, fall asleep at my desk in the afternoon. If I was planning to give a presentation or drive a long distance the following day, I dipped into the supply of

Valium that Barry had picked up for me the day before he died. But drugs, which offered quick and easy sleep, were an infrequent and last resort.

I was aware that serious depression can lead to suicide and requires professional help. Eventually I did see a psychologist but not because I consciously considered taking my life. As someone constantly apprehensive of finding a threatening lump or blemish, who sees each ache and pain as a dreaded sign of impending illness or malignancy, I cannot say I actively planned suicide. Nevertheless, on mornings when lying in bed listening to news, traffic and weather over and over seemed a better alternative to getting up only to face another depressing day, I can't say the possibility of ending my life didn't pass my mind. I thought of times in the past when I was depressed and why - my job was not going well, at least one son was having trouble or causing trouble in school, the plumber failed to show up, the baby sitter cancelled, the sun failed to shine for days, it was January. Each problem seemed big at the time, together they were overwhelming but I found ways to overcome them. I could do so again.

The last time I had been regularly depressed was half a lifetime ago when I was a young mother. After Barry was born, I did not work for a year and a half while I cared for him and attended evening classes while studying for my master's degree. I should have been the happiest woman on earth. I had a handsome husband with a good job who thought I was pretty terrific, a beautiful healthy son, devoted parents and good friends. Yet my life seemed so inadequate. I didn't care much for housekeeping. I tried to be a good mother but couldn't spend the entire day amusing my child. With him on my lap or in his crib, I read book after book. Just before Jay was due to get home, I would plop Barry into the playpen and run around like a maniac picking up toys from the floor, washing the breakfast and lunch dishes and looking for something quick and easy to prepare for dinner. When I seemed a bit frazzled as my husband walked through the door, I told him about the tough day I had at home trying to get all my chores done. Jay was no fool and he probably didn't believe a word of it but it was not in his best interest to disagree. Among the books I read was Betty Friedan's *Feminine Mystique.* (Friedan, 1997 reprint) I identified with the yearning expressed in the book by college-educated women for a life beyond an immaculate kitchen and a good-looking husband who returned every evening to a beautiful meal in a well-ordered home. I longed for creativity and intellectual stimulation but my life was consumed by laundry - sorting socks, folding sheets, cooking and cleaning. No matter how much I scrubbed, the dirty fingerprints instantly reappeared on the light switch. Crumbs sprouted under the kitchen table and dirty sneakers lined the back hall.

I volunteered to do good works. Although I helped to raise thousands of dollars for worthwhile causes, and sat on the Board of Directors of several important women's organizations I did not see this as my professional mission in life. I resented spending hours putting together the centerpieces for the gala ball even though they were important in making the event a success. I went into cold sweats each time I had to call members asking them to buy whatever we were selling for that year's fundraiser. Even the Board meetings were disappointing. Hoping to make weighty decisions and construct five-year plans that would achieve goals and objectives, I sat through meetings using my problem-solving skills to decide which desserts to serve at the annual dinner and whether mailings should go out first or third class.

There's more, I kept telling myself. My malaise came as a surprise to me since this was the role I was educated and groomed for from early childhood. I didn't start out to be a career woman. My parents' only goal for me was to marry the right man. My mother instilled in me the desire, not to be successful myself, but to be the wife of a successful man, successful meaning rich. I would bask in the light of his accomplishments. College did little to change my aspirations. At Mount Holyoke, a woman's college which, we were told, offered an education equal to that of the finest men's colleges, we were prepared to become capable wives, mothers and civic leaders. A career was something one did, however briefly, until ready for these more appropriate goals. Most of us bought into the plan. The object was to have the engagement ring on the finger by last semester of senior year.

My first hint that the life of a happy housewife might not be for me came during my junior year in college when my mother had surgery and I was called home to take care of her, my father and brother. They required three hot meals a day: a cooked breakfast – corn flakes would not do, a casserole or warmed up leftovers for lunch and a full course dinner. An inexperienced cook, it seemed my whole day was filled with kitchen chores. I no sooner got breakfast served and cleaned up than I had to start preparing lunch. Day after day, it was the same routine.

Cook, cook, cook then try to get some housework done in between. "Is this what married life is like?" I asked my mother. "It does have a certain rhythm to it," she responded, not wanting to discourage me.

When I eventually assumed my destined role, the 1960's housewife, my early doubts were confirmed. It was not the life I wanted. I had a master's degree. I felt over-qualified for the job I was doing. I wanted an identity separate from wife and mother. I hired a sitter and went to work part-time as a counselor at a university. My job offered challenge, an opportunity to use my training and a focus. On the days when I didn't work, I cared for my son and went about my chores with a new dedication. I was committed to being a career woman.

Working in an academic setting was easier than returning to the corporate world. I had a flexible schedule and summers off. Still, when my boys were small, I was not popular with my friends and neighbors for doing this. They thought I was neglecting my family responsibilities. "We hated you," Julie confessed many years later after she, too, had returned to a responsible job using her MBA. Working women were controversial. My husband's role as a provider was suspect. To protect his image, he bragged about how much it cost him to send his wife to work. Day care as we now know it, was non-existent, but I always found a way for my sons to be well cared for while I worked. A series of sitters came to the house, some more kind and patient than others, until we finally found Mrs. Meers, a woman in her sixties. She loved my boys as if they were her own and cared for them until they were taller than she was. Barry and Andy grew up to be independent and confident young men, with a somewhat different view of a woman's role than they would have had with a mother at home full-time.

Returning to work after the deaths, I became very proficient at building a wall between my private and my professional self. When I presented a workshop, I had to face a roomful of people who had just lost their jobs so they weren't feeling so well either. Yet they looked to me for the assistance and encouragement that I was hired to provide. Before Jay died, I used to include stories about him in my talks but I erased his presence from my presentations in fear that someone would ask about him and I would have to tell my story. My employers trusted me to do a professional job despite my fragile emotional state, yet going out to new settings filled me with apprehension. Administrators and workshop participants are sometimes curious about the outsider who has come in to help them with their problems. They could not know that I needed help badly with my own. If there was talk of family I remained silent. The hurt was too new and I resisted discussing my family with strangers. My co-workers in the office were kind and understanding, bending over backward not to say the wrong thing, which they usually accomplished by saying nothing. They smiled at me and asked how I was in a tone that was different from the way they asked others. "How are you?" they asked with the emphasis on the middle word. I knew they didn't really want an answer so I told them what they wanted to hear. "I'm getting along all right," I said and they replied, "That's good," or something equally neutral and that was that.

One man periodically invited me to join him for lunch. He would ask me candidly how I was doing and I knew he actually wanted to know. I would tell him the truth. Talking about my feelings helped. As time passed, I began to dip my toe into the pool of disclosure ever so slightly, testing the water when I felt I might find an understanding acceptance. With another widow, with someone who had lost a child, a common bond made conversation easier. The fear of new situations, a definite occupational hazard for a consultant, gradually decreased. Soon I found it easier to look someone in the eye and say, "I am a widow." Stories about my husband gradually crept back into my presentations. In a one-to-one conversation, I might confide to a participant that I had a son who died, but mentioning Barry in a workshop is something I still cannot do. Someone suggested that telling my story would provide inspiration to those who have lost their jobs, helping them to overcome their adversity. But it doesn't work that way. I tell them about the man who made 155 networking phone calls to get a job. I tell them about the 68 year old sales clerk who went to secretarial school and got a good job as an administrative assistant. These are the stories that inspire them. Mine would be too depressing.

When people ask me how I deal with depression, I tell them I have found no single solution but would be happy to accept suggestions. One of my friends recommended a visit to a medium or psychic which was how she communicated with her dead daughter. She felt strongly that her daughter had received her messages and was trying to speak with her. She encouraged me to try to contact Jay and Barry. Several people have spoken of "sixth sense" experiences they have had - hearing voices, seeing shapes. I have not had such experiences and I am just too literal a person to believe that I can actually communicate with those who have left the earth. I occasionally speak to my husband and son but I would be pretty nervous if they spoke back. That is not to say that I think communicating with the dead is not possible for others. Mourners have to grasp for each bit of happiness they can find, taking whatever path will get them there. Sometimes, close to sunset, Jay and Barry send me a small rainbow in the western sky, not a spectacular semi-circle in bold Technicolor, just a short band of colored ribbons that attach themselves to a passing cloud, a sign to show me they're looking out for me. That's how we communicate, through a veil of tinted mist that collects in the evening sky. The little rainbow makes me smile. That's one of the ways I deal with depression.

Fortunately, I did not develop additional problems related to my losses as some mourners confided they had. One woman spent hours buying things through the Internet late at night when she could not sleep and is now deeply in debt. Another gained weight after her husband and sons died and is overprotective of her remaining children. Some people stay at home, uncomfortable and insecure in the outside world. Others are always on the move. I was in the latter category. In their sympathy notes, friends in distant places extended invitations to visit. I accepted most of them. My travels were therapeutic. Getting out of the house distracted me and helped me to forget, if only for a minute. I visited friends throughout the northeast, favoring those who lived on the seacoast or in the mountains. They treated me royally, offering not only beautiful surroundings and good food but warm companionship. I volunteered for business trips that took me out of town, even to areas not normally considered attractive destinations. My co-workers wondered why I would savor such assignments. The secret was I turned them into sightseeing trips.

Traveling gave me the opportunity to get into a different life, a new set of challenges. Arriving in the airport at a new destination, I went to the tourist information desk for maps and brochures of the area, and I chose the most interesting among them. In my rental car with unlimited mileage, I went to famous places like Niagara Falls and some I might never have seen such as Pennsylvania's Laurel Highlands, an area of natural beauty and historic interest. I visited palatial residences that have become museums, factories that are condominiums, and train stations that are shopping malls. I toured university campuses, admired magnificent gardens and wept at vast empty green fields that were sites of tragic Civil War battles. If the business trip was scheduled for one day, I turned it into two or three, paying for an extra night or two at the hotel. I attended professional conferences and seminars if they were held at an attractive resort. When the meetings were over, while others relaxed at the pool, I became an instant tourist. "You went to EPCOT three times in four days?" my colleagues inquired, implying that I should have outgrown such behavior by now.

In addition to the overnight travel, I always found day trips worth the effort. I left work at 4:30, went to New York to see a show and returned home at midnight, knowing the alarm would go off at 6:00 the next morning. I went to the Jersey shore, sometimes after a work assignment that brought me within an hour's drive. I love the shore at sunset when the wind calms down, the fishermen are out on the jetties and the sand catches a pink glow during that minute before daylight becomes twilight. Relaxing at the end of the day, I walked on the beach, sat on a rock dangling my toes in the frothy water and ate a crabmeat sandwich, coleslaw and French fries on the side. Then I drove back to a house that, like a beacon, continued to beckon me home but offered such a cold greeting when I arrived. I wish I could say that all this running around helped to make me feel better. My frequent flyer mileage accumulated and I put thousands of miles on my car seeking an elusive happiness that would not come.

8

Cycles

Until I was thrust so suddenly into the abyss of grief, my assumptions about death and mourning were naive. I knew that sadness had come to be my partner but I underestimated its depths and the length of its duration. We have become used to the "quick fix," the television solution where problems are solved in fifty minutes. We have difficulty accepting that some things take time, and recovery is one of them. I associated mourning with a group of activities that included attending a funeral, going to the cemetery, wearing dark clothes, saying prayers at certain times, lighting candles, crying, and perhaps attending a support group or seeing a psychologist. I assumed I would eventually resume a normal life, not quite healed but almost. A few years ago, a widow and I were discussing our lives over lunch. I told her that I had read a book saying that the death of a child is the worst possible loss. "No wonder I'm such a mess," I said, in a matter-of-fact tone that did not betray my anguish. "I incurred the worst possible loss the day after my husband died."

"You're not a mess," she answered.

"How do you know?"

"You're functioning, aren't you?"

"Yes, I am functioning, but how? Animals function. So do cars."

Functioning is a goal I can achieve but I want to believe there's more. I realize now that while mourning has its rituals and activities, the psychological aspect of grief continues long after we put away the dark clothes and return to our supposedly normal lives. These so-called stages that we go through are not exactly something we predictably outgrow, like adolescence or mid-life crisis, but are recurring states that become part of who we are. I spoke with a woman whose husband had died four months before. When I remarked that she must still be in shock, she replied that she had already left shock behind her. According to what she had learned in her bereavement class, shock lasts for two months, followed by ten months of grief, suffering, pain and mourning. After the first year, one reaches accommodation, conciliation and the search for a new identity. This seemed a little pat for me. I would like to see the edges blurrier, the time frames less structured. I cannot imagine waking up one morning and suddenly realizing that I had used up my ten months of mourning and had to move on.

In Hope Edelman's book *Motherless Daughters* she wrote: "Here's what I learned about grief...: It's not linear. It's not predictable. Someone did us all a grave injustice by first implying that mourning has a distinct beginning, middle and end... It's not real life. Grief goes in cycles, like the seasons, like the moon, ... one ends and a new one begins, slightly different than its predecessor, but with the same fundamental course." (Edelman, 1994) In mourning more than one person, I was caught up in the seemingly endless ebb and flow of grieving, going around and around like a rat on a treadmill - denial, anger, acceptance, anger, denial and so on, over and over. People whose single losses span many years consider themselves victims of multiple loss because, like me, they are trapped in grieving cycles that continue with no resolution in sight. Each new death brings on its own cycles of grief which overlap the previous phases, making resolution or recovery all the more distant. If I can never be my old self again - the person I was before my loved ones died, how do I know who my new self will be and who will help me to create this new self?

Psychologists and authorities on grief and mourning use various words to describe the state we are supposed to reach when we have come to terms with the deaths of our loved ones. Kubler-Ross defines acceptance as the last stage. (Kubler-Ross, 1969) Others use acceptance as the beginning of the mourning process. Yes, I accept that my husband and son are dead. Now what? I need a plan and a destination. I want to know how I will recognize a better place when I have reached it. These are some of the words experts use to describe the process of grieving and the result I am supposed to achieve: adjust, accommodate, reinvest, resolve, reorient, redevelop and recover. Friends and acquaintances, even relatives may use the term "getting over it." Six months after Barry died, a relative asked me how Ellen was doing. I responded that she was "extremely unhappy." "She isn't over it yet?" the man asked. He seemed surprised. I was amazed when several months later, he inquired again whether Ellen was "over it."

Mourners who have suffered painful loss know we will never "get over it." We seek other terms to explain that psychological place we live in. In the years since my husband and son have died, I have adjusted and adapted, accommodated and resolved but like most who have suffered tragic loss, I have not recovered. Recovery seems to imply that at some point, like winning a board game, or finding one's way out of a maze, there will be an escape route from the circle where an exit suddenly and magically appears and I will come out at the other end, the winner. When people I spoke with used the word "recover" the sense was usually negative: "I know I will never recover from the loss of my two sons," Wendy said. If recovery implies returning to the intact psychological life I had before my loved ones left me, I probably will never get there. The best I can hope for is an awareness that my grief may diminish but will never disappear. Like a scar that remains after the wound has healed, I can live with the scar but am different because of it. "I cannot help with your book," a woman e-mailed me, "but I can understand your suffering. Of course you will never get over it." It is doubtful that anyone truly gets over the death of a loved one but people cover their wounds and go on with their lives.

If complete recovery remains an elusive goal, I can, nevertheless, aim for a level of functioning that will lead to a happy and productive life. I think of the process as rebuilding. When my foundations crumbled, my psychological house was in ruins. I had to start from the ground up, brick by brick to build a new life. It took a long time to get to the first floor and I may never build a skyscraper but with each new layer I can look at where I've been and see where I still have to go. I can create a design for my new structure, making it bigger and more ambitious as I get stronger and better able to build. I can do some of the job alone but usually I need help. I asked other mourners, "What helps? How do you ease the pain?" They found various ways—some predictable, some unique. What works for some, does little for others. As my mother always reminded me, one man's meat is another man's poison, and a woman's too.

Devoted and caring family and friends are the most common source of support. Without family members available, my support comes totally from friends who continually amaze me with their generosity. From dinner invitations to rides to the airport, calls, notes, e-mails, I am blessed with the attention of those who were there not just on the first day when emotions ran high but for the long haul. I remember the small gestures, the singular acts of kindness that may have been routine to the giver but gained significance in the good they generated. On a cold Sunday afternoon not long after Jay and Barry died, my friend Helene called to ask if she could come to take a walk with me. She lives about 20 minutes away by car, but she left her husband and drove over. Shielded by down and wrapped in scarves we took a brisk walk around the lake, trying to make conversation as our words came out in frosty puffs that blew away on the chill wind. We were friends in college and renewed our friendship when marriage and our husbands' jobs brought us to the same state. One would think we have little in common but perhaps it is our differences that keep us going. She's a Midwesterner, one of five children. An accountant, her skill is numbers, mine is words. She loves opera, I love ballet. She walks, I swim. I don't remember what we talked about on our walk but I remember feeling better when I got home.

Some women who were barely acquaintances in my prior life have become good friends. I have learned, more importantly, that friendship is earned. Considering aid from others my entitlement, I waited for people to help and befriend me. I thought I deserved such treatment considering all I'd been through. Like Blanche in "A Streetcar Named Desire," I was dependent "on the kindness of strangers." But strangers and friends as well disappear quickly unless a reciprocal relationship develops. I am grateful for the hospitality and generosity of others. When Jay was alive, he was my best friend. I enjoyed the relationships I had with women, but they were not the necessity that they are now. Sharing friendships with those who have supported me has become my reward.

I have known for most of my life that I am not a person who takes well to groups, a trait I shared with my husband. Although we enjoyed the company of other couples, we did not seek out such companionship as often as we might have. Friends often called us to go to a movie, which surprised me whenever they did it. I did not consider a movie a social experience because so little conversation takes place throughout the evening. True, we discussed the movie and whatever else was occurring in our lives over coffee afterward but, to me, sharing a dinner would have been a more pleasant opportunity for getting together. We, on the other hand, usually went to movies and most other places alone.

Being part of a group was not something that came natural to me so seeking a support group was not an option that immediately came to mind when I needed help. I was aware of The Compassionate Friends (TCF), a national organization of bereaved parents because my friend Julie was very active in her local chapter. As the group's leader, she spent hours on the phone speaking with grieving parents, often following a long day of work and sometimes in the middle of the night. She edited her chapter newsletter which she frequently sent to me. Over and over, I read the beautiful articles and poetry written by parents whose dead offspring ranged from newborns to adults in their forties. I asked Julie why she devoted so much time to this cause. She said that attending TCF meetings had taught her to live with the pain of her daughter's death. In redefining her life, weaving the torn pieces into a new tapestry, she wanted to find new meaning and purpose. Her work with TCF gave her that purpose. If someone from The Compassionate Friends had reached out to me, I might have attended but I, who am so resourceful when I need to get somewhere or buy something, somehow never found the interest or the energy to look for a group. Even if I found one, I could not image walking into a roomful of strangers and telling my story.

Another problem rested with the type of support group I would attend. I could not find one for people like me who had lost more than one person in a short period of time. I feared being the only recent widow in a group for those who had lost children or the only bereaved parent in a group of grieving spouses. I thought they would not understand my losses, or that they would see me as someone trying to surpass them by doubling their loss. In a book I read later, a widower said a support group did not work for him because there was a feeling of "one-up-manship" about it, each one trying to outdo the next with his or her loss. Perhaps that was what I feared about telling my story. I had to seek a different path to healing.

Sometimes informal groups are as helpful as organized ones. I remember the ad hoc, on-the-spot mourning groups that developed among my parents' elderly friends as they lost spouses, siblings and lifelong friends. When my parents moved to Florida, they bought a condominium in a new development for senior citizens. Their friends and neighbors were lively, vigorous couples in their sixties who had moved south, confident that they had found an earthly paradise in which to enjoy their retirement. Having left their families "up north," they formed strong attachments to one another, sitting at the pool on lazy afternoons, playing cards and trading stories about their health, their successful sons-in-law and extraordinary grandchildren. They attended shows in the Recreation Center on Saturday night, played golf and shuffleboard, took occasional trips to Palm Beach and Nassau, and grew old together. Within ten years, ambulances visited the complex with unsettling frequency and so did death. Eventually funerals outnumbered parties. Each death reduced the resources of those who remained. The camaraderie of the gin rummy games was lost and fewer remained to drive a neighbor to a doctor's appointment. Those sitting around the pool became unofficial bereavement support groups. They discussed the deaths not only of those they knew but of lost relatives and friends who lived in other places. They helped one another to grieve until gradually younger people moved in and the cycle began to repeat itself. I had no such close community to help me cope with my grief but found help from those whose interests intersected mine in other ways.

My strength and consolation came from exercise. I love two sports—skiing and swimming. For me skiing is a challenge, a sport I could hardly consider to be relaxing. Much of the time I am either nervous, terrified or wondering why I have spent so much money on an activity that provides such a short amount of pleasure relative to the amount of time traveling and preparing to do it. But when I am making my way down the mountain, my concentration on the task is so complete that I can think of nothing else. My troubles are the challenges of the minute. The only thing that matters in my world is getting through the next set of bumps, over the icy spot and down the steep part. When I get to the bottom I feel such exhilaration. That's why I ski.

Swimming is for relaxation. On one of my ski trips to the Rocky Mountains, I stayed at a hotel with a heated outdoor pool. After a day of skiing, I couldn't get into the pool quickly enough. With the outside temperature hovering in the 20's, I lay on my back in the 90 degree water, looking at the sky and the white mountains in the distance, while all the concerns of the day drained out of me. Slowly I paddled around in the water with never a thought about how I looked. I only knew how I felt, enjoying the unsurpassable combination that had been my day -

the exhilaration of skiing and warm cocoon of my swim.

Swimming has been my therapy, physical and psychological. If I could not swim laps several days a week I would lose my sanity. I swim at YMCAs where the smell of chlorine reached through the lobby to the front door and I hang my clothes in scratched metal lockers—high school style. I swim in college pools, at luxurious hotels with expensive health clubs and elegant locker rooms. I swim in icy mountain lakes so clear I can see the bottom fifty feet out from shore. I swim at sea level and at 8,000 feet, in the Atlantic, Pacific, Mediterranean, Adriatic, Gulf of Mexico and the Dead Sea. The setting doesn't matter. When my body hits the cool water, my cares drain away. When I swim laps, there is no sound but my own breathing and the beat from my steady kick. I love the quiet and the solitude.

I learned to swim when I was four or five at a small pond near my home in Connecticut. My mother took me to swim every day during the hot summers. She pushed my brother in his carriage as I trailed along. Part of our walk was along an abandoned railroad track. A fearful child, I worried about what would happen if a train came along, but one never did. I guess my mother knew that. My fears were not unfounded. In a town with so many trains, children were taught how to be safe. Don't play on the tracks. If you are crossing the tracks and your shoe becomes caught, leave it there.

On Sundays we drove to Hammonasset State Park, a sandy beach on the Long Island Sound. Usually with a few other families, we stopped along the way to buy fresh-baked blueberry pies from a farm. The pies were warm, and the savory smell of them wafted from the trunk of our car into the back seat where my brother and I sat with our sand pails and shovels jostling for space. Our next stop was a picnic area under the trees in a pine grove. The trees provided a cool shelter from the hot sun. The children chased one another while the women put oil cloth tablecloths on the heavy wooden picnic tables. The men started a fire and pumped delicious ice cold water from one of the wells. Because this was our Sunday dinner, although eaten at midday, my mother brought a cooked beef brisket and potatoes in gravy that she heated in an iron pot over the charcoal fire. A friend who grew up in New York City told me her mother performed the same ritual when they went to Coney Island, carrying her pots on the subway to get there.

I loved the salt water and gentle waves at Hammonasset and the cool white feel of the Noxzema cream that my mother put on my shoulders when I had a sunburn. Every year I had a new metal pail and shovel with a painted picture of boats and waves on the outside and a lining as blue as the sea. Pails like mine are in antique shops now, still new and shiny unlike the rusty ones my mother threw away at the end of each summer. I wore rubber beach shoes at all times to protect my feet from hot sand and rough stones. A little cotton pinafore covered my bathing suit. Returning to the furnace-like heat of the un-air conditioned car at the end of the day, my father opened all the windows and my brother and I quickly fell asleep in the back seat. Our summer swimming rituals always ended abruptly in August when polio struck and the pools and parks became deserted. How I hated those hot, late-summer days when, deprived of the water, I was limited to a small, dusty backyard because of a disease I only vaguely understood. If I complained, my mother told me about the dreaded sickness that put children into iron lungs or on crutches, if they lived at all. When I was older, I went away to camp where I became a good swimmer and eventually a swimming instructor.

Swimming was always for me either a job or something that I did to cool off during hot weather. I did not consider it my major form of exercise and swam in the winter only when I was in college and was required to choose a sport to meet the physical education requirement. For years I worked in colleges with beautiful pools and never went near the water. One day a professor who swam regularly encouraged me to try the university pool at lunch time. Not surprisingly, I loved my lunch hour swim and went back for more. For half an hour each day, I swam a combination of strokes because I wasn't strong enough to do the whole thing in crawl, or freestyle, as it is now called. In the next lane, the Dean, a powerful swimmer, swam 35 lengths (1/2 mile) of perfect freestyle. I admired her swimming and told her I could swim only about 12 laps of freestyle. "If you can do 12 you can do 35," she said. And she was right. Each day, I increased the number of freestyle laps until, I too, was swimming 1/2 mile of steady freestyle. Like people who run outdoors in thunderstorms and blizzards, I became a compulsive swimming addict.

When I changed jobs and no longer had access to the university pool, I joined a health club at a hotel and have been there since. The exercise machines do not interest me, but the pool has kept me sane and healthy as well. The whirlpool and the locker room are communities. The early morning crowd arrives when the doors open at 6 a.m., exercise and leave, showered and in business clothes by 8:00, followed by women who do water aerobics. The afternoon group of retired men and women sit in lounge chairs chatting or reading the newspaper that the hotel provides free to its guests. The school teachers come after 3:00, and I belong to the after work group who exercise during evening commuting hours. Health clubs are good for networking and I always recommend them to job seekers. I advise them to go between 5 and 7 p.m. when people arrive after work. Let everyone know you're looking for a job and see what develops. A lot of matches, both business and romantic, are made in health clubs. People feel good about themselves after exercising and the aura spreads.

For companionship and a different type of water exercise, I attend an evening water aerobics class. After a work day where I have been the instructor, it is good to be the pupil. A core group of us, five or six women, has been together for years. Instructors come and go, additional class members come and go, but every Tuesday and Thursday from 6 to 7 p.m., our little group is there. Although we barely know each other's last names, we know each other's life stories. We recommend doctors, restaurants, vacation spots, and shopping bargains, share recipes and household tips, (soak your stained blouse in dishwasher detergent) and rally when someone needs help. When Jay and Barry died, my water aerobics class sent a card signed not only by them but by all the pool members who knew me. We do all this while improving our quads and biceps. We have come from work with our complaints and we continue to complain in the pool—the water is too cold, the pace is too fast, we don't like the arm exercises, the showers are moldy, we want better towels. Instructors put up with us, as do the lifeguards who are younger than our children. We share life's joys and tragedies while relaxing in the hot, bubbling whirlpool or drying our hair over the communal sink. When we leave, we feel healthy and renewed, before going home to complain again about how tired we are.

Although friends and exercise provided support, I knew I needed additional help to address my grief and handle all the difficulties I foresaw in my life ahead. I was depressed all the time. There was never an hour, there were barely ten minutes, when I did not think of my dead husband and son. It seemed as if a cloud of woe surrounded my head and I could not see anything beyond the cloud. Two of the most obvious sources of help were medication and professional counseling. Taking an antidepressant medication might have been a solution but I didn't want to start out that way. There was, after all, no easy solution. If I started on a medicine, I would be on it for a long time, perhaps for the rest of my life. I did not see a life change on the horizon that could suddenly make me so happy that I would be able to leave the pills behind.

I called my insurance provider, a managed care organization, to inquire about counseling. I learned that my policy included mental health coverage. The representative referred me to an agency that screens individuals before recommending therapy. I wondered who they screened out. Calling for help represents a need in itself. I didn't know how disturbed I was expected to sound. The screener on the phone had a soothing voice. Her name was Grace, which seemed a lovely name for someone in her position. She asked why I needed counseling and I told her. She then proceeded through a list of standard questions, an oral test to determine what kind of help I needed and how desperately I needed it. She inquired whether I had thought of harming myself or others, a euphemistic way of asking if I was about to murder someone or kill myself. She was so sympathetic that I thought <u>she</u> was going to cry. Grace said I qualified for immediate counseling and suggested names of therapists in my area. They were either psychologists, social workers or nurse-practitioners. With the HMO paying, no high-priced psychiatrists were on the list. I chose a psychologist whose office was nearby and I promised to call to make an appointment. A few days later, the psychologist called me saying she had heard from the agency that I needed help. Perhaps I had failed the screening test. Was I suicidal or homicidal? We made an appointment for the following evening.

Dr. Keating was an attractive woman in her early forties, with blonde hair and even features that showed no trace of ethnicity. Like many Americans, I try to place each new person I meet into a category: black, white, Asian, Indian, Italian, Irish, Hispanic, Polish, Jewish. I used to be quite skilled at classifying people, but the task has become more difficult. With mobility, intermarriage and adoption, the old stereotypes are blurring. I initially labeled Dr. Keating as Midwestern, but it turned out she was a Southerner who had lost her accent. She shared a suite of offices with another psychologist and a social worker who specialized in eating disorders. Coincidentally, the social worker had been in an outplacement workshop I delivered after she lost her job at St Agatha's. I was happy to see that she had established her own private practice. I was always concerned about meeting someone I knew in the common waiting room, but I went at night when the other practitioners did not have office hours so that never happened. Given my psychological state, I had no need to be embarrassed about seeing a psychologist but I didn't know what I would say to someone else waiting there. I also did not want to be the subject of gossip in our small town where word would spread fast that I was not doing as well as I seemed to be because Susie's husband saw me in the waiting room of the "shrink."

Dr. Keating's office was a large room comfortably furnished like a family room in a private home. The carpet was pearl gray and a small sofa was covered in a gray and pink fabric. She indicated that I should sit on the sofa and she sat facing me in a chair that, in my memory seems about 10 feet away, but perhaps it was closer. The distance made her feel remote. I told her how Jay and Barry died. She took notes as I was speaking. She asked information about my background, work, and family members. She wanted to know how I got along with my parents and brother as a child, and later as an adult. I didn't understand the need for such discussion and how it related to my current difficulties. As if I was sitting in a job interview or applying for a loan, I dutifully answered all the questions. She asked about my relationship with Jay, which seemed to make more sense. She wanted to know who made decisions, what we argued about, how we solved problems.

Then in a very soft voice she asked, "How did you feel when your husband and son died?"

How did I feel? It reminded me of a reporter's question at the scene of a disaster— fire, bus crash, earthquake. "Excuse me, ma'am, but what were you feeling when they pulled your child from the wreckage?"

"How did I feel?" I repeated the question. "How do you think I felt?" I answered, getting angry and raising my voice. "What kind of question is that? I wouldn't be here unless I felt terrible."

Actually it is a fairly standard question. I asked the same question later on when interviewing people for this book. Dr. Keating ignored my outburst. She explained in her soft even way that she was a "feeling" person and some of our relationship would deal with feelings. I calmed down and told her that I felt awful—I was devastated. She suggested that if I found such questions uncomfortable I might want to work with another psychologist. I did not want to change after just one session, and I was confident that our conversations would be more productive for me in the future. I made an appointment to see Dr. Keating again in two weeks.

We had five meetings authorized by the insurance company over the course of several months. I began to understand that Dr. Keating's role was not to provide long term therapy or psychoanalysis but to offer practical suggestions for coping with problems and making my life more productive. Some of the things we discussed seem like common sense to me now, but at the time I was not using common sense so Dr. Keating directed me toward behavior that would help me to heal. When I complained that I was depressed because I had done nothing social all weekend she told me to plan ahead—something I was not used to doing. I like to be spontaneous, to see what might come along as the weekend approaches. Maybe go out for lunch or to a movie. In my old life, these were not things that had to be planned ahead because I always had an available escort. Jay and I often went out at the last minute depending on our mood, who might be performing in New York at the time, or even what was on TV. Now I would have to do things differently. This was part of adapting, one of the steps toward rebuilding.

I called weeks ahead to schedule weekend meetings with women— some married, some single. If I saw a notice for a concert I wanted to attend, I made plans to go with a friend. I planned lunches and dinners out. I made sure the calendar always included at least one weekend event, even if it meant going alone. I became so scheduled that often I was busy all weekend. The scheduling helped. It was something I had to learn how to do. It became routine. Eventually spending a weekend alone no longer depressed me and I occasionally welcome the opportunity.

Dr. Keating and I discussed social life. From the time that I was a teenager and became aware of the opposite sex, the words "social life" to me indicated an involvement with men. I told her that I saw a beautiful long velvet dress in a department store and felt sad because I would never again wear such a dress. Even if Jay had lived, I might never have needed so formal a dress, but on my own I knew that opportunities for elegance would be few. She suggested volunteering for a philanthropic organization that would have fund raising benefits where I would wear a formal dress. I took her advice and volunteered for several organizations. This has opened new doors, channeled my energies in constructive ways and I have enjoyed the activities. But the formal events are usually balls that require major contributions and an escort. I have attended none.

We never discussed Barry. I kept waiting for her to bring it up, but she didn't. Her mission was to teach me to function on a level that enabled me to continue my life, without becoming a menace to myself or others. On that level, our conversations were quite productive. Occasionally I wanted more. I thought I was dutifully working my way through the stages of mourning. I told her about my anger toward Jay and the doctor, but that I could not summon up a single angry thought toward Barry. I wondered if I had missed something or if the anger would arrive at some later time. Dr. Keating replied in her calm, soothing way that everyone did not go through every stage of grief. I felt relieved that I didn't have to find a way to become angry at Barry. He probably would have told you that I did that enough when he was growing up. And he would have been right.

My meetings with Dr. Keating lasted for several months because I stretched them out. Knowing that my insurance would pay for only a limited number of visits, I hoarded them, like a box of favorite chocolates. When I used up the allotted number, the screening agency recommended that they continue but the insurance company turned down the request saying I was no longer eligible because this was a "pre-existing condition." I knew this was a mistake but it took six months to straighten out the problem. My coverage had been refused due to a clerical error made by their employee. "Sorry for any inconvenience," the HMO said. By that time, I was busy with other things and never returned to the psychologist. It was nine months after the death of my husband and son and I had reached a dead end. I was stuck. Except for attending a support group, I had done most of the things that Dr. Keating suggested. I had also done everything that common sense as well as all the authorities on death and mourning suggested: keep busy, stay involved, help others, reach in, reach out. Why hadn't it worked? My upbringing and education stressed cause and effect relationships, do this and that will happen. Work hard and reap the reward. I had worked hard and yet I was still so sad. I realized then that grief and I were going to live, side-by-side for a lot longer than I had anticipated.

Work is considered the magic potion, the bromide that cures all ills. Everyone told me to work and keep busy. Work provides a structure and an income, a place to go to every day, to be among co-workers, to have a measure of control in a life gone berserk, to do something well and be rewarded for it. The job can be a refuge after a tragedy but is not the cure-all we hope for. At the time of Jay and Barry's deaths, I was working as a consultant for a few human resources consulting firms. My job assignments ranged from one day to months. Occasionally, I provided individual counseling to people who had lost their jobs, but usually I conducted job search workshops in settings that ranged from glossy corporate headquarters to dusty factory workrooms. I enjoyed the work although it provided no security, no benefits and few opportunities for creativity. I gave some thought to finding a permanent job that paid better and offered health care insurance, but during the first few months of widowhood I had no time to look for a job. I knew well that finding a good job requires solid research and a strong campaign. I couldn't begin a job search because I was too distracted just trying to cope. Looking back on it now, I could have contacted people I knew in high places at major companies but looking back is a lot easier than doing it at the time.

Just as I find long lost things in the house when I am not looking for them, I was offered a job quite by chance. A woman who worked with me at an outplacement firm took a permanent job with a consulting company that served as a contractor to government agencies. She worked at a Career Center in an area that suffered from chronic unemployment. There was an opening for a counselor, and she wanted to know if I was interested. The pay was terrible and the commute was long, but the job provided benefits: paid vacation and sick leave, medical coverage and a pension plan, not to mention a fax machine and a copier.

After going for the interview, I described the job to Laura, another consultant. We were presenting workshops at a factory near the docks in Newark. I have conducted programs in state-of-the-art corporate settings with audio-visual systems that drop down out of the ceiling at the press of a button and shiny tile bathrooms with marble counters and full length mirrors. In the cafeterias, employees look out on ponds with fountains and can choose from a vast array of delicious foods at company-subsidized prices. Parking is underground so employees can leave their coat in the car when it is raining and never have to scrape the snow off their car when they leave at the end of the day during a snow storm. On a permanent basis, I would love to work in such a beautiful environment, but for a two-day workshop, I'll take the factory. In a factory I might not get a flip chart or markers that work, but I find some great hard-working people who hand me their problems, expect me to fix them, and are especially grateful when I do.

The factory where we were leading the workshops didn't have a cafeteria. People brought their lunch or bought food from the lunch wagon that showed up around 11 every morning. Laura and I ate at a local lunch spot, the kind of place where the waitress has hair that is either too red or too black and a hard luck story as long as your arm. They serve great eggs, any style, at all hours of the day. At this place, the tables were red Formica and the booths were a stiff vinyl that had gone out of style thirty years ago. The restaurant could have jumped right out of a 1950's movie, except it was real and working people ate breakfast and lunch there every day.

"Don't take that job, you're going to hate it," cautioned Laura. "You're not hurting for work." She continued to lecture me as I ate my Western omelet sandwich. "You're going to miss the freedom of consulting, the variety, and the option to turn jobs down. You're going to be bored in that place."

"Yeah, I know, I know. You sound like my mother. I don't care, I'm going to take it." I accepted the job.

The Career Center was on a busy thoroughfare in a tidy, working class neighborhood of small, well-kept houses and local merchants. Run with county and Federal funding, the Center provided counseling to the multitude of people who lose their jobs and never receive the type of job search assistance that outplacement firms provide. The people who used the services were assembly line workers, forklift operators, bookkeepers and clerks hoping to improve their lot, striving to move up a step on life's ladder. They had worked for banks that had merged, a large pharmaceutical company acquired by an even larger pharmaceutical company and the textile factories that had once employed thousands before moving their operations to Alabama or Mexico.

The Center offered these people a place to come to, to conduct their job search— to check out the want ads, use a computer and copier, send a fax and meet with a counselor. But more important, it served as a screening agency to send unemployed people for government sponsored training. Although I realized after the interview that the job was not right for me, it offered an opportunity to help people in a way that my corporate work did not. If Jay were alive he would have told me to take it as he had previously advised me to accept offers for safe, routine jobs offering no prospects for growth or creativity. I always turned those jobs down. This time I took the job so I had no one to blame when I ended up frustrated and unhappy. Given my state of mind, I probably would have disliked any job.

The first day, I sat in my small, windowless, basement office. The building was built into the side of a hill so the back offices were underground. They were musty when the weather was good, and wet when it rained. The ceiling leaked and the carpet was always damp. I looked around and wondered what I was doing there. Then I remembered the vacation pay, sick leave and medical insurance although I'm not sure that was what really mattered at the time. I think what I wanted was the structure. I wanted a place to go to every day where there was stability, where people knew my story and I knew theirs. Like the Cheers Bar, I needed a place where everybody knew my name. I wanted the comfort of a neighborhood where I could do errands on my lunch hour, have an office with my name on the door and a business phone number where I could be called during the day. Maybe variety wasn't what I needed at the time. I needed a home, even if the one I found was more "handyman special" than it was House and Garden.

My co-workers were energetic, enthusiastic, intelligent people who sincerely cared about and went to great lengths to help the people who sought our assistance. We spent a good deal of time complaining about the management and the convoluted government regulations that controlled everything we did. The paperwork was endless. A procedure that could be done in two steps required four and everything moved at a snail's pace. But we were committed to our job and worked hard to achieve our goals. My job became my mission. I felt that I was doing the work that Barry never lived to do. I believed that I was put in that place, at that time, to give people a chance at a new life. Barry wanted to help people who had nowhere else to turn and I was doing it for him, carrying on where he left off.

There is power in what I do although some may not see it as such. Having the ability to change someone's life is a strong responsibility. When I was a job placement counselor at a university, I received a call from an architect looking for an assistant. I referred a recent graduate who not only got the job but met his wife who was working there at the time. If I had referred a different person, many lives would now be different. My work can also be rewarding, not financially, certainly, but in the satisfaction I receive in knowing that I have made a difference in someone's life, given her or him the confidence to pursue a goal and to succeed.

Like teachers who learn from their students, I also learned courage and perseverance from some of the applicants who came to the Career Center for help. Anne had lost her bookkeeping job and needed computer skills to get a new one. She had been a widow for 15 years. Her husband died suddenly when they were both in their thirties, leaving her with three small children and no insurance. Needing a job, Anne cleaned houses during the day while her children were in school. When they were older, she found an office job as a bookkeeper. Her proudest achievement was sending all her children to college. I arranged for her to attend school to learn computerized bookkeeping. Most people who went to retraining programs went to school full-time and waited until they were finished to look for a job but not Anne. While she attended school, she spent every Sunday searching through the want-ads. On Sunday nights, she stayed up until midnight typing cover letters to send out with her résumé. Her diligence was rewarded when she landed a good job six weeks before completing her training. The school allowed her to finish at night while she worked full-time during the day. Anne sent me a lovely note thanking me for helping her to get a job but the benefit was the other way around. I learned survival skills from Anne. She was one of the hardest working people I've ever met and she never gave up.

From another of my clients, I learned the importance of self-esteem. Iris was a wisp of a woman in her twenties, although she looked like a teenager. She first came to the Career Center during the summer. Weighing no more than 90 pounds, she wore a tiny shirt that left her midriff exposed to below her navel where her jeans shorts began. All of her scant clothing could have been made from two dish towels. Her mousy brown hair, which she wore in a pony-tail, did nothing to enhance her pretty face and pale, smooth skin. Iris had lost her job as a purchasing agent for a company that manufactured bongo drums. Most people came to the Center to apply for training which they saw as an entitlement, although it wasn't. Many were aggressive, sometimes abusive about their right to this training. Iris came to get help with her résumé. Because she never asked for training, I assumed she was not interested in it. When her resume was complete, Iris started looking for jobs with little success. I asked her if she was interested in training, perhaps a computer course that would enhance her skills. Her face lit up. "Could I go to school?"

she asked, her eyes widening, like a child being offered an ice cream cone. "Of course you can," I assured her.

I called a few schools for her, which counselors normally didn't do. Our workload was so high that we required the applicants to do the investigating. Because her unemployment benefits were about to end, we were able to circumvent the paperwork and she went to computer school within a week. Soon after finishing school she got a purchasing job in the office of a hotel chain. She was so excited, she brought her boyfriend to the office to meet me. He was a motorcycle guy, covered with tattoos and rings. Earrings, nose ring, eyebrow ring. Although it was summer, he wore a leather jacket decorated with silver studs. He shook my hand and thanked me for what I had done for Iris. I was flattered. I had never met a motorcycle guy before. I wished them well and off they went, zooming down Main Street on his Harley.

When I was Iris's age, my aspirations were not much higher than hers. Expecting me to become a secretary as she had been, my mother told me I would never get a job unless I knew shorthand. During my senior year in college, I took a non-credit shorthand course taught on campus by a man from a nearby business school. Following graduation, several of my college classmates attended a summer secretarial program offered by Radcliffe College, the women's college associated with Harvard. Women with degrees in economics and French literature went to Harvard to learn to be secretaries. My course was briefer. I learned to write "Dear Sir" by making squiggly lines on my steno pad. Many years later, reading the poet Sylvia Plath's autobiographical novel *The Bell Jar,* I laughed to see how similar her experience was to mine. She attended Smith College, another of the Seven Sister schools. During the summer, her mother tried to teach her shorthand so she could support herself after college. She wrote: "[My mother] stood at the blackboard and scribbled little curlicues in white chalk while I sat in a chair and watched...The only thing was, when I tried to picture myself in some job, briskly jotting down line after line of shorthand, my mind went blank. There wasn't one job I felt like doing where you used shorthand. I told my mother I had a terrible headache and went to bed." (Plath, 1971)

When I went to New York to look for a job after college I too hoped I would not have to apply for a job that required shorthand. Beyond that, I was not too selective. I wanted a job that would pay the rent until a man came along who could afford to support me. I hadn't figured out at that time how I would avoid the drudgery of cooking three meals a day because the romantic idea of being someone's wife was still foremost in my mind. In 1958, female college graduates who didn't become teachers, nurses, secretaries or nuns could find jobs for incredibly low pay at advertising agencies and publishing houses or for insurance companies which paid better. I answered help-wanted ads for Female College Graduates and made the rounds of employment agencies and insurance companies. Traveling about the city, I always wore white gloves, even in the subway.

A woman at an agency who interviewed me while eating a sandwich at her desk, sent me to an interview for a job as Miss Gray, working for the Gray Line which ran excursion boats on the Hudson River. The Gray Line also owned buses and the interview was in a shabby office at the old Port Authority Terminal. The man who interviewed me was a very nice, fatherly type although he wasn't old enough to be *my* father. As Miss Gray I would wear a gray suit and jaunty little hat like Katharine Hepburn wore in 1940's movies when she "went to business" as my mother used to say. I would sit behind a counter at one of New York's fancier hotels, selling tickets to Gray Line boat trips. The fatherly man offered me the job, which paid surprisingly well, and then asked why, with my education and background, I would want it. He may have changed my life. I realized that I had to aim higher, that accepting any job because it paid the rent was not good enough. I turned down the job, thanked him and concentrated on the insurance companies. Years later, sitting across the desk from Iris, I remembered the importance of aiming higher and vowed to do better than my current employment.

Despite many successful outcomes at the Career Center there was a lot of sadness as well. People who had every right to be sent for the training that could have changed their lives were kept waiting interminably until they finally gave up, returning to minimum wage jobs that barely paid their bills. I found the job depressing most of the time, yet I kept putting off the decision to leave. Finally, the choice was made for me. My job was cut due to a reduction in Federal funding. It was comic. As a "displaced worker" I was eligible to receive benefits from the very program I was working in. Most people are devastated by losing a job. I was relieved. By letting me go, my boss gave me the push I needed to get out and look for something I wanted to do. I called the outplacement firms that I had left the year before. One that was starting a big project offered me a place on the team. I left the Center on Thursday and started a consulting assignment the following Monday. It was part-time, no benefits, no permanent office with my name on the door and I was thrilled. Walking into a planning meeting that first day, I felt as if I was breathing fresh air for the first time in a long while. Getting out of that dank basement office, I actually was breathing fresh air both literally and metaphorically.

Being in a business setting gave me a new confidence. Although I would not have as much opportunity to help people on an individual basis, the project I would be working on involved some travel and conducting workshops for large groups of people who had to make some difficult decisions regarding retirement. I felt a new professionalism about my work. Like Iris, I was soaring down the road on a Harley. Proud as I was for reaching this point, I had deceived myself into believing that a new workplace would somehow signal the end of mourning, that I would come out of the grief cycle healed. But it was too soon for a miracle. I wasn't so much surprised as disappointed. I simply re-entered the cycle in a different place and went on from there.

9

Changes

If widowhood is about changing roles, my husband's death turned me into a business woman. As beneficiary of Jay's estate, I inherited a bank account, IRAs, stocks and bonds, unused travelers checks, frequent flyer mileage and a year-old Ford Taurus station wagon. I had to do something with all of them, either transfer the title to my name or sell them. I also had to pay my husband's debts. These were not tasks that could be delegated to lawyers, accountants and brokers. With the exception of a lawyer to write the will, the legal and financial matters that I dealt with could be done by a layman. The transactions were time-consuming but not hard to do. I did them because I wanted to take control, to demonstrate to myself that I could handle matters that were routinely done by my husband. Even more important, I was involved in a process that kept me focused on short term goals. If I kept busy with little things, I could concentrate on small frustrations instead of the larger pain that permeated my life. The process left little room for ambiguity. The decisions were black or white. Plug in the numbers, change the names, write the letters, make the phone calls. While I was making the small decisions, I wouldn't have to think about larger ones.

At times I felt frustrated and defeated when what should have been simple transactions stretched out for weeks and months. My anxiety increased daily as I realized that my husband and son would never again be there to help me with my problems. Along with the normal frustrations of clogged traffic, obstinate computers, endless minutes navigating telephone menus, ("thank you for your patience, your call is important to us") my days seemed to be filled with conversations with error-prone clerks and small bureaucratic minds that impeded my progress in accomplishing the tasks I had set out to complete. I was still in my "victim" stage, believing that I was entitled to small favors, but these functionaries neither knew nor cared that I had suffered great tragedy. Understanding my personal needs was not part of their job. They had difficulty enough understanding my business needs.

The banks were the worst. Among my chores on a busy Saturday morning, I visited a branch of Jersey Central Bank to combine two of Jay's Individual Retirement Accounts into one and transfer the ownership to my name. The bank's storefront office was in the next town in a strip mall it shared with an Italian restaurant, a curtain shop and a paint store. When I arrived at 11 a.m., I found the last empty chair available to customers who were waiting to see one of the two people working on the "platform" that morning. The man next to me, who had been there for 20 minutes, was trying to amuse a whining toddler. In this case, the child was right. The wait was interminable. I felt like whining too. After 45 minutes, I met with Sharon, a slim, attractive young woman wearing a sweater and jeans. I handed her the two IRAs, telling her how I wanted them handled since I knew the routine, having recently completed it successfully with a brokerage firm. She spent a lot of time with her computer inputting data and pulling up screens. Finally she told me that what I wanted to do was impossible.

I told Sharon that another financial institution had completed a similar procedure. She suggested that I leave the accounts with her, she would call the IRA department on Monday and mail the new accounts to me when completed. By then it was well past noon and the bank had locked its doors. Only one other customer remained—a man who seemed to be negotiating a loan with the manager. Sharon and I signed and exchanged several forms. She unlocked the door with a key to let me out. I had been at the bank for an hour and a half. The enticing smell of pizza wafted through the parking lot helping to distract me from the nagging feeling that Sharon and I were probably not finished doing business. What Sharon should have been able to complete during my first visit took two more visits and was settled only because of my irate phone call to a regional vice-president. I told myself I didn't deserve so much frustration and turned my attention homeward.

We had started construction of the new master bathroom six days before Jay's heart attack. (I was still part of a "we" then, but the bathroom project was all mine from start to finish.) The room was months in the planning. I had consulted an architect, a few plumbers and several building contractors. In bulky winter clothing, I sat in showroom bathtubs to test their length. I swung my arms around in stall showers to be sure they were wide enough and brought Jay along to test them for height. Eventually, I chose the components of the bathroom of my dreams. The space would be open and airy compared to the cramped bathroom we had shared since moving to the house 17 years before. Although the work continued after Jay and Barry died, the process took place without me. Occasionally I made a decision. New construction requires so many decisions on things I took for granted when moving into places where someone else did the choosing long before I got there. I chose light fixtures, doorknobs and moldings. At 10 o'clock at night I wandered around a vast home supplies store, comparing faucets and handles to those I had seen at the plumbing supply store that had closed hours before. Periodically I wrote checks. Slowly the new bathroom took shape while I continued to sleep in the small guest room down the hall and use another bathroom.

Eventually the bathroom was finished except for paint and wallpaper, which I had not chosen. The room was clean and new but I had lost interest in it. The master bedroom was still dusty from construction and the carpet was stained from the feet of workmen. For months the rooms sat unused. In my new widowed state a small room with a single bed was adequate. Truthfully, I could not bring myself to move into the room where my son spent his last night, where the last time I saw him he lay dying at the foot of my bed. I wanted to close off the room as they do in horror movies. The curtains would decay and cobwebs would cover the furniture for decades until a young, unsuspecting couple would move in to open up the space while heavy organ music played in the background. I wanted no part of the bedroom that my husband and I had shared for so many years.

Like preparing my first dinner alone, and developing the film that remained in my camera from our last Thanksgiving together, I knew that eventually I would have to summon the courage to move back into that room. Building the new bathroom was an achievement. The bedroom could be warm and welcoming once again. I could not change the past, only the present. I had to move back. A few months went by until I finally decided I had spent enough time feeling sorry for myself. As long as I occupied the house, the master bedroom and bath would never again be lived in by man and wife, but I could turn them into lovely rooms for a woman. Normally I love to choose wallpaper. I spend hours looking through every book in the wallpaper store. I bring home samples of paper to tape to the wall, and heavy, bulky books that I hold up, trying to picture the room in stripes or flowers. This time I had no enthusiasm for the job. For the bedroom walls I chose a creamy beige and for the bathroom, a simple gray wallpaper that looked as if it belonged in a dentist's office. I found a painter to do the job. Then I vacuumed out all the construction dirt and hired someone to clean the carpet. Finally I asked a neighbor to help me install new curtain rods. I hung delicate white lace curtains that filter the sun and billow in a breeze.

I made up the bed with a favorite antique quilt and moved back in. That night, I filled the tub with bubbles, sank into the hot water and turned on the whirlpool. The room smelled sweet and comforting. The window and the mirror steamed up until I was engulfed in a cocoon. As I dipped beneath a foot of foam, I felt like Julia Roberts in "Pretty Woman" luxuriating in my tub. How proud Jay would have been to see me in my new bathroom. I was proud too. I had obtained the estimates, chosen the fixtures and the surfaces, hired the contractor, worked with the carpenters, tile men, electrician, plumber and painter, and paid the bills. When the wrong vanity was delivered and installed while I was at work, I had to fight with the supplier to take it back, even though the carpenter had taken a piece out of it to install the heater. I was sad that Jay never got to use the room because I know he would have loved it too.

Women have told me how lonely they felt sleeping in a half-empty bed. Some slept on their husband's side so that his side wouldn't be empty. As the ad used to say, "You can't fool Mother Nature." I was very aware that I was alone in that bed, no matter which side I slept on. I bought a fluffy down comforter which I covered with a white coverlet. On chilly winter nights I love to climb into bed and snuggle under my comforter but let's face it, nothing will ever replace sleeping next to a man I love. Having my bedroom back represented a big step in rebuilding my life. I had accepted the reality of living there alone. The room became the refuge I needed. I looked forward to getting into bed with a good book at the end of the day.

My job at the Career Center was in a good location for running errands on my lunch hour so I had in place all the ingredients needed to begin the process of converting Jay's stocks and bonds to my ownership. I collected the stock and bond certificates from the various spots where Jay had stored them and visited a brokerage firm for advice on how to proceed. The broker I met with told me the firm would handle the transfers for $65 a stock. The transfer procedure is tedious but not difficult. Considering that I had ten stocks to transfer, I decided to do the job myself. When I contacted the transfer agents for each company, I was surprised to find that each required different procedures for the transfer, some simple, others tangled in complexity. I spent many lunch hours obtaining the required notarization and signature guarantees on the stock certificates.

The bank branch I dealt with was in a neighborhood of modest houses that were immaculately kept. The small front lawns, two green squares on either side of a cement walk, were neatly cut, the hedges trimmed and the sidewalks swept. From Thanksgiving to well after New Year's Day, plastic snowmen stood guard on snowless patches of grass. In this hardworking area, people may have owned company pensions but were unlikely holders of stock certificates. At the bank, my stock transactions made me unique. For a stock to be transferred to my ownership, a financial institution had to stamp the stock certificate with a medallion stamp. The branch manager was the only one authorized to use this type of stamp. A congenial man, he came to know me as "that lady with the stocks."

After obtaining the stamp, I drove back to my office eating a sandwich in the car, photocopied all the forms, added the death certificate and letter of administration and went to the post office to send the originals by registered mail. The post office closest to my job was in a former shopping area that had lost its customers and prestige to the suburban malls. It stood grandly on a corner opposite a parochial school where uniformed children played ball in the asphalt school yard. The exterior of the post office boasted marble columns, but the once spacious lobby was gone, the room divided by cheap partitions and shared with community offices and a senior citizen center.

Harry, the friendliest postal worker in the world, always greeted me with a big smile. He called all the women "honey" in a way that made the ladies want to hug rather than slap him. I always waited in his line even though it was longer than the line of the worker standing beside him. The first time we met, he eyed my home address on the envelope, a town 20 miles away. "You work around here?" he asked, wondering whether I was likely to become a regular customer. He knew everyone in the neighborhood, and by their mail he knew about their lives as well—who mailed packages to relatives in Italy, who was paid in cash and bought money orders to pay the bills and who needed registered mail, return receipt requested, to gain ownership of her dead husband's stocks. "How many more of those ya gonna mail?" he would inquire each time I came in.

"Almost done," I kept telling him. I plugged along at my own pace. The shares of one stock had been "escheated to the State of New Jersey as unclaimed funds" and took almost a year to recover. Sorting through years of records and files, I found an occasional uncashed check and even a stock certificate that I assumed to be worthless but turned out to be a stock I could sell although it was worth far less than it had been several years before. I sold it and claimed the proceeds as a tax loss. I plodded along, weaving these tasks into my bereavement routine, my grief work. Here was denial: maybe one morning I will awaken to find this was all a bad dream. My husband will be there beside me wondering why I am so happy to see him. Back again was anger: I found a stock certificate that, unknown to me, Jay had reported lost many years before. He obtained a replacement certificate and sold the shares. The paper in my hand was worthless, but I did not find out until I had spent hours tracking down the information.

Like a dog that has been bred to chase rabbits, the compulsion to settle the estate was imprinted in my genes. I gained a perverse enjoyment over outwitting the government and corporate employees who stood between me and my goal. Five months after Jay's death, a letter addressed to him arrived from the Bureau of the Public Debt, Department of the Treasury, Box 1328, Parkersburg, WV. Why was the Bureau of Public Debt in West Virginia? I surmised that the Federal Government had not decentralized to achieve greater efficiency but that the influence of a powerful U.S. senator had brought jobs to his constituency in return for aiding Midwestern farmers or building a new dam on the Columbia River. My hand shook as I apprehensively opened the envelope wondering what major offense my husband had committed to attract the attention of the Bureau of Public Debt. I feared responsibility for great sums and was relieved to see that the letter referred to U.S. savings bonds that had recently matured. The Public Debt was the debt of the Federal government, not my debt. The timing of the letter was coincidental since I had not informed the Bureau of Public Debt of Jay's death. The bonds were among his papers in the safety deposit box and I had put them aside to deal with after I completed the transfer of the stocks. As a piece of good fortune, or so I thought at the time, the letter I had just received gave me the information I needed to proceed. Jay had owned one of the bonds since he was a teenager along with his mother who had been dead for 20 years. For that one, I had to produce her death certificate as well. I wrote to the Bureau of Public Debt, Department of the Treasury, Parkersburg, West Virginia, informing them of my husband's death.

Seven months later I received a response from the Examination Branch, Division of Transactions and Rulings, also in West Virginia. People who know little about New Jersey except what they learn from the media or see as they travel the New Jersey Turnpike in the eastern part of the state have a stereotypical view of a foul-smelling landscape filled with oil tanks and strip malls, inhabited by a population that says "Joisy" and lives in cookie cutter houses ten feet apart. They never see the rolling hills and tiny farm communities, the 500-acre horse-country estates or the miles of beaches with sand so fine it sticks between your toes for hours before you realize it's there. I harbor a similar, and no doubt, unfairly narrow view of West Virginia. Although I have visited parts of the state that were green and prosperous, I imagine a population of exploited coal miners who live in hollows with inadequate sanitation and poorly fed children. In the middle of my picture is a vast government facility, The Bureau of Public Debt, where hundreds of government workers toil away in gray cubby holes not far from mine shafts where workers emerge soot-covered at the end of their shift. The seven month delay in responding to my letter did nothing to dispel this image, although I have learned since that a Federal government facility in any state would probably have taken as long. The letter explained the steps necessary to complete the transfer or redemption of the bonds. I assembled all the papers and mailed the hefty packet to West Virginia. I later received new bond certificates and a check for one that could not be renewed. The process took 10 months. Perhaps I was lucky.

Earlier in the year, I had encountered the bureaucratic mind at another Federal agency. The Social Security Administration pays a one-time benefit of $255 to a surviving spouse or other beneficiary, a sum that is laughable considering that the average funeral costs more than $4000. Several weeks after Jay's death, I received a phone call from a Social Security employee saying that the agency had been notified by the funeral home of the death of my husband. The representative was calling to arrange a personal interview at the regional Social Security office to determine my eligibility for the $255. We agreed on a day and date. I later received a letter in the mail confirming my *telephone* interview for that date. The letter listed the original documents that I would have to produce at my telephone interview, saying copies were not acceptable. Along with its other powers, I assumed that the government has psychic powers that enable it to see original documents over the phone.

A few weeks later, I received another letter from the District Manager of the regional Social Security Office. It said: "We were recently notified of the death of your spouse and there may be benefits due you from Social Security. Please complete the enclosed application so that we may determine your eligibility for a one-time benefit of $255 from your spouse's Social Security record." The letter made no mention of my scheduled appointment. It seemed to have come from another source, maybe a different Federal government. I completed the application, mailed it off with the death certificate and received my $255 by mail. I tell you this because it was typical of the frustrations I continued to endure at a time when I wanted my life to run smoothly. Perhaps I was naive in expecting that government officials would welcome my requests and deal with them cheerfully and efficiently. Although most of my days were dull and uneventful, I remember the adversity with a pride that comes in conquering it.

I tried to find ways to make my life less worrisome. Since cars can be a source of anxiety when they don't work properly, I decided that by owning two I would be guaranteed at least one functioning vehicle at all times. After transferring ownership of Jay's wagon to my name, I kept it although not without considerable guilt about the extravagance of owning two cars. If I had one washed, I drove it only on sunny days, using the other in the rain. If one was low on gas, I drove the other. I depended on the wagon to get me through the snow in the winter, but when spring came I offered it to Andy who was driving a jaunty little red pick-up truck that he had bought a few years earlier. A gray station wagon that belonged to one's parents was about the last thing a single guy wanted to be seen driving around town in, but I convinced him of its safety, of the luxury of its air-conditioned spaciousness in the stifling Virginia heat and of the extra cash he would gain from the sale of the truck. He kept the wagon until he moved to an apartment in downtown Philadelphia where a car would be a liability. Then he brought it home and I again owned two cars.

The last time I had sold a car, the purchaser bought it on the first day the ad was in the paper. Jay drew up the agreement and I typed it out on the computer. It looked very official but something handwritten probably would have done the job. When it came to selling one of the cars without Jay to help me, I was timid and reluctant to do it myself. I went to the cemetery and asked for his help. I knew that somehow the right negotiations and procedures would pop into my head if he helped me with his logical thinking. I don't recall his giving me any practical advice but I left the cemetery a little more confident about my business skills. I went to a few car dealers who offered me so little money that I became indignant. Anger and greed are good motivators. The wagon seemed to be the more marketable of my two cars so I put a FOR SALE sign on it and eventually made a deal. I printed out Jay's agreement, still in my computer from the previous sale. The process was not as easy this time, but the couple who bought it had two little boys who happily jumped into the back seat and I was glad to see the wagon go off to its new home.

While I struggled with my transportation on land, my eyes were also on the skies. Jay's most recent statement form Delta Airlines showed a frequent flyer mileage balance of 56,071 miles. My own current balance with Delta was 27,900. Combined they would add up to a tidy sum. I sent a letter to Delta with a death certificate, requesting the transfer of all mileage to my account. About a month later I called Delta to verify that the transfer had been completed. I spoke with Karen who told me that my current mileage balance was 55,980.

"Have you transferred my husband's mileage to my account?" I asked. She put me on hold. "We transferred that mileage on April 2," she announced cheerfully when she returned.

"My previous balance was 27,900 and my husband's was 56,071. How could the new total be 55,800?" I asked.

"That's what the computer says," Karen replied.

"I don't care what the computer says," I told her. "You are telling me that the new total is less than my husband's mileage was before you added it to mine."

"That is correct," she said. "What is correct?" I was losing my temper. There was a pause. "The correct total is 55,800 miles," she insisted.

"Look at it." I shouted into the phone. "Forget the computer. Look at the numbers. Tell me how you can add 27,990 and 56,071 to get a total of 55,800?"

"I can only tell you what the computer says." The woman was perhaps trained to say that and not to think or speak about obvious discrepancies.

"Karen," I said, getting angrier by the minute, "do you have a piece of paper and a pencil in your cubicle? Add 27,990 and 27,990 and what do you get? 55,800. Instead of transferring my husband's 56,071 miles to my account, Delta has doubled my own mileage."

"I guess the computer made a mistake," she answered, sounding defeated.

She told me to call corporate headquarters in Atlanta. She then sweetly thanked me for calling Delta, asked if there was anything else she could do for me and hoped I would have a nice day. Eventually the computer corrected its error and awarded me the mileage.

Since Jay and I were both self-employed, we paid for our own health insurance. To reduce costs, I decided to join a health maintenance organization. I called the doctors that I used most frequently to ask them which plans they belonged to. Only one company responded to my request for an individual plan so I chose them by default. The general practitioner who is my primary care provider or gatekeeper is a member of a sizable medical group. He wouldn't know me if he tripped over me in the hall outside his office. The bureaucratic nightmares I have been through, with everything from approval for surgery to obtaining a flu shot, have been horrendous. My HMO's rates have increased 25% since I have had the coverage while benefits have been curtailed. Too young for Medicare, too old to find a well paying full-time job with health benefits, I am caught in the American health care nightmare.

Seeing the difficulties I encountered by the absence of Jay's will, I was determined, for Andy's sake, to have a current will. I went to a local lawyer who drafted what I would call a "boilerplate" will. I bequeathed my money and all earthly possessions to Andy. I wrote a Living Will concerning my wishes for medical treatment if I should be incapacitated and not able to make decisions regarding life support. I put one copy of the will into my safety deposit box and left the other with the lawyer.

A few years later, as Andy and I were about to take a plane trip, I wondered what would happen to my estate if we were to die together. My will had no provisions for such an occurrence, which according to Carol, my lawyer friend, should be part of a standard will. I made an appointment to see Jerry, a lawyer who had worked in the same office as Jay when they were young attorneys, not long out of law school. Although they had gone separate ways, they had remained friends. The last time I saw Jerry was at Jay and Barry's funeral. Jerry's law firm was in a shiny new office building on land that was a dairy farm when my boys were young. A small working train circled the farm. On weekends, Mr. Walker the farmer, sold train rides to the delight of generations of youngsters and their parents who rode in open cars behind the miniature steam engine which blew its whistle as it passed barns, horses, and cows. Now the only remnant of the property's agricultural past is the building's address: 2 Walker Farm Road. I walked through the plant filled atrium to the glass elevators. Like a deluxe hotel, balconies circled each floor overlooking the atrium. The law firm was on the third floor. Its front walls and doors were glass, like a store where customers can peer through the windows before deciding if they want to shop.

Sitting behind a broad mahogany desk, a male receptionist greeted me in the entry room. I have seen male receptionists at old line New York law and accounting firms with oriental rugs on the floor and dark paneled walls hung with oil portraits of founding partners. With no lack of females available, I assume that the young man I now faced was there to create a touch of class and a modicum of conservatism not readily apparent from the glossy setting. In the waiting area, a silky leather sofa and two matching chairs surrounded a heavy glass coffee table. The burgundy colored carpeting was thick enough to show footprints. The receptionist directed me to hang my coat in the closet. He called Jerry. I settled into one of the smooth leather chairs. Tan from a recent trip to Florida, Jerry came out to meet me. If we were meeting for the first time, I would have guessed his age to be late fifties but the face I saw was the one that I knew when we were all young, when we saw each other at the annual holiday office party, children in diapers crawling after one another under the massive board room table, dropping crumbs on the costly Scandinavian carpet. Jerry gave me a hug and escorted me to his office which had large windows and was furnished in modern decor, all plum and gray. On the desk were pictures of grown children, older than Jerry and his wife Rose were when we all first met.

He called in an associate who would actually write the will. "She charges less than I do and her qualifications are excellent," Jerry assured me. The three of us spent an hour discussing my assets and how I wished to distribute them when I die. My new will covers all contingencies—if I die before Andy, if he predeceases me but I am unable to write a new will, if we die together. There are provisions for trusts, charities and a Living Will. I had to designate a trustee to manage the trust for Andy in the case of my premature death. Jerry suggested choosing a "trustworthy" person (I now know where the word comes from), who lives nearby and would be willing to take on such a responsibility. I called David, Jay's best friend, who said he would be honored. I was grateful. Jerry strongly recommended that Andy write a will as well, but people in their twenties seldom find the motivation for doing so. When Andy has an heir, my will can be revised. Until that happens, I am confident that my estate is in good order.

Within about six months, the job of transferring the assets and putting my business affairs in order was practically done. The process kept me going and brought small satisfactions. Each stock certificate that came in the mail was like a little diploma with my name on it, a reward for completing a procedure that involved research, writing, perseverance, and endurance. I have taken college courses that required less dedication. As my list of things to do got shorter, I became stronger seeing what I had accomplished. I was happy for my independence and relieved by the lack of major mistakes.

I credited some of my success to a certain amount of divine providence that was granted to me. During the early months of my bereavement, I believed I was living within the protective circle of many prayers. Numerous people had offered to pray for me, from the nuns at a college where I once worked who had some credibility in this area, to friends who, as far as I knew, were far removed from any religion. "You are in my prayers," they wrote on their condolence cards. When I met them on the street or in the supermarket, they said their prayers were with me. I was in no position to doubt them or to refuse such offerings. I used these prayers as vouchers. When I needed a parking space or hoped for a normal mammogram, I reminded God of all the prayers that well-wishers had said for me. "Please help me out here," I asked God and frequently my prayers were answered. I needed my vouchers to move me forward. I still had business to attend to.

ജഗജഗജഗജ # Part III ഗജഗജഗജഗ

A Slow and Cautious Way

Money

B y late summer, nine months after Jay and Barry's deaths, some of the raw pain was gone. I cried less often and had progressed from thinking of my dead husband and son every minute to thinking of them every hour. Although I had a full-time job and numerous additional responsibilities, I was still directing most of my energy toward the greater task of coping with loss. Mourners occasionally become "stuck," unable to take even the tiniest steps that will help them to rebuild their lives. I wasn't advancing, but I wasn't sliding backward either. I kept hoping to reach a level of adjustment that never seemed to come. Instead, each day brought an old memory and an old hurt, a new challenge and a new sorrow. Despite the constant anguish with which I lived, I continued to concentrate on my financial responsibilities. The actions required of me provided some focus and direction.

With the estate settled, taxes paid, and most of the assets transferred to my ownership, I felt I should develop a plan for my financial future. I was afraid I would drift along spending my money until, who knows, it would run out. I didn't want to end up old and poor, living out my days in the county nursing home among other indigent widows. During my married life, I probably should have developed a financial plan, but it didn't seem necessary. I never accumulated any debt beyond a monthly credit card bill and if any money was left over I deposited it in the bank. I didn't need a plan for that. "Don't buy it if you can't afford it," was my mother's standard advice, absorbed during the Great Depression when she was a young woman. We are shaped not only by our times but by the times of our parents.

My mother grew up in a farm town on Long Island, about 50 miles from New York City. Her father owned a clothing store in town and some land in the area which he'd bought "on speculation" according to my mother. Had his speculation survived the Depression, he would have been a rich man, since the land is now covered with housing developments and shopping malls. But in the 1930's when the farmers couldn't pay their bills in his store, and there were no takers for the land, my grandfather lost much of his income and his land as well. My mother couldn't afford to attend college so she went to work in New York where she boarded with a widow to avoid the three hour train ride each day. My parents were married during the worst part of the Depression but my father always had a job.

My mother was never poor, not even close, but she maintained what is now called a Depression mentality and passed it on to me. "Waste not, want not." "A penny saved is a penny earned." I grew up with these homilies. Most of my generation did. Although we should have absorbed the post World War II optimism generated by the prosperity of the 1940's and '50's, many of us still drag behind us, like so much baggage, our parents' fear of being poor. "Live within your means," Mother said and we did. Jay's income provided a comfortable life. He made the decisions about when we could afford a bigger house or a new car. I made the decisions about whether we could buy the antique chair from the barn in Massachusetts. I worked for professional fulfillment and what used to be called "pin money" but is now known as discretionary income. With my small salary, I bought little luxuries for myself and saved the rest, investing in CD's—bank certificates of deposit.

During the 1970's, banks offered double digit interest rates on CD accounts and, to be competitive, sweetened the deal with gifts. Whenever I saved enough to meet the minimum deposit requirement, I opened a CD, earning as much as 13% interest as well as a new toaster, a pair of gold earrings or Corning dinnerware. CD's are insured so I was not taking any risks with my money. That would come later. In the 1980's, lower interest rates fueled the expansion of the economy and the golden days of high interest rates for savings accounts ended. I needed to find a better way for my money to earn money.

A stockbroker I interviewed for a newspaper article told me that by investing in the stock market he doubled his money every two years. I was intrigued by this concept. Although the world of finance was completely unknown to me I decided that it was time to invest my money. To do this I needed advice and the first person I asked was my husband. He told me to keep my money in the bank. He was conservative with money, as with attire. Since I didn't have a lot of money, he recommended keeping it where it was secure. I didn't take his recommendation. Instead I started reading the investment columns in financial magazines—Fortune and Forbes, Business Week and Money. Writers in these magazines recommended establishing a financial portfolio that included diversity and balance, stocks for growth, bonds for security. They all stressed a long-term approach, standard advice for dealing with the bumps and troughs of the market. Go for the long range and stay the course. Don't try to time the market. A long-term approach was not a problem for me. I was looking far into the future when my money could help Jay and me to buy a vacation home, travel and have a comfortable retirement.

All the advisers start with the fact than any investment strategy must include an assessment of one's tolerance for risk. I don't know whether risk and fear are gender specific, whether men are more likely to take physical risks than women, and whether either sex is more willing to take financial risk because each risk is different. When someone asks for my opinion on whether he should accept a job offer he is considering, I respond with a question. What is the worst that can happen if you take the job and what if you don't? I ask myself the same questions when I am fearful.

One day I watched three squirrels scamper up a tall oak tree. Almost to the top, they ventured out one after another onto a sturdy limb. From there the first squirrel jumped to the branch of a neighboring tree. The second followed. The third squirrel paused and looked. It inched a little closer to the end of the limb and looked again assessing the distance it would have to jump. It hesitated briefly, turned around, ran down the tree and climbed the next one. It ended up in the same spot as the others but by a slower, safer route. I wondered why the squirrel was afraid to take a jump that two others completed successfully. Why are people afraid to fly, swim, drive or risk their money? We all know that some fear is sensible, it keeps us safe. Other fears are irrational. We fear what we cannot control. Yet, despite my fear of being poor, I was ready to risk some of my hard-earned money. Buoyed by the optimism of the Reagan economy, I was ready to plunge in.

When I chose to invest my money in something more speculative than certificates of deposit, I approached the stock market understanding the risk, willing to accept it and hoping for prosperity. I decided that mutual funds would offer an entry-level approach for an inexperienced investor like me. With an opportunity to buy a small piece of many companies, I could invest in the blue chips as well as in small companies about which I knew nothing. The closest I had come to blue chips in the past were actual blue chips. Jay had a set of red, white and blue chips that we used to play poker with friends. The blue cost the most. I knew that.

Coincidentally Barry, who was then a senior in college, started a part-time job at a large, respected mutual fund investment firm in Baltimore. He suggested that I call their information line for advice. The man who answered was knowledgeable, extremely helpful in answering the questions of a novice and made no attempt to sell anything. I decided to buy funds the way I might have bet on a horse, because I liked their names and what they promised: "long term growth," "growth and income," "new American growth". I bought bonds for balance and for diversity, an international stock fund because a conservative and well-informed man I worked with told me it was a good investment. I figured he wouldn't steer me wrong on an investment. The outlook seemed so promising I never considered that I would actually <u>lose</u> money. When some of my stock funds suffered losses after the 1987 stock market crash I forgot that I was supposed to invest for the long-term. I sold some of the stock funds, transferring the money to bonds. This, as things turned out, was not a good move, but I was still a novice and made an occasional mistake. Eventually my stock funds regained their previous levels and went on to new heights. My investments became part of the longest bull, or rising, stock market in U.S. history. (How do I remember which is bull and which is bear, a falling stock market? Bull has a "u" in the middle for "up".)

When Jay died, I was not rich but I had an assortment of assets—stocks, bank accounts, mutual funds, a pension fund from my employment and insurance money. I also had many expenses. I had never developed a household budget or a long term financial plan. I had no concept of how much money I needed to live on for a year, what luxuries I could afford and the amount of money I would need to accumulate before I could retire. It was time to meet again with Jack. He told me to prepare a record of all my assets, as well as income and expenses. I collected the latest statement from each investment and bank account, a copy of my retirement plan, a lists of stocks with the amount of shares and current value, information on my house—mortgage, taxes and current appraised value. I sat down at the computer, created a spreadsheet and entered all the figures. Accounting spreadsheets are not a skill of mine. The one I created was not as an accountant would do it (in fact, he had difficulty understanding it) but it was a document that I could understand and continue to use. I tried to evaluate my possessions (a 50-year-old piano, antique Victorian chairs that had belonged to my mother-in-law, china vases that I received as wedding gifts that are still in the boxes they came in) and finally came up with an amount that was probably too high. I totaled my yearly expenses, anticipated my annual income and projected future expenses.

With my total worth neatly spread out on paper, I made an appointment to meet with Jack, my accountant, to discuss my financial future. Having prepared my tax returns, he was familiar with my financial situation but the information needed for taxes presents only a part of the picture. Now we could look at the panoramic view so that he could help me with my financial plan. We had never discussed the cost of developing a financial plan ahead of time or what the process would be. I naively trusted professionals who seemed eager to help me and assumed the rest would work out. That was my first mistake.

In outplacement classes we do an exercise called the nine-dot puzzle. Participants have to connect nine dots arranged in a square of three rows and columns, using only four lines and without lifting their pencil from the paper. I tell them there is a trick to it. After they struggle for a while, I illustrate the correct answer on the flip chart. The trick is to extend two of the lines beyond the boundary of a horizontal or vertical row. "You didn't tell us we could go outside the row," they complain. "That's right," I answer. "You made the assumption that you could not." In a job search, as in other aspects of life, making false assumptions can result in lost opportunities. I went to my meeting with Jack assuming that we had similar, if not identical goals - to help me manage my financial future in a way that would be comfortable and appropriate for me. I expected that his fee for this service would be commensurate with the value received.

It was a warm summer evening and Jack had his shirtsleeves rolled up although his tie was still firmly in place. Other staff members were working as well and the reception area smelled residually of pizza.

"What is your goal?" Jack asked when we were seated in his office. "Where would you like to be?"

"In a little house by the water where I can write," I answered without hesitation. I had not planned on giving that answer. I was amazed at my audacity in expressing such a vision for myself. It was a dream sitting in the back of my head that suddenly found words. One of my early ambitions was to be a writer after my eighth grade teacher told me she expected me to write a book. Not wanting to disappoint, I did - forty years later. Established in my career as a career counselor, an occupation that did not exist when I was in eighth grade, I wrote a book on how to find a summer job. I achieved my fifteen minutes of fame as the authority on summer jobs and was interviewed by the media whenever they needed a summer jobs expert. My parents in Florida saw me on TV. I visited dozens of radio stations, from the glamorous NBC in Rockefeller Center to small local stations where the furniture was held together by duct tape. At NBC I felt like Alice in Wonderland, looking around in the elevator and walking down the corridors, hoping to rub elbows with someone famous. I was as likely to see a celebrity on the street as I was in that building, but that didn't keep me from trying. After my interview, walking out of a secure entrance, I passed two women in the lobby watching the door for famous people.

"I wonder who she is," one said to the other as I strolled past trying to look famous. I'm nobody, lady. A gaper like you. A housewife from New Jersey who hoped to be introduced to Tom Brokaw in the hallway and met the college intern instead.

As for my desire to live near the water, my love of swimming is matched only by my desire to look at water and listen to it. Oceans, streams, brooks, rivers, canals, waterfalls, lakes, ponds, fountains and pools draw me as a moth to flame. I will eat the most mediocre food if the restaurant overlooks the bay. A walk on the beach, the heavy noise of the surf, the cool evening sand on my toes provides a healing no therapy can equal. I love to see how the ocean becomes gray or blue with the changing light, how the first early morning rowboat sends shock waves across the flat surface of the lake. At the beach, I watch the ducks, gulls and cormorants dive for their sustenance while children bob in their pink plastic tubes and container ships creep wormlike along the horizon. I know a woman who moved to the east coast from Denver where she grew up. She longed to see mountains. She missed the way the morning sun turned the peaks lavender and the evening sun set behind the foothills. She felt disoriented without mountains as if she couldn't find her true direction. Her spirit required mountains as mine does water.

"Let's see if we can make that happen," Jack replied in response to my dream as he began to analyze the assorted collection of information that I presented him. The appointment lasted about an hour. I am not sure now what I expected the outcome to be. I hoped for a magic plan that would tell me what my income would be, how much I could spend on clothes, travel and lawn care, what stocks I should buy and when I could begin to think about the house by the water with my writing desk in an upstairs window. I did not feel that such a plan was beyond my reach. I was involved in the same wishful thinking that my job search clients express when they come to me looking for magic solutions.

"Just give me a list of companies that are looking for my skills and experience, not too long a commute and with a better salary than I was earning," they say. I tell them that I will help them to understand who they are. By helping them to define their skills and goals, I will give them the tools to make their own list. They look disappointed. They want me to do it for them. So here I was looking for the same magic solutions. Tell me what to do and make it happen. What I could not imagine was the bizarre result this kind of thinking would get me.

Jack promised to review the material and develop a financial plan. He called a few weeks later to say the plan was ready. I was excited about this and we set up a date and time to meet. He then asked if I would mind if Bob Rienzo joined us for the meeting. I assumed this was a member of his staff and agreed to meet with Bob as well. I was again making assumptions. As a lawyer, Jay never made assumptions when it came to business. That was my second mistake. It took me a long time to learn.

My third mistake was wearing the wrong clothing to the meeting. I usually wear business clothing when meeting with individuals with whom I am going to do business. Whether buying a car or getting a quote on installing a new floor, I find that wearing a jacket and skirt rather than a sweater and slacks will get me different treatment. I carry a small briefcase with a pad of paper inside so I can make notes. The same pad would fit easily into my purse but the brief case is more impressive. When a woman appears in a sweatsuit she may be a judge, engineer or the superintendent of schools, but the assumption is that somewhere, behind the scenes, a man is controlling the money. In 1986, when I looked for a new car and I wore my casual clothes, only one auto dealer sat down and spoke with me. The others handed me brochures and told me to return with my husband when I was ready to buy. Women now are taken seriously by car dealers. Some actually are car dealers, but even today it helps to dress for success on occasions where money is going to be discussed.

For the meeting with Jack, I broke this rule. We were scheduled to meet at 5 on a hot Indian summer day in September. I rushed home from work, quickly took off my suit, pantyhose, and black pumps. Following the meeting I planned to go to the health club for my usual lap swim so I dressed for sport, not business. I arrived at the meeting wearing a short sleeve shirt, summer skirt and sandals. Jack, as usual, was in a white shirt, tie intact. He greeted me with his broad smile and ushered me into his office where Bob Rienzo waited. Bob stood up when I entered the room. He wore a well-cut navy suit, a red power tie, designer eyeglasses, and shiny tassel loafers. He had an expensive haircut, good teeth, excellent eye contact and a firm handshake. He looked like a talk show host. Compared to Jack's casual demeanor and my sport clothes he was too perfect.

Jack said they had developed a financial plan for me and Bob handed me the plan. Titled *Financial Planning Considerations for Sandra Schocket*, it was bound in a spiral binder with a heavy clear plastic cover. "Presented by Jack Ward, CPA and Robert Rienzo, Jr., September 1995," it said on the title page. Inside were 55 pages describing my financial situation including graphs and pie charts in four colors. The stated objectives of the plan were retirement planning and estate planning. The retirement planning portion offered an adequate assessment of where I was in the fall of 1995. A portion called Analysis included "financial condition" models projecting my cash flow to 2019 when I will be 83. No recommendations were included for changing or improving my current asset mix. The focus of this Financial Plan was not managing my money while I was alive but protecting it from taxation when I am dead.

A section called *Long Term Care Impact* pointed out that I currently have no plan to protect my assets from "potential catastrophic expenses associated with long-term convalescent care." With the cost of services provided by nursing homes averaging $22,000 to $44,000 annually, the report indicated that people paying long term care costs on their own could be financially devastated by these expenses.

The Estate Planning section began with the title page Family Income Trust W/GST , followed by Leveraging Your Gift, QPRT, and The Economics of Gifting. This part covered the mechanisms that can be established for denying the IRS a major portion of my estate when I die while saving the maximum amount of dollars for my heirs.

"Are you healthy?" asked Bob.

An odd question, I thought. I wondered why Bob would be concerned about my health, but I told him my health was good.

"Good," he said, and recommended a concept called "Gifting" which required that I pass a physical examination. Suddenly what he was recommending became clear. By purchasing an $800,000 life insurance policy with an annual premium of $23,672 for ten years I could protect my heirs from inheritance taxes. The "gifting" was my outlay of almost $250,000. It was like the "courtesy" calls that telemarketers make at dinner time. Now I understood Bob's role. He was a financial advisor and also a life insurance salesman. He was one of the 98% of financial consultants selling a product—the very group that Jack had warned against when we met six months earlier. By this time the meeting had gone on for more than an hour. The room seemed to be getting smaller and hotter. The information in the report was far more than I could grasp, understand and make a decision on at that point. I needed a break. I needed to sit down by myself in a quiet place with a tall glass of iced tea and digest the figures page by page. My mind started to wander away to the pool where I could silently swim endless laps putting worrisome money matters out of my head.

"Now we are ready for the implementation phase," said Jack, opening a whole new topic when I was ready for a quick closure. "A plan is only as good as what you do with it. It is important for us to implement this plan *as soon as possible.*" He strongly emphasized the last four words.

"What do you think of gifting?" Bob inquired, still looking cool in his Wall Street clothes. I was the only one sweating.

I told him I would consider it but did not feel ready to make a decision ($23,672 annual outlay sounded a little steep to me, considering my salary wasn't much higher than that).

"How about long-term health care insurance?" he asked, taking another tack. He pointed out annual nursing home costs would be $50,000 or more when I need such services. "I own a house," I replied. "When I'm ready for a nursing home my son can sell my house. Your statistics say the average nursing home stay is 2 1/2 years. The sale of my house will cover that." Bob looked surprised but didn't answer. "This may not be as easy as I thought," his look seemed to say.

"What are your objections to going forward with this plan?" Jack asked. There were the words "going forward" again.

"I want time to read it, think about it, get some other advice."

"Whose advice?" Jack continued pressing.

"Maybe a lawyer, a financial advisor."

"Lawyers don't know about this. I had a client who got bad advice from a lawyer and lost a lot of money." Jack's tone of voice was not kind. I had never seen him so defensive.

"I'm smarter than that," I answered. I was beginning to feel small and insignificant, like a little girl in a room with two grownups. If I had worn my navy suit, they would not have treated me this way. If I were a man, they definitely would not have treated me this way. The plan was in my lap and I nervously kept finguring the corners of the pages. "I can't do any more today," I said suddenly and stood up. "Maybe we can set another time. What do I owe you?"

"Bob and I have invested a lot of hours in this," Jack said. He didn't mention an amount of money. When I tried to pin him down he said that the entire plan, including implementation would cost no more than $1000. I wished I had done my homework and had a basis for comparison. Given the 55 pages, colored graphs and number of meetings this did not seem out of line. What did seem out of line was the badgering, the hard sell, the implication that I was not able to make my own financial decisions or to consult others as qualified as those in the room. In any business situation, I am wary of a professional who is uncomfortable with a second opinion or who exerts pressure for a speedy resolution. I was very angry, hurt and, even worse, afraid I was going to cry. Crying would have been a disaster. I would have looked like a weak and helpless female when I wanted to show these two men that I was as strong as they were. Jack pushed for another appointment, the sooner the better. I wanted to put it off. We agreed on a date a few weeks later. Jack seemed disappointed but tried to hide it and Bob was no longer smiling. I shook hands with both men, and left, clutching the plan to my chest.

My head was spinning as I walked down the stairs leading to the outside and my release. I felt manipulated and blamed myself for getting into a situation where everyone would come out a loser. I wondered what Jack and Bob were saying about me. Had they underestimated my ability to think for myself or overestimated my vulnerability? The evening was still surprisingly warm for September and the humidity hung in the air. I drove to the health club hoping that Paul would be there. Paul is the unelected "mayor" of the health club, although if we had an election he would surely win. He knows everyone's name and life story. Ask him about his travels or Notre Dame's football team and you probably will not escape for half an hour, but he's also a good listener. As a retired bond salesman, he is knowledgeable about finance and I knew he was the person I needed at that moment. Luckily, he was sitting in the hot tub at the far end of the room, chatting with two women when I arrived. "Wait," I shouted from across the room. "Don't go anywhere, I have to talk to you." I changed into my bathing suit and was in the hot tub in five minutes. The two women had disappeared. I described my meeting with the accountant and insurance salesman.

"What should I do?" I asked. "I took the plan. Do I have to meet with them again? Did they give me good advice?"

"This is what you tell them," he said. He joined his thumb and four fingertips together, put them to his lips and flicked his wrist as if he was blowing a kiss.

"What does that mean?" I asked.

"It means get lost," he answered. "You're not obligated to them. I hope you didn't pay them."

He made me laugh and I felt a little better. I jumped into the pool and began to swim. With my tight fitting rubber cap and goggles, my bent elbows pointing upward, I looked like a large aquatic bug. Up and down the pool I went, arm over arm, three kicks to each stroke, head to one side, breath in, face in the water and blow out, three more strokes, head to the other side, breath in, blow out. The rhythm was delicious and hypnotic. The water was cool on my face and I could feel the stress leaving my body. At times like this, I missed Jay the most. When I got into trouble, he always knew what to do. He fought my battles and rescued me from bad decisions. I never realized how hard it would be doing it all on my own. I have always had great respect for single mothers knowing what a difficult life they lead—driving all the car pools, making all the decisions, calming the fears and nursing the hurts. How fortunate I had been to have a husband who was a good father to our boys, who shared the joys and pains of raising them. Being alone at my age was nothing compared to raising children without a partner, but that doesn't mean it was easy.

By the time I left the health club, my hurt had turned back to anger. I wanted a financial plan and knew the one I had was useless despite its pie charts and four-color graphs. Later that evening I called Carol to tell her what had happened and ask her advice on what to do next. She was surprised that Jack had shared my financial situation with Bob without my permission. Information between an accountant and client is confidential. Revealing it is breaking a trust. Jack should have given me Bob's name as a referral, not included him in the meeting. The decision to meet with him should have been mine. Carol suggested that I call Jack and tell him I was disappointed that he would disclose privileged financial information. As for buying a life insurance policy that would help my heirs to pay inheritance taxes, Carol did not recommend it. "Cancel the appointment, pay the bill and find yourself a financial planner and a new accountant," was her advice.

I called Jack the next day. His tone had changed completely. He apologized for not consulting me before bringing Bob in but defended Bob as "the best I've worked with." He pushed again for implementing the plan. Given all the work that goes into it, he said he found it frustrating if a plan ends up gathering dust. I wondered what his stake was and why he was trying so hard to persuade me. I assumed he shared a piece of Bob's fee if I bought something. I cancelled the meeting we had scheduled saying I needed more time, and told him I wanted no further meetings that included Bob Rienzo. I requested an itemized bill of expenses. The bill never came and subsequent tax reform has changed the rules, making much of the plan obsolete. Most people would have looked for a new accountant, but I did not because I believe that Jack is a good accountant. He continues to prepare my tax returns and advise me on tax related matters. He is always available and willing to answer questions when I call. In this situation he showed poor judgment and I can forgive him for that. The following winter, when we met to discuss my taxes, he apologized again. We no longer talk about this incident, but I know he remembers it, probably with regret, each time I visit his office.

Eventually I found a financial advisor to manage the insurance money I received. He has created a portfolio of investments that include blue chip companies, smaller growth companies and, at my request, bonds for safety. He earns an annual fee based on a percentage of the total funds he manages. We share the same goal—if my money increases so does his commission. He is honest and I believe works in my best interest. He keeps me informed on how he is investing my money and I receive a monthly statement from the brokerage firm that handles the transactions. Managing money is a time-consuming business and to do it well requires skill. I am happy to pay a qualified professional to do the job.

Each widow's financial situation is different, and the decisions I made may not be appropriate for someone else. I chose not to invest in long-term health-care insurance, but I frequently recommend it to others. With nursing home costs continuing to increase, such coverage may soon be necessary for everyone. I was fortunate that my husband's life insurance was generous. Nevertheless, if I had not worked almost without a gap since college graduation, my financial status would have been considerably different. My pension and savings, along with my current job, enable me to have a comfortable life. I often wonder how I would have supported myself if I suddenly became widowed and had no marketable profession. I think I would have gone to secretarial school, learned all the newest computer skills and applied to every large corporation that offered good benefits. A well-qualified secretary can always find a job.

I have counseled hundreds of women who were looking for the next step. Some improved their skills through education and training, gaining new qualifications as well as the confidence and self-esteem to succeed. I know that many of them went on to new jobs, careers, even marriages. I met them when they needed help. They did not know that I needed help too but in many cases, they helped me as much as I helped them.

Learning to be Single

The first year is the hardest, I heard repeatedly. Life would be easier after I experienced "the firsts" without my husband and son—Valentine's Day, wedding anniversary, the birthdays of those who died and those who lived, a winter of shoveling snow and a summer of cutting the grass. It was true. The first year was all anxiety but this first year business is a little over-rated. The second year was hard too. Knowing what to expect helped because I could prepare for it. I struggled through my income taxes the first year; the next it was a breeze. Sometimes preparation was not enough. Well in advance of any snow, I hired a man with a truck and a plow to plow my long driveway so I could drive out after a storm. Men with plows are at a premium where I live and I considered myself lucky to have found one. But when we had a major blizzard that winter, he never showed up. I felt so lonely and isolated watching my neighbors whose driveways had been cleared, driving up and down the street, doing their errands when the best I could do was wade through hip-deep snow to get to the curb. It was like the grief cycle. My snow plower had abandoned me. I was angry and wounded. That blizzard taught me the importance of fending for myself, and the necessity of having a back-up plan.

I thought I had learned the skills I needed to survive the threats of nature until, a few years later, Hurricane Floyd struck. I made the necessary preparations—bought candles, flashlight batteries, milk and tuna fish. Unless a tree fell on the house, I was in little danger of harm, but I remembered the hurricanes when my family was here, when I felt protected by my husband's strength and confidence. My sons had kept me busy and the whole experience had the air of adventure, like camping out. This time, when the power failed I sat alone in the eerie darkness of an empty house. The hurricane arrived a few days before the Jewish High Holidays so I had on hand the 24-hour memorial candles that we light on the holiday to commemorate the anniversary of family deaths. Some people light one candle for all their loved ones, but I had bought four, one for each parent, Jay and Barry. As night fell, I used the memorial candles to light my way. They reminded me of my solitary place in the windy darkness. The following morning, still without power, a neighbor helped me to open manually my electric garage door and a friend with electricity stored some of my perishable food in her refrigerator. The "firsts" were all challenging and preparation was useful but nothing helps me to prepare for Barry's birthday or having no one to kiss on New Year's Eve. Both of those events remain uncharted territory, year after year.

Some life changes were immediate but others took longer. Being alone required vast adjustments in ways I could not have imagined when I was married. When people asked Jay how long he was married his usual response was, "I've always been married." We met in our early twenties and married a year later. I have not been single since I was 23 years old and I was a different person then. First, I had to learn the language—to become an "I" instead of a "we". The "we" response was so automatic, I could not remember ever being an "I".

"How long have you lived in your house?" "We've been here 15 years."

"Are you taking a vacation this year?" "Yes, we'll probably go to Maine for a week."

I often hear people who speak of themselves always as "we," as if they have no individuality. Losing my husband has taught me to speak for myself. For me, saying "I" instead of "we" was not too difficult. I mastered the language within a few weeks. Becoming an "I" was something else. That did not happen until after Andy left. He had come for three days when his father took ill and stayed for a month after events turned tragic. While he was here, he was my support. He provided structure and the facade of normalcy. I shopped for food and made dinner every night. He ran errands and did household chores. Together, we cleaned closets and made decisions. We went to the synagogue on Friday nights and stood to say the prayer for the dead. On the day Andy decided to leave, I was presenting a job search workshop at a consulting firm not far from home. Andy called to ask if he could meet me for lunch. He had never done this before. Perhaps he was feeling the pain of separation, of going back to his home as a different person, diminished by the loss of his father and brother. Maybe he was thinking of my being alone. We ate sandwiches in the cafeteria and traded small talk about his trip. A typical mother, I told him to drive carefully, eat the food I had packed for him, and to seek counseling that was available at his university. When we had finished eating, he hugged me longer than he usually would and walked quickly down the long hall to the elevator. I watched his tall narrow frame become smaller as if he was disappearing into a picture with converging lines like the ones in psychology textbooks used to teach perspective. Then he turned the corner and I was looking down an empty hall.

When I returned to the office, I had a room full of people waiting for me to help them through their job loss crisis so I had little time to feel the sudden wrench of Andy's departure or to feel sorry for myself. When leading workshops I have to be upbeat and positive. I have to listen to the fears and concerns of the participants and be responsive to their needs. I have no time to think about myself or my own troubles. The people in my workshops are in pain, they look to me to offer the encouragement that will help them to heal. "Of course you will find another job. It's just a matter of time." My group and I completed the tasks that would get them closer to their goal. After work that day, I spent an hour swimming at the health club so by the time I got home, most of the evening was gone.

The impact of my new solitary life did not strike until the weekend when I awoke on Saturday feeling as alone as I had ever felt in my life, the same pit-of-the-stomach loneliness I felt when my parents drove off leaving me at college. I waved from the front steps of the dorm trying to feel brave as their car pulled away, through the green of the campus and then out toward the highway. I wanted to run after them yelling, "Take me home, this is all a mistake, I don't like this place." Instead I went upstairs and began to unpack. I have asked women and men, professionals and leaders in their field, homemakers and captains of industry, to describe times when they have felt most lonely. Most included being left for the first time at camp or college. I hadn't felt that lonely again until now. The reality of my new life began to become apparent, like an instant photograph that develops slowly before one's eyes. I had nothing social to do all weekend. No place to go and no one to talk to. This was different from the times when Jay was away and I made plans to meet friends on a weekend or when I traveled and ate meals alone away from home.

There is a distinction between being alone and being lonely. Many times in my life, I have chosen to be alone and enjoyed the luxury of solitude, but having someone to come home to made the difference. Traveling alone, eating alone in a restaurant when I was married, I stored up impressions in my head, selecting the memories I would share with Jay when I returned home. At home alone when he was away, I did the same thing. I managed my chores without him but I kept my stories to share along with the pile of magazines waiting for him to read. I filtered my experience through his eyes as well as my own, and sometimes through Barry's as well. At times, I couldn't wait to call Barry to tell him about a person I met or conversation I had. Neither of them was very far away in my mind, even if I was alone. Any separation was only temporary but in my current state I could feel deep within me a different kind of solitude, born of loss and despair.

First, the little things affected me. If I wanted the newspaper and a fresh bagel, I had to go out and buy them. On the weekends, Jay always did that. No more breakfasts in my bathrobe. Over coffee, we each read our sections of the paper along stereotypical lines, he the sports section and I the human interest stories—Doctor Carves Initials on Woman's Abdomen After Caesarean Delivery, Executive Missing Following Stock Fund Plunge. The highlight of my weekend was always Saturday night. Jay and I usually went to a restaurant on Saturday night, or I prepared something for dinner at home that I didn't have time to make during the week. We went out to a movie or brought one home. Saturday night is supposed to be special, a night to entertain or be entertained. In the 1940's, when the men were away at war, there was a song called, "Saturday Night is the Loneliest Night of the Week." Written from the perspective of the woman waiting at home, the song laments the emptiness of a Saturday night without a man. When I was in college, not having a Saturday night date to look forward to dampened my whole week. Suddenly, I was back in the same situation. I survived that first weekend alone by doing the things I would have done if Jay were away on business but I did them with a different attitude. I rented a movie, ate take-out food, went swimming and felt sorry for myself.

Living alone frightens many people. I know women who have never had their own room. A sister, a roommate, a husband always shared their space. They cannot conceive of a life alone. A widow whose adult daughter lives at home told me she fears her daughter's leaving because, alone in her house, she would cease to exist. With no one to respond to her conversation, she would be like the proverbial tree that falls in the forest. I was not afraid of, or disturbed by, solitary living. I had done it before. Although robberies are not uncommon in my neighborhood, I believe I am safe from live intruders. My fear is not of man but of beast. I have some experience in this regard.

On a lovely, warm summer night, as I relaxed reading in bed, a bat flew by. I jumped out of bed, screaming like a banshee and ran around slamming doors to the bedroom, trapping the animal inside. In my mind, it grew to be the size of a winged prehistoric creature from Jurassic Park. I ran downstairs and called the police. No help there. They told me to turn off the lights and open all the windows in the room where the bat was. With that advice I would have had a dozen bats in the room instead of one. In the morning, after a sleepless night on the couch, I found an exterminator willing to come. Still in my nightgown, I called a friend to help me brave the trip upstairs so I could get some clothing. We stalked up the stairs, she directly behind me, like two cops about to confront a dangerous criminal. I dashed into the bedroom and grabbed my clothes while she hovered in the background. The exterminator found the culprit behind a picture in my bedroom. I slept downstairs for three nights before I found the courage to return to my bed. The camel crickets were worse. Large black things that hop like grasshoppers invaded the house, from cellar to attic. I never knew where the next one would appear—in the kitchen, the garage or the bathtub. It took two exterminators and many months to rid the house of them. Having faced all these creatures once, I think I might do better the next time. They unnerved me so because they attacked when my coping skills were at their lowest. The previous time we had a bat in the house, Jay handled it. That's what husbands are for.

While training myself to become an "I," I also had to learn how to talk about my "children." Andy and I were at a dinner party when a woman at the table asked me if I had any other children. I hesitated for a minute. Our host, seeing me floundering, jumped in and said, "No, she doesn't." The woman must have wondered why I myself couldn't answer such a basic question. The host probably told her after I left. The next day I called my friend Julie. " How do I tell people how many children I have?" I inquired. Her response: "I say I have three children but only two of them are living, and then I change the subject." She pointed out that by saying I have only one son, I am denying Barry's existence. But sometimes that is the easier answer. Genevieve Jurgensen wrote about the death of her two little girls in an automobile accident and the two children she subsequently had. "At the square with the children, I was not like other mothers...If another woman wanted to talk to me, I had only two options: a bright facade which devastated me...or a truth that was socially unacceptable. ("These are my two younger children. The elder ones died four years ago.") I would always be out of place." (Jurgensen, 1999.) Telling strangers how my husband and son died puts me in an awkward position and pains me in the telling. The setting isn't always appropriate. The person asking and I may never meet again so I feel no need to share my life story with her. She may think she is asking a perfectly simple and straightforward question and will not be prepared for the melancholy response. When someone becomes a friend, or engages me in a way that I feel comfortable, I tell him or her about my other son, the one who died when he was 30.

During the first few months of bereavement, I had difficulty relating to other people. Not an hour passed when I did not think of Jay and Barry and feel the open wound of their deaths. I knew that others saw me in that way as well. Like other victims of singular fortune, whether good or tragic, I have become a one-story person. Our losses define us, whether we write the definition or someone else does. Columnist and author Anna Quindlen wrote, "My mother died when I was nineteen. For a long time, it was all you needed to know about me: ... "Meet you in the lobby in ten minutes— I have long brown hair, am on the short side, have on a red coat, and my mother died when I was nineteen." (Quindlen, 1988) I have become "the-woman-whose-husband-and-son-died-within - 24 hours." Although I have done many things in my life, I am identified by only one. It is what people think of first when they see me. It is like having a visible scar that people don't talk about and pretend they can't see when, like a light that is blinding them, it is the only thing they do see. I might as well be wearing a billboard.

My losses have become my identity. Some people want to talk about it. Like reactions to large tragedies— the Challenger disaster, the death of Princess Diana, people want to tell me exactly where they were when they heard the news. Julie was shopping in Barnes and Noble on a Sunday afternoon when she called home to speak with her son. He told her that a mutual friend had called to tell her Jay and Barry had died. Sometimes, over lunch or dinner, a friend wants to tell me her end of it—how she heard, who she called next. It may not be the first time she has told me. I realize that this is her need, not mine, but I have arranged for us to get together for a meal that I hoped would be pleasurable for both of us. Do I politely let her go on with her story while I sit uncomfortably picking at my food, my appetite suddenly gone? Usually I do not. I ask her to postpone the discussion until after lunch and quickly change the subject.

People still ask me how I am getting along. Others no longer ask, assuming I have "gotten over it" and moved on to other things. We maintain a facade. Yet I know as soon as I leave the person I have been speaking with will turn to the person next to her and say "She is the woman -who -lost- her- husband- and- son- within- twenty- four- hours." "Really, how is she doing?" With new acquaintances I have no label. When conversation turns to family, I remain silent. A young widow I know took early retirement from her job and moved to Colorado where she became a ski instructor. There, she says, she is known only for who she currently is, not as the wife of a man who died young. She suggested that I move away, to a place where my story will not follow me, like someone in the witness protection program or the captain of the high school football team who never lived up to his potential. I don't know what my tag line was before my husband and son died although I must have had several. Women with children the ages of mine remember me as the woman who worked when she should have been at home with her children. The lifeguards at the lake know me only as the lady with the big red, white and blue tube. To many I was Jay's wife and Barry's mother. They are the identities I have lost. I think about starting a new life but I have a suspicion that no matter where I go, my ghosts will follow. My new acquaintances will tire of hearing me talk about Andy and sooner or later, someone will ask if I have any other children. I will again become the woman -who-lost- her- husband- and-son- within- twenty- four-hours. Like a sailor with a picture of a ship tattooed on his arm, it is the identity I will bear for the rest of my life.

During the first year I cried a lot, loud heart-wrenching sobs. I still cry occasionally, but they are quieter tears. It's difficult to predict what might trigger a cry. Julie sobs when she hears the song, "I'll be Home for Christmas," grieving for her daughter who will never spend another holiday at home. I cried when I saw a little boy ask his older brother to help him tie his shoe and I cried when the song "He's Not Heavy, He's My Brother" came over the loudspeaker system in the supermarket. I cried for both my sons, the one who is gone and the one who will never again have a big brother. Seeing a man patiently waiting while his wife tried on clothes in a woman-only store brought tears as did watching my neighbors on a Saturday evening get into the car together to go out for dinner, something so routine they did not realize how lucky they were to do it.

The big sobs usually come only once a year. During the Jewish holiday of Yom Kippur a special service is held to remember the dead. For everyone, this is a sad service. For me it is doubly so. The first year I cried so hard I had to leave, compose myself in the ladies' room and return with a fresh supply of tissues. Each year I hope the service will be easier to bear. I try to muffle the sobs but my shoulders shake and people around me look on uncomfortably wanting to help but not knowing what to do. "Are you all right?" they ask me when the service is over as I try to calm myself. "I felt like hugging you," a woman told me, but she was sitting too far away for hugs.

About a month after Jay and Barry died, I overheard a woman in a workshop I was giving telling another participant that her husband had died unexpectedly during minor ear surgery. I cornered her during a break, anxious to hear her story and share mine. She was the one who told me about "the firsts." I asked for advice on getting through them. "Look at family pictures," she recommended. "They will help you to remember all the happy times you shared." At that time, looking at pictures would have been extremely painful. I told her so. It has taken me years to be able to look at pictures of Barry and Ellen's wedding.

"What helps?" she asked. "What makes you feel better? Find a way to do those things." I had known her for only a day but she gave me her address and home telephone number in Maryland. "Call me anytime, day or night if you need help," she said. I never called her, but it was her willingness to be called that helped me so much as well as finding someone whose experience was similar to mine. I thought about the concept of what helps and have already talked about the most common methods: friends and family, support groups, counseling, medication, exercise.

Within the past few years, the Internet has opened up a vast support network enabling grievers to "speak" with one another not just locally, but internationally with anyone who shares their language. A librarian referred me to the Internet when I was seeking bereavement books. I found not only books, which numbered in the 100's, but an amazing variety and depth of on-line offerings. The many websites related to grief range from helpful to hokey. Individuals with questionable academic credentials offer bereavement counseling for a fee. One business sells custom handmade teddy bears "that reflect your deceased loved one's personality as much as the clothes they wore." An illustration shows a bear wearing a tuxedo shirt and bow tie like that worn by the deceased, presumably an entertainer.

Well-organized and well-run bereavement websites provide a useful service. I found discussion and support groups, bulletin boards and chat rooms for a broad variety of losses: loss of spouse, sibling, child, only child, adult child, newborn, suicide, violence, substance abuse and, yes, multiple loss. The research I had sought earlier to understand my place on the bereavement scale was here in raw form on the Internet. I found the people whose losses were similar to mine. I felt as though I had opened a door into a vast room of those who have survived tragedy and there was a chair waiting for me. Individuals were seeking advice as well as helping one another. At the multiple loss site, the stories made me weep. There was Patrick, whose parents and younger brother were killed in an automobile accident on the way to visit him; Beth, who came home from work to find her entire family murdered and Amelia, whose 14-year-old son killed her 12-year-old daughter. They presented a Biblical litany of woes, a scale by which to measure one's own. There was a surrealism to this—people sharing their sorrows with strangers whom they cannot see or hear, whose names and locations they sometimes do not know, and being comforted in return. In addition to the posted messages with opportunities for response, there are chatrooms with scheduled meetings. These are the ultimate virtual support groups. Someone in Florida reaching out to someone in Oregon. A woman in Oklahoma communicating daily with a woman in England whose common bond is the death of their sons.

I spent a great deal of time on the Internet telling people about the book I was writing and asking for their help. I received more than 25 responses. Some helped me not only with the book but with my life. They gave me the confidence I had lost when my family members died.

They encouraged me to continue, and to tell their stories which they hoped would help others. I still keep in touch with several of them. I wish I could have helped them more.

Slowly, I started to reassemble my life, like trying to glue back together a much loved bowl that has broken. I might get it to look good, with the cracks hardly showing, but every time I dust it I know they are there. I had to redefine my attitude about being alone. I could make decisions about this. It was under my control. I could determine whether I wanted to do something on my own or seek companionship. Sometimes my decision relates to transportation. I didn't realize that single people drive so much. Where I live most public transportation is aimed at getting commuters into and out of New York City. Traveling from town to town by train or bus could take hours. Jay did many errands that cut down on my driving. He always drove when we were in the car together and he did most of the driving on long trips. Now just being in the passenger seat is a luxury. Riding in the High Occupancy Vehicle lane is heaven. Friends scold me because I have not yet bought a cellular phone for use on long trips. They remind me that my car could break down when I am alone on a dark highway late at night. Like locking the barn door after the horse has run away, one of my mother's favorite expressions from a past more rural than hers, I will buy the phone when experience tells me I should have owned one all along.

When I first became a widow, I did no cooking. I ate Chinese takeout, frozen dinners or leftovers from restaurant meals that I brought home in little plastic containers. This lasted for a few weeks until I tired of the diet and wanted some good home-cooked food even if I had no one to share it with. One Saturday I went to the fish market and bought a beautiful piece of salmon. I sautéed it with a little olive oil and some basil leaves I had grown and frozen the previous summer. I cooked some rice and made a salad of Boston lettuce, radicchio, black olives and sliced mushrooms. I bought a fresh Italian roll. I set it all out with a glass of white wine, looked at it and burst into tears. It seemed so pitiful— an elegant dinner for one. Beautiful dinners are supposed to be for at least two. Look at the television commercials: two attractive people are sharing a romantic dinner, white tablecloth and candles. Occasionally in movies, the woman prepares a dinner for two and the guy doesn't show up, or he shows up hours later after she has become drunk on the wine. In my case, the guy would never show up. I stared at the food for a while. I had worked hard on that meal. I was hungry and it was waiting. I dried my eyes and ate my first dinner cooked for me alone.

Since then I have eaten thousands. I probably spend too much time cooking for myself. In winter I cook soups and stews—the comfort foods that remind me of a time when the boys were growing. They ate so much I had to learn to cook in larger quantities. As teenagers, they asked why we never had hash anymore. Because hash is made from leftovers and we never have any leftovers, I told them. Now I have plenty of leftovers because I have not managed to scale down some of my favorite dishes to an appropriate portion for one thin woman. The freezer is full of food I prepared from recipes designed for eight. I have learned to enjoy my summer meals when I can be more casual. I buy corn and tomatoes picked that day from a neighboring farm. I open a can of tuna fish and eat on the porch where the light lingers long into the evening. It is a quiet and peaceful time. I watch the sun lose its brightness and the lake turn bronze. The birds gather for their nightly meeting in the oak tree. I enjoy my solitude. My dinner is not the hectic end-of-the-day dinner I once had with people coming and going, one arriving late, another running off early, but it suits my schedule. I have adjusted.

Holidays and special occasions were a different story. Weeks ahead, I worried about how I would spend them. I dreaded being alone at times when family is so important. Like the Pilgrims, my first Thanksgiving was the hardest. It was the anniversary of the last time our family was whole and happy. With its key elements of family, food, and gratitude, Thanksgiving is a difficult time to be alone. I decided to go to New York for the day. Hundreds, maybe even thousands of people spend Thanksgiving alone in New York. I knew I could find an open restaurant and maybe a Broadway show. At the last minute, a neighbor invited me for dinner. As if I had walked into a Saturday Evening Post cover, I entered a Norman Rockwell holiday, the kind I remembered from my childhood when we celebrated the day with my aunts, uncles and cousins. Although we were Jews transplanted to New England, you would have thought from the food that we had come on the Mayflower. My mother and aunts were excellent cooks. Whoever was the hostess that year served a turkey that looked like a magazine advertisement. There was the usual variety of colorful accompaniments along with homemade apple and pumpkin pie for dessert. The table gleamed with rarely used silver and crystal. The dishes had gold rims. I reveled in this elegance that was hauled out only once or twice a year. We were just the right size family to fit around the dining room table with all the leaves in, so we children did not have to sit at a separate table. I wore my best clothes and ate until my mother told me I would burst if I ate any more.

I did not wear my best clothes to my neighbor's house because she told me that dress was casual. A pity. I would like to have dressed up. Otherwise, everything was traditional. Her family had all assembled and her table was beautifully laden with glorious food. When her husband said grace, thanking God that they could all be together to share the goodness of Thanksgiving, I was afraid I would sob out loud and embarrass everyone. A tear or two rolled down my cheek but soon the food was passed and I was distracted from my sorrow. I was thankful that I wasn't alone. I was privileged to share the day with a lovely family. And the meal was delicious.

One year, a woman I knew from work invited me to her house for a Passover seder. The seder is a special festive meal, including a service that commemorates the Jews' flight from Egypt. It is as important a feast to Jews as Christmas dinner is to Christians. My family came together for elegant seders when I was a child. In my own home, I too made lovely seders which we shared with friends and family. I always looked forward to this annual celebration and found it a difficult time to be alone when I had no one to share it with. The woman who invited me was single but she had assembled 18 people for the holiday meal. After introducing us to one another, she seated us at a long table, actually a collection of tables in the living room of her condo. She led the seder service, usually a man's function, and served a lavish meal. It was a joyous occasion and she seemed happiest of all to be able to share her hospitality with so many people. The solution was so simple, why hadn't I seen it? Waiting for an invitation was not the only answer. I too could fill my house with people. The following year I had my own seder. Andy came with his girlfriend. I invited Christian neighbors who had never attended a seder. I led the service. It is customary to set a glass of wine on the table for the prophet Elijah and to open the door during the service to welcome Elijah to the table. When we opened the door, I felt that in spirit Jay and Barry were also joining us. We lifted our glasses to all of them.

Seeing that I could do it, I hosted luncheons and dinners, brunches and cocktail parties. I offered my home for meetings. I learned new recipes and put out the silver and china. At first it was not easy. When Jay and I entertained, there was always that pause about an hour before the guests were due when he would turn to me and ask "What next?" Usually we had spent the day in busy, sometimes hectic preparation, he doing errands, picking up last minutes ingredients at the market, buying the wine, mowing the lawn or shoveling a path to the front door through the snow. I did last minute vacuuming, shined the bathrooms, set the table, washed the salad and fed the boys early, while keeping an eye on the roast or the gravy. After a quick shower and less time spent on my appearance than on that of the house I was almost ready. When he asked "What next?" I gave him the short list of last minute chores that make the difference between looking relaxed when the first guest arrives and rushing frantically through the final half-hour thinking that lack of organization will definitely ruin the evening.

The first dinner I gave without him, when I reached the one-hour point, I could almost hear him asking "What next?" I wanted to tell him to put out the folding chairs and make sure that the front lights were on. I wanted him to ask me again the names of that new couple and whether he should turn up the air conditioning. When guests arrived, Jay would serve drinks while I kept the conversation going and fussed with hors d'oeuvres. At my first solo dinner party, one of the men offered to serve the drinks as though he had been doing it all along. When we sat down to eat, Jay's place was empty, like a mouth with a hole where a tooth used to be. I had only invited couples. Poor planning. We all sensed his absence but the party went on. We ate, drank, laughed; it was a start. I was glad I did it. I enjoy entertaining and have learned I don't need a partner to bring people together in my home. I invite my friends, get the house ready, do the cooking, and serve the meal. My guests do their part, carrying the heavy trays, serving drinks, bringing dessert, moving furniture. I know that being alone is an option only if I want it to be.

Although I was learning to be single, I wore my engagement and wedding rings for months after I was no longer married. In the late 1950's when I became engaged, engagement rings were big and fancy, the diamond set high in platinum with tapered baguettes on each side. My engagement ring and, later, its matching wedding band, were like trophies. They certified my entry to the first rung of the ladder of success despite the fact that my in-laws, and not my husband, had paid for them. Living and working in New York, I flashed my rings wherever I went. I sat in Carnegie Hall watching the light from a hundred bulbs glint off the facets of the diamond. I wore them to the supermarket and walking through Central Park. I cannot imagine wearing such jewelry in the subway now, but I did so then without concern. A decade later, the jewelry looked dated. The diamond that shone so beautifully when I was a bride became dull and cloudy with housework. It was the 1970's. I worked on a college campus where ostentation was out. The students and some of the faculty wore tie-dyed clothing and peace signs. My rings were out of place. I put them into the bank vault and for $12 bought a plain gold band that I wore for years. After the turbulent times, when elegance began to creep back into fashion, I had my diamond reset into a simple gold setting which looked fine with the gold band. These were the rings on my hand when I decided it was no longer appropriate to wear them. By our fingers do others know us. I did not want to be seen as someone's wife when I was working so hard to establish myself as an independent, single woman. The engagement ring would not fit on my right hand so I put it back into the vault. At first, my ring finger looked strangely deformed and barren, yet there was a freedom to having an unadorned hand. Psychologically, I had removed a huge piece of my previous life, simply by taking off the two pieces of jewelry that symbolized that life. I occasionally miss my beautiful diamond ring and one day I will have the stone set in some other way.

The act of removing my rings set up in my mind the possibility for me to develop a life involving the opposite sex. My head told my heart that I was free. But my heart had other intentions. It wasn't ready to get broken again or even to consider the possibility of opening up to a new individual. To survive the tragedies and travails of my life, I have developed a shell that shuts out the good along with the bad. I have become fiercely independent, not to mention a bit selfish. Giving up my independence would not be easy. A good relationship takes a lot of work and I don't know if I have the energy. I remember something I saw on television when the American prisoners returned after seven years of captivity in Vietnam. A reporter interviewed the wives. Most were overjoyed to see their husbands, but one expressed doubt. "I've had that bed to myself for a long time," she said apprehensively. I think the bed symbolized something more - an autonomy she feared losing. I can understand her concern.

Psychiatrists refer to a "phobic response to marriage" experienced by women who lose their mate without warning. A few years after Jay died, a woman told me she was surprised I had not remarried. "Remarried," I responded with some amusement. "I haven't even had a date." Marriage was not my concern, but I would have considered lunch, maybe even dinner. In my previous single life, men called all the time. "Janice (or Arthur or Joan) told me to call you," they would say. "Would you like to go to a movie?" That was how I met my husband. He and Charlotte, whom he grew up with, were on the station platform in Trenton, NJ, waiting for a train to take them to New York where Charlotte and I shared an apartment and Jay went to law school. She suggested to Jay that he might like to meet her roommate. I expected that to happen when I became a widow but it never did. I read recently that widows outnumber widowers four to one. For the men, it's a buyer's market. On my own, I have met a few likely dating candidates, nice men who seemed compatible, but I have always said the wrong thing, said "No, sorry I'm busy," when I should have said, "Not this time but how about a rain check." As a teenager I knew what to say. It's a skill I have lost.

I have also met some unlikely suitors. There is a saying, "Be careful what you wish for." I often wish for someone to ski with, an occasional dinner partner, a person other than me in the driver's seat. I know many congenial women who fit the bill but the chemistry isn't the same. On a ski lift in Pennsylvania I met a man my age, a bachelor, who was an excellent skier. He was a chef at a local country club. I'd never have to cook again. We spent a few hours skiing together. Before leaving, he asked for my address so he could send me a post card from Florida where he was about to visit his mother. My friend May, a widow, told me never to give out my name or phone number, although I'd make the exception for Kevin Costner. My skier friend seemed pleasant enough and harmless, but definitely not someone I'd want to spend time with if skiing was not involved. After some hesitation because my instinct said no, I gave him my name and address telling him I was not looking for a romantic relationship but would be happy to ski with him again. I figured that was the end of it. Four days later he sent a valentine, then a postcard and gaudy refrigerator magnet from Florida. He started calling. First he asked me to ski, then to go out to dinner. I refused. When someone is that persistent, I become suspicious. It's the old "I wouldn't want to join a club that would have me as a member" syndrome. My mistake was telling him when we first met that I lived alone. My imagination went wild. I couldn't sleep at night. Perhaps he had been rejected before. Chefs have knives. He knew where I lived. He could kill me. I piled furniture in front of the door before I went to sleep at night. The next time he called, I told him I had someone else. He didn't believe me. Instead, he sent delicious chocolates. Despite my lack of interest in my suitor, I enjoyed those chocolates. The letters and phone calls continued. He told me how much he missed me, and this was based on one meeting. I began screening my calls. When Andy came to visit, we changed the recording on the answering machine. Andy's deep voice told callers to leave a message. My friends and colleagues were curious to know who was suddenly answering the phone at my house, but I had found the solution. The skiing chef stopped calling. Can you blame me for being wary of men?

Still, I occasionally miss male companionship. The problem is I cannot define what I want this companion to be. An escort but not a lover. A friend who appears like a Genie at my bidding and goes back into his bottle when I become tired of his company. No man is going to put up with that. I told some friends that what I want is a regular date, a well-dressed man who comes to pick me up, takes me out to a nice restaurant where we engage in charming conversation, then leaves me at my doorstep after paying the bill and leaving the tip. My friends spent the next ten minutes laughing. "I am waiting to be rescued," a single friend confided. "Aren't we all," I replied.

I know what I miss. I miss having someone tall walking along side of me. I miss a strong male hand extended when a slope is steep or a step is high. I miss an arm around my shoulder. It's the small things. The things I accepted so easily when they were my daily custom. I have asked widows what they miss most. "My husband buying me a gift that I would not buy for myself," said one friend. For the Chanukah we celebrated just before Jay died, he bought me a large box of Perugina Baci chocolates. They are a luxurious Italian version of Hershey's kisses— incredibly rich chocolate with an almond inside. Baci means "kiss" in Italian. Each candy comes wrapped with an individual love note. The box sat unopened for months but as spring approached I knew I had to eat the chocolates before the warm weather spoiled them. Sadly, I read each little love message as the chocolate dissolved in my mouth. I knew Jay wanted me to have those chocolates and I thought of them as kisses he had sent me. A few years later, for a special occasion, Suzanne and

David gave me a beautiful woolen shawl, so soft and large that I could wrap myself in it. It is the only truly luxurious gift I have received since Jay has not been here to buy one for me. I love the shawl. Even if I'm only walking around the house with the shawl over my shoulders, I feel elegant. I could have gone to the mall, bought that shawl and charged it, but the feeling would not have been the same. There's something about a lavish gift that makes a woman feel special, and putting it on a credit card doesn't have the same effect.

Most widows agree it is the everyday life they miss the most. The things we most took for granted are suddenly the most painful in their absence. I miss being loved more than I miss making love. I miss having someone who knows exactly what I mean, sometimes before I finish my sentence. I miss having a background of shared experience. A twenty-six-year-old woman I know lost her husband on their honeymoon. She attended a bereavement group where widows her mother's age described their grief. "They had years of living an everyday life, she said. "I never had one day."

My psychologist and I discussed dating. During my early visits we had talked a lot about feelings but we were past that. Of course, she was aware that I had feelings and was struggling to cope with them. But my visits were limited by the insurance company so she was trying to give me practical tips to help me get on with my life. She knew of several women who met husbands through the personal ads in newspapers. I have always been intrigued by the personals and read them regularly in the local papers, even when I was married. "Handsome man, 5'10", 58-years-old seeks beautiful woman, 30 - 45, for long, caring relationship." I dismiss these ads immediately. The men my age are looking for younger women and I'm too old to be a trophy wife. In a friend's bereavement group was a man who placed an ad in his small-town paper. He received more that 100 responses. He called the likely ones to arrange an interview in *their* home. Talk about nerve. I know women who have developed relationships with men they have met through the personals and I have heard some horror stories. Occasionally, like a help-wanted ad where my experience exactly meets the criteria, I see a personal ad where I'm actually what he's looking for: tall, slim, non-smoker, 60-ish, athletic, good dancer. In the film "Mary Poppins," the children write an advertisement describing the qualities they seek in a nanny. Their request miraculously wafts up the chimney, and floats through the air into the hand of Mary flying about under her umbrella. Fitting the requirements, she gracefully descends to claim the job. I haven't taken out my umbrella yet and I doubt I ever will.

Nevertheless, I love the success stories. Traveling alone on Maryland's beautiful Eastern Shore, I checked into the historic inn where I had a reservation. A wedding was taking place on the back lawn. Guests were seated and a string quartet played, but I had difficulty identifying a bride and groom. I was making assumptions again—looking for a young couple in white gown and tuxedo. When I finally spotted the bride, it was a woman in her 50's who wore a turquoise dress. The groom, also middle-aged, was in a gray suit and blue shirt. That evening I found myself sitting next to the bride on the inn's broad porch. Congratulating her on her nuptials, I told her I was a widow, hoping she would tell me her story. She too was a widow. Her new spouse was a business colleague of her husband's whose wife had died. They met when he came to her husband's funeral two years earlier. One thing led to another and now they were married. She said her first husband had been cremated, his ashes scattered in Chesapeake Bay. As she and her groom drove over the Chesapeake Bay Bridge on the way to their wedding she called out to her dead spouse, "Bob, you'll never believe what I'm doing." She encouraged me to be open to new possibilities. It certainly worked for her.

Recognizing that I may be single for a long time, I have to find ways to make my life enjoyable and productive. When I have an empty day, and a female companion is not available, I head for New York. I go to New York when I am depressed. I know that I will come home feeling better and I am never disappointed. While some find the city overwhelming, expensive, dirty and frightening, I find it a never-ending source of enjoyment and exploration. I love the museums, Central Park, the theater, ballet, libraries, baseball at Shea Stadium, the U.S. Open tennis matches, street fairs, small restaurants, big stores. I know where to find a dinner special for $9.95, how to get free theater and concert tickets and which museums stay open late on weekends. In New York I can be anonymous. Alone in a restaurant, I look around and see several others at tables for one. In the suburbs, the only solo diners are businessmen in hotel restaurants and truck drivers at road stops. While I don't enjoy eating alone, I know ways to make the meal more pleasurable. During good weather, I eat at tables outdoors where there is always something to look at. When that option is unavailable, I try to sit at a table near a window so I can view something other than the neighboring diners. I don't bring a book or newspaper. Men do that. They're more insecure eating alone than women are. I eavesdrop on conversations. I was eating lunch at a former Irish bar that was trying to become a trendy restaurant, but its neighborhood had not yet caught up. Two women who seemed a little down on their luck were at the next table. "Did I tell you that I changed my religion?" asked one. "What did you become, a Buddhist?" asked the other. "No, a Protestant," said the first. "I used to be Catholic, but there's a Protestant church near where I live now. They serve great breakfasts."

I go to New York because it is my closest city but Boston or Philadelphia would do. So would Chicago or San Francisco. Cities are a good place for single people to wander around in because there we become invisible. I tried to find places that would help the wound to heal. I rejoiced when I found them: a corner in an art museum that offered up a view of a painting so breathtaking it brought tears to my eyes, a chamber music concert in a mansion with marble pillars and crystal chandeliers, or a brassy Broadway musical comedy to make me smile. One of my best New York places is a lovely garden where I can stroll through a grape arbor beneath a Roman colonnade. I know New Yorkers who have never visited this garden, removed as it is from the pulse of the city. On Saturdays and Sundays, wedding parties line up to be photographed while their white limousines await on the street outside the tall gate. Children chase one another around a large seasonal flower display where spring tulips give way to summer's marigolds and fall chrysanthemums. There are benches for resting beneath rows of trees that arch overhead, cooling the paths on the hottest days. A writer sits scribbling into her notebook. A student sketches. My favorite spot is the English garden, an acre of flowers, the pinks, blues, whites and purples on one side so as not to offend their flashier cousins, the oranges, reds and yellows across the way. Tall pale grasses rise against dark green hedges. In the center of my garden is a small reflecting pool where pink and white water lilies float. A bronze statue of a little girl holds a bowl of water which gently overflows into the pool below. Birds perch and drink from her bowl. Kneeling beside her a little boy, perhaps her brother, plays a flute. I sit under the broad beech tree that shades this oasis and listen to the water splash gently into the pool. I know of no more peaceful spot than this beautiful space in a northern corner of Central Park, bordering Harlem. In this charming retreat I find solitude, reflection and repose.

During my first sad winter as a widow, I visited indoor flower shows where I found strength and sustenance looking at the colorful blossoms tricked into displaying their brilliance in the dead of winter. Spring brought joy and heartbreak. I went to parks and public gardens where I could walk through miles of flowering cherry blossoms and admire endless daffodils and tulips. But how could I reconcile this new growth and flowering, this annual renewal of nature's cycle with the fact that my husband and son would never experience another spring? Jay would never enjoy the blooms of the lilac tree that he had so carefully pruned the previous fall or smell the fragrance of hyacinths that he had helped me to plant in November. I watered the garden with my tears that spring. The flowers didn't care that they were fed with salt. They bloomed in spite of it. They tried to tell me that they would survive and I would too.

ॐ౮౮ॐ౮ॐ౮ॐ **12** ౮ॐ౮ॐ౮ॐ౮ॐ౮

Good Works

I needed to be a part of something. I felt that Jay and Barry's unlived years were a challenge to me. I wanted to use my time to do the good deeds that they would have done if they had lived. I wanted, as well, to involve myself in a larger sphere where the troubles of one person would seem small. I thought that I could do this through religion and by volunteering for good works. According to Jewish custom, mourners attend services, rising to say *kaddish*, the prayer for the dead, for a year following a death. I have read that the original purpose for standing was so they could be singled out among the congregation as people who needed help. Now, in some congregations, everyone stands for this prayer to remember the deaths of the six million Holocaust victims who have no one to mourn them. I faithfully attended religious services to say *kaddish* after Jay and Barry died. I stood for two years since my mourning was double. The synagogue I attended was not new to me because Jay and I had prayed there occasionally but we were not members. I did not see a familiar face, but the music drew me in. Whether soft and lyrical or august and stirring, the melodies brought tears to my eyes. Some of the tunes were strange to my ears but others were common to services of my past. I had learned them in Sunday school in Connecticut.

I went back in my mind to the time when I was a little girl singing those songs as I sat in the synagogue with my mother. A few years later, I sang them at summer camp. Friday nights were special. To welcome in the Sabbath, the campers, all girls, wore clean white uniforms, crisp cotton shirts and stiff, starched shorts fresh from the laundry. Even the most mischievous among us looked like angels as we rose and lifted our voices to God. I sang the songs again as a young woman in my mother-in-law's synagogue. She always claimed I went to services only for the sing-a-long. And I sang them as a family member with my husband and two sons. "Do you always have to sing the harmony?" my sons asked, annoyed at my improvisations. Yes, I had to. It was a compulsion. I've been singing harmony since I was in second grade. Finally, alone as a widow, I sang the harmony in a place where nobody knew me, where technically, since I had not paid my dues, I did not belong. While others stood singing fervently, I rummaged in my purse for a tissue hoping no one around me would notice the tears rolling down my cheeks. I need not have worried. Most people pretended to ignore the sniffling woman who showed up regularly to worship among them, invading their space, making them uncomfortable, daring them to take an action as insignificant as saying hello. The only people who spoke to me were the Rabbi's wife and the president of the temple. The others kept their distance. At the reception following the service, I was invisible. I didn't mind. Their lack of friendliness suited my mood. I cannot deny that my outlook might have changed had I been welcomed into a more caring environment. A friendly handshake or someone asking my name would have made a difference. But I communicated with God, availed myself of the cookies and coffee they provided and left them talking with one another.

For about a year I tolerated their behavior and failed to change my own, for I was equally at fault. I was still in the stage where I expected indulgences from others and neglected to recognize my own responsibility. To improve the situation, I did two things. I did the first because my mother, long dead, spoke to me. "Don't be a *shnurer*," she scolded. Yiddish is a language rich in words that describe the human condition. My parents used Yiddish when they could not find an English word that conveyed an idea as accurately and succinctly, as one they knew in Yiddish. A *shnurer* is someone who tries to get something for nothing. With the exception of the High Holidays when I purchased a guest ticket, I could attend this temple, or any other, for that matter, without paying a cent. My mother was telling me to put up the cash. I filled out an application, wrote a check and became a member of the congregation.

The second thing I did was to join the choir. After becoming a temple member, I was eligible and the choir director approached me about joining. By attending services so frequently, I had learned most of the songs and some of the harmony as well. Still, I waited months to acquire enough bravery to make the call to the choir director. Volunteering to sing required considerable courage from someone with as average a voice as mine. I was relieved to learn that no audition was required. The choir was looking for altos and my ability to sing the alto part was qualification enough.

I have had a lifelong fear of auditions since I was a freshman in college and auditioned with Miss Cutlass, the choir director, for a place in the freshman chorus. When I finished singing, she mumbled something, told me to stand aside and asked the next girl to sing. Behind me in line was a student from my dormitory who began to sing in a gorgeous soprano voice that filled the room with such magnificent sound that everyone turned to listen. It was far different from my meager attempt. When Miss Beautiful Voice had finished, Miss Cutlass turned to me haughtily, as if I had just spilled ketchup on her music. "That's how you're supposed to sing, Sandra," she snipped. "Of course, I guess I just forgot," I should have answered, but I was too scared. The memory of my humiliation at the hands of Miss Cutlass has remained with me. My temple choir was a more welcoming group and the director has never asked me to sing like a gifted soprano. To those who had only seen me wiping away tears, I became a person with a name. The choir gave me a legitimacy. Its members accepted me immediately as one who could contribute to the group. Strangers in the congregation talked to me. I cried less frequently during the services because I had a job to do. I couldn't sing and cry at the same time, particularly not with the whole congregation watching. Religion provided a community and a sense of spirituality. Singing to God helped my soul to mend.

I am not alone in this. Many mourners told me that their spirituality and firm faith in God helped them to overcome their grief. They found solace in their strong Christian belief that their loved ones are with God. They know they will all be reunited some day and their faith has been a great source of strength to them. Jews are a little vague about the afterlife so a firm conviction about where we go when we leave this earth was not part of my upbringing. I would like to think of Jay and Barry together in heaven, shooting a round of baskets, making jokes. Every once in a while they take a look down to see how Andy and I are doing. On a black starry night I look up and picture them, each sitting on a separate star, his legs hanging over the edge, eating an ice cream cone, calling to one another,

"Hey, did you see the shot Michael made the other night?" "Do you think the Giants will make the playoffs?" I know this is whimsy but it helps me to smile.

As a widow, I had to forge a new Jewish identity. I have had several. My parents considered themselves religious Jews and when I lived with them, I was religious as well, or I should say I was a more observant Jew than I am now. My mother kept a kosher home. She prepared only foods that she bought from a kosher butcher but, schizophrenically, in restaurants we ate shrimp cocktail, T-bone steaks and Chinese food cooked in the same pots as the pork we were forbidden to eat at home. We had numerous sets of dishes and silverware, everyday services for dairy and meat, others, the "good" china, for guests—and still more for Passover. Before Passover my mother cleaned, scrubbed and swept all cookies, crackers, crumbs, cereal and bread from the house. She lined the shelves and counter tops with clean brown paper. She packed up all the dishes, utensils, pots and pans used during the rest of the year, put them into the cellar and brought out another complete eating and serving system that we used for seven days until the whole process was reversed.

Being Jewish was not easy in Meriden because there were so few of us. We had one of everything—one synagogue, one kosher butcher, one "Jewish-style" bakery. Not only did I grow up in a world without television, I grew up in a town without bagels. Although the bakery had challah and holiday treats such as hamantaschen on Purim, we had to go to New Haven, 20 miles away for bagels. Occasionally my father made the trip on a Sunday morning. Before the interstate came through, New Haven was not the quick zip down the highway it is now, but an all-morning affair. Bagels and lox were the ultimate luxury, a delicacy to be savored.

Out of 300 students in my high school class eight of us, mostly girls, were Jewish. There were five or six boys who were a year older. We first met as small children in Sunday school and grew up as a unit, going to parties and dating each other. One couple actually married after college but the rest of us grew bored with one another long before that. The schools were open on the High Holidays. When I returned to school after being absent on Yom Kippur, the holiest day of the Jewish year, a teacher scolded me for not doing my homework. I pointed out that it was a religious holiday, but she said that was no excuse. At Mount Holyoke, it was the same story. The quota for Jewish students was 10 percent, a statistic that was neither published nor acknowledged by the administration but we all knew it. We could count. The college did not recognize the Jewish holidays in any way but synagogues in the area invited Jewish students to attend services. Freshman year, I had dinner with a family in Holyoke, a nearby town, and attended services with them at their temple. The next day was Yom Kippur, a day of fasting. After not eating for 24 hours, my first meal was the regular dinner served in my dormitory. The main course was ham. Although I enjoyed ham at other times of the year, a food that is forbidden to observant Jews did not seem appropriate for breaking a fast on Yom Kippur. With my innate Jewish sense of guilt, I was sure I would receive a terrible punishment from God if I ate the ham. I ate the salad, mashed potatoes and dessert but skipped the ham. I was used to making my way in a Christian world and did not expect accommodations to be made for me. The college catalogue said that Mount Holyoke was "a distinctly Christian institution" and I came anyway. This was just another inconvenience.

After leaving my parents' home, my religious observance diminished. For many years following our marriage, Jay and I did not belong to a synagogue. We were still under the umbrella of our parents' synagogue affiliations, not members but welcome, for a fee, at High Holiday services. When we were not willing or able to travel to where they were, we always found a local congregation to attend as High Holiday guests. Sometimes it was an Orthodox *shul* and the services were conducted all in Hebrew. We sat patiently feeling we were making our annual commitment to religion and to God along with the other once-a-year Jews who crowd into the temples for Rosh Hashana and Yom Kippur, then disappear into their secular lives for another 363 days. I did not keep a kosher home as my mother had done. We lived in a small Manhattan apartment and there was no room for all those dishes and pots. I know more observant Jews would have found room but I wasn't interested.

When it was time for Barry to attend Hebrew school, we joined a Conservative congregation. We lived in an area with many Jews and could choose our synagogue from among several. We tried them out and chose one because the Rabbi delivered excellent sermons and the members looked like us - not too rich or too poor. We felt we would be comfortable there. This was when my life most closely resembled that of today's "soccer mom." I was always different from the other mothers because I worked, but my jobs were part-time, allowing me to participate in my children's lives as carpool driver and homeroom mother, although I drew the line at baking brownies. For school parties or Cub Scout outings, I told my children to volunteer only for the carrots and celery, if paper plates and napkins were already taken. Once a year, I made an exception for the temple. As a member of my new congregation's Sisterhood, the woman's organization, I joined other mothers in someone's kitchen to make hundreds of potato pancakes for the children's Chanukah party. I also attended evening classes to learn to read and speak Hebrew. This was my second attempt at the language. When I was a child, our rabbi, years ahead of his time, started a Hebrew class for girls. I went for a year, but the class never went beyond that because we all lost interest and quit. With that minimal background, I could identify a few letters of the Hebrew alphabet and pick out some words during the prayers. I welcomed the opportunity, as an adult, to start again. This time I learned not only to read but to speak haltingly in the language when we visited Israel on the occasion of Barry's Bar Mitzvah.

When we moved to our current town, our theological choice became religion-by-carpool. By then I worked full-time and could drive only the return trips from Hebrew classes which the children attended two afternoons a week following public school. One Jewish family in town belonged to the Conservative synagogue in Highmount, about 10 miles away. We joined that synagogue. The other mother picked up my children and took them to Hebrew school twice a week. After work, I drove everyone home. This arrangement lasted for a few years until her daughter celebrated her Bat Mitzvah at 13, which concluded her afternoon classes. Andy still had two more years to attend and I was without a carpool. Several families in town belonged to a Reform temple, also in Highmount. By joining there, I would have the luxury of driving the home-bound leg only once a week instead of twice. So for reasons that had nothing to do with religious belief or observance, we became Reform Jews.

We belonged to that Reform temple for many years, but when Andy's religious education ended, we found ourselves attending services less and less often. Eventually, we dropped out. For High Holiday services, we were able to purchase guest tickets at a closer Reform temple. We went there as well to say the *kaddish* on the anniversaries of our parents' deaths and for occasional Friday evening services. I enjoyed the service because the rabbi had a gorgeous singing voice and there was an emphasis on singing as part of the service. It is the temple where I now sing in the choir. As in most suburban congregations, a great deal of the activity is focused on the education of the children and on fund-raising. As a single woman, the social activities—dances, progressive dinners and weekend trips do not interest me. What drew me in, in addition to the religious services, was the education and I did something so amazing that, at times, even I could not believe I would embark on such as endeavor.

I read in the temple bulletin that a class was assembling for an adult Bar or Bat Mitzvah. Where I grew up, a Bat Mitzvah, the female equivalent of a Bar Mitzvah for boys, did not exist. My Jewish education culminated in a confirmation service at age 13. There are no laws preventing a Jew from becoming a Bar or Bat Mitzvah at any age after 13 and I knew a few adults who had done so. Among them was Jay's friend David who, several years earlier, in an enormously moving service, became a Bar Mitzvah. As a child in Poland during the Holocaust, he hid in a cellar with his mother and brother while his father worked in forced labor. Despite their deprivations and suffering, his father taught him to read Hebrew, but he never had a formal Bar Mitzvah. As a prosperous suburban man with a beautiful wife and grown children, he accomplished what Jews did not dare even dream about under Nazi domination. His journey was longer and far more difficult than mine, but he was an example to me.

I had another example. Her name was Lillian Morris. In Meriden there were two Jewish women, sisters-in-law, with that name. To distinguish them, they were known as Big Lil Morris and Little Lil Morris. Big Lil wasn't very big, but she was taller than Little Lil, who was barely five feet tall. Meriden's second synagogue, built in 1908, was an imposing three-story Italianate edifice that I remember as old and ramshackle when I was a child. The sanctuary, where services were held, was on the second floor. Although the congregation had left its Orthodox roots years earlier, women continued to sit in the third floor balcony where Orthodox tradition assigned them. In Conservative synagogues, women and men pray together, but in Meriden perhaps no one had dared, or bothered, to change the status quo.

During my childhood in 1940's Jewish women had not yet found their voice. I sat with my mother in the first row of the balcony, looking over the wooden railing at my father, brother and the boys I knew from Sunday school praying below. Small, white-haired men wrapped in prayer shawls that covered them from shoulder to ankle, stood a few feet from the front wall. Hunched over wooden lecterns where they stored their books, they prayed loudly, swaying back and forth. These men were known as old man Goodman and old man Katz, titles bestowed upon them denoting their position in the congregation. One of them, the grandfather of a girl in my class, drove down our street periodically in a horse-drawn wagon calling out "Rags we buy" in a strong Eastern European accent. The business he had started years before had developed into a thriving scrap metal company run by his sons, but the old man stuck with what he knew best. I was afraid of him when he came by with the horse, but in the synagogue he held a place reserved for the respected elders.

One year, on the High Holidays, I sat in the balcony in my new fall dress that was too warm for the weather, trying to pay attention during the long service. Along with most of the congregation, I didn't understand the portions that were read in Hebrew. Most people didn't sit through the service from beginning to end, but came and went according to their whim. When a World Series game coincided with the holidays, my father and his friends snuck out of the service to listen to the game on a car radio. Squirming with impatience, I was looking forward to the time when I could go home. Suddenly there was a stir from the first floor. All the men were twisting around, turning their heads and pointing as if a celebrity had just entered the room. The women in the balcony were twittering like birds on a wire at the end of the day. I asked my mother what had happened. "Little Lil Morris just walked in downstairs and sat with her husband," my mother exclaimed.

I was shocked. Didn't Mrs. Morris know that sitting downstairs with the men was a sin? I expected the pillars of the balcony to collapse and the whole congregation to be killed because of what Little Lil Morris had done. In Sunday school I had colored dozens of pictures of Biblical buildings crashing to their ruin due to the transgressions of my ancestors. Within a few minutes the congregation recovered and the service continued to its conclusion. Happy to have survived, I followed my mother down the stairs and into the vestibule. The women surrounded Little Lil, like a team member who had just scored the winning basket. They wanted to know why she did it. "Because I wanted to sit with my husband," she told them proudly. I don't know whether her act was spontaneous or whether she had planned it with her husband's support. But using a term that came later, she was a role model and she changed the world of which she was a part. Soon all the women sat with their husbands, either in the sanctuary or in the balcony. Eventually, the congregation built a new temple, all on one floor, and Little Lil's accomplishment slid into history.

When I signed up for the Bat Mitzvah class, I did so as David did, because it was unfinished business from my past. I wanted the learning that accompanied the event and I wanted to improve my Hebrew language skills. Twice I had learned Hebrew and forgotten most of it. By attending services so frequently, my Hebrew had improved, but I wanted to read more fluently. I wanted to prove to myself that I still had the ability to do it. But there was another item on my agenda. I wanted to tell the Lil Morris story. Lil Morris was my Rosa Parks. Rosa Parks sat down in the "whites-only" section of a bus in Montgomery, Alabama because her feet were tired and she started a revolution. A historian told me that Miss Parks did not take her momentous step at the spur of the moment. She was selected and trained for the part. It doesn't matter to me why she did it. She had the courage and strength to volunteer for an act that clearly put her life in danger. Lil Morris did not endanger herself or the rest of us, despite my childish fears, but she was brave and unafraid of change. To me she was an inspiration, and I never forgot her. I wanted to give a sermon about her at my Bat Mitzvah.

Four women attended the first session of our Bat Mitzvah class. Our temple had a new rabbi, a woman willing to be flexible with the requirements and lessons that would enable us to reach our goal. We spoke about why we wanted to have a Bat Mitzvah. Two of the women had little Jewish learning despite being active temple members for many years. They came to expand their knowledge of Judaism. We had all seen our brothers and sons celebrate their Bar Mitzvahs, and we wanted to celebrate a milestone that had been denied to us as teenagers. We chose a date for our service and discussed a book, *The Red Tent* by Anita Diamant, that the rabbi had assigned to us to read. The book, a novel, is about the four wives of Jacob, one of the founding fathers or patriarchs of Judaism. Its narrator, Dinah, is Jacob's only daughter. Following our first meeting, the rabbi asked us to keep a journal. I wrote:

"Four women of a certain age have come together to study Judaism. Our instructor is not quite young enough to be our daughter but almost. She is the Rabbi so she is in charge, but she is also studying us, trying to fit our needs, wants and schedules into a framework that will be acceptable to Jewish tradition and to us. We established some guidelines and chose a date for our Bat Mitzvah. It is uncanny. A most bizarre coincidence that the Torah portion for our date is the same story we have been reading in the "Red Tent." Dinah, who tells the story, considers all of Jacob's four wives her mothers. With us, our rabbi has four mothers as well."

Eventually two of the women dropped out. I was grateful to Marion, the one who remained, because I would not have had the courage to do it alone. We chose to have the Bat Mitzvah as part of a regular Friday evening Sabbath service rather than a special Saturday morning service as most 13-year-olds do. For almost a year we met with the rabbi to study the Torah portion that would be read at our service. We discussed news events pertaining to Judaism, examined our beliefs and our place as Jewish women in the Christian world that surrounds us. We each prepared a short sermon related to the Torah reading. Marion talked about Leah's unconditional love for her husband Jacob although she knew he loved Rachel, her sister, more. Marion compared this to the love she and her husband shared since meeting as teenagers in high school. Her husband, sitting in the first row, wiped several tears from his eyes as she spoke.

I did not talk about Lil Morris. Deciding to make it more personal, I talked about bargaining with God as Jacob did when he found himself alone in the desert and needing help. Jacob dreamed that God came and stood beside him. God promised to watch over Jacob until he could return to that spot. His descendents, God said, would cover the earth. When Jacob awoke, he vowed that if God protected him on his journey, he would keep his end of the bargain and would worship the God who had safeguarded him. I told the congregation that I would like to bargain with God to have again, the Fourth of July when my family and I went to New York. I acknowledged that there are wishes that an all-powerful God can grant and some that are beyond God's power. An all-powerful God could give me my day but suppose the God we bargain with is more human, more like us, more of a partner who can grant small favors than a fairy Godmother who creates miracles. The God who stood beside Jacob in his dream promised a deal. I'll keep you safe if you come back to worship Me. I know that the God I worship cannot grant me my day, but until I read this Torah portion, I was not aware that maybe God needs something from us, although that need may not be apparent to us, just as we need something from God.

In addition to my sermon and other readings, my goal was to read four Hebrew prayers during the service. At home, I practiced them endlessly until I could say them as speedily as the average 13-year old. I tried not to think of this whole event as a big deal but I knew it was. Andy flew in for the weekend. David and Suzanne came. So did Carol and her sister from New York. A woman from my water aerobics class came with her husband as did some of my neighbors and many of my Mount Holyoke friends and classmates. Marion and I were so nervous we were practically sick. We certainly had a better appreciation of what youngsters go through in the same situation. We both did beautifully. When I finished the last of the Hebrew prayers, even though my sermon was still to come, I knew I was home free. My sermon was in English. I could handle that. Everyone was very proud of us that night. I knew Jay and Barry would have been proud too, but if Jay were alive, I would not have done it because we did not belong to a temple and probably never would have joined.

The Bat Mitzvah represented a milestone of another sort. For a year or two after Jay died, I continued to live my life as half of a suburban couple, but gradually I have branched out. Doing the Bat Mitzvah was one of the ways in which I asserted myself in my new life. I had taken on a new Jewish identity among the other new roles required of me. Previously, my primary Jewish role was wife and mother. I maintained a Jewish home, observed the holidays and accompanied Jay to the synagogue when he went to say the *kaddish* for his parents. I drove the Hebrew school carpools, cooked the potato pancakes and planned the Bar Mitzvahs, but until necessity required it, I had never walked into a religious service by myself. At my current temple, I am a single member, not someone's wife or mother. Some members know my story but most do not. I wanted to stand in front of them, read my Hebrew and be recognized as a Jewish woman of learning. In addition, I wanted to regain my confidence. I needed to accomplish something for myself unrelated to the death of my husband and son. The Bat Mitzvah offered me the opportunity to be proud of myself. That others shared my pride was a bonus.

Mourners seek many routes to healing and religion has been one of mine. I found others as well. Public service, projects that aid the common good and living memorials are some of the ways that people find to ease the pain and to pull good from bad. For as long as I can remember, I have been a volunteer, doing good works for this or that organization. Since I left campus, I have assumed alumnae leadership and fund-raising positions for my college. I am a member of the Environmental Commission in my town. Nevertheless, I was open to other possibilities where I could make a difference. As if in response to my need, I received a letter from the New York City Ballet seeking individuals to augment its volunteer corps. Ballet has been my passion for as long as I can remember. I have held season subscriptions to performances for more than thirty years. Jay accompanied me and professed to enjoy it but his head nodded and he dozed off soon after the lights were lowered. We went on Sunday evenings and when a performance coincided with the Superbowl, I found a friend to go. Since his death, I have gone alone. Until I received the letter seeking volunteers, I was not aware that the ballet offered such an opportunity. I nearly jumped at the possibility of doing something that would put me in the same environment as the ballet dancers whose on-stage perfection I so admired.

My earliest childhood fantasy was to be a ballerina. In Meriden, there was no professional ballet. I doubt that there was a professional group in all of Connecticut when I was growing up. The only ballet I had ever seen was in the movies and at the dancing school recitals that my mother took me to each spring in the high school auditorium. Girls my age, my classmates, danced in little pink tulle dresses made by their mother or grandmother. In lipstick and rouge, they shone like fairy princesses on the stage. How I longed for dancing lessons, but my mother did not drive, had to care for my little brother and somehow never worked it out. I was obsessed with ballerinas. I drew them over and over in the sketch books that we were required to keep for art class. When I was 15, a friend from summer camp invited me to her home in New York. She took me to see the New York City Ballet. I was enchanted. Maria Tallchief, an American Indian with beautiful cheekbones and jet-black hair, danced "The Firebird" in a red costume with flame-colored feathers on her head. What magical dancers these were—women of great grace and athletic ability who looked as fragile as the china figurines that spin on the top of music boxes. Their partners were handsome men who leaped higher than horses. The music and costumes were glorious. I had seen a few Broadway shows, and even the Rockettes, but, for me, ballet surpassed them all.

Now, on the far side of my life, I was being invited to take part in this enchanting world that I had admired from a distance for so long. With my letter in hand, I attended a meeting for prospective volunteers at the New York State Theater in Lincoln Center where the ballet performs. Like a job fair, heads of all the committees were there to tell about their needs and requirements. Because I was working full-time, I could join only committees that offered evening and weekend hours. I chose to write for the Newsletter Committee and to be a hostess during intermissions when ballet benefactors are invited to a reception room where they may chat, sip a glass of wine and munch on snacks. Being a volunteer required an interview with the Director of Volunteers. I left work early one day and made the trip into New York where I proceeded through the stage entrance— me, entering the New York State Theater through the stage entrance, past the security desk to the volunteer offices on an upper floor. While my interview was going on, dancers, accompanied by a pianist, rehearsed in a studio down the hall. Occasionally I looked up to see one of them, who appeared so remote and unreachable on stage, casually strolling by in tights and a tee shirt. I could hardly concentrate. This was heaven.

My work with the ballet boosts my morale. I especially love being a hostess during performances of "The Nutcracker" at Christmas time when little girls in velvet dresses that could be straight from Edwardian England and their brothers in navy blazers, come to the reception room. We offer them handfuls of colorfully wrapped candy, sugary cookies and a sweet punch in little paper cups. I remember when I brought my boys to see "Nutcracker," each when he was four or five. Their eyes grew wide with wonder during the scene where the Christmas tree magically grows larger on stage, eventually becoming more that 20 feet tall. When my boys grew too big to be interested in ballet, I borrowed a seven-year-old child from the neighborhood and took her. I always thought that I attended ballet for the entertainment value only, but I have come to see that my interest has a spiritual element to it that transcends mere enjoyment. The combination of beautiful music and the pure movement of the dancers brings me to a level where healing can occur. My volunteer work adds to that healing.

I love opera too, but most operas leave me saddened. Although I enjoy the magnificent voices and elaborate scenery, I cannot leave the performance feeling happy when everyone has died tragically on stage. I stick with the silly, happy ones involving mistaken identities, lost lovers suddenly united and the whole chorus on stage to sing the finale in major key. Many ballets have no story at all and those that do rarely end in death so I can enjoy them without shedding a tear. I have loved classical music since I first heard it as a child. Jane Goodman, a piano teacher, moved into the second floor apartment of the house next door. I stood watching in amazement as the movers hoisted her grand piano through an upstairs window because it was too big to carry up the stairs. I used to sit on the gravel driveway beneath her living room window listening to her play. When I was 10, my parents bought a second-hand baby grand piano so I could take lessons. The piano was the most beautiful piece of furniture in our house. The day it was delivered, my mother sat down and played a composition that she still remembered from when she took lessons. The music was "Country Gardens" by Percy Grainger, an Australian-American composer. She played it again and again until my brother and I made up words to it. I was impressed because until then I had never seen my mother do anything artistic or athletic. She did what all the mothers did: cooked, cleaned, did laundry, played cards with her friends and went out occasionally. This musical talent that she suddenly displayed made her seem very special. Now that I had a piano, my neighbor became my piano teacher. After a year or so, my mother and I played duets for piano, four hands.

On a cold Saturday morning, Jane and I took the train to New Haven. I was dressed in my best clothes—a skirt and blouse, woolen coat with a velvet collar and my dress-up shoes. I was at the in-between stage, too old for leggings and too young for stockings. My legs froze above my little white socks. In a paper bag, I carried a chicken sandwich on challah bread, left over from our Friday night Sabbath dinner. From the New Haven railroad station we took a bus to the Yale University campus. We were going to a children's concert performed by the New Haven Symphony at Woolsey Hall. As we walked through the campus I stared in awe at all that surrounded me. I had never been on a college campus. The Yale students were the tallest and handsomest boys I had ever seen. The buildings were magnificent beyond my imagination - stone structures that stretched for blocks unlike anything in Meriden or even Hartford.

Woolsey Hall was the most amazing of all. Inside was a huge auditorium, with columns of golden organ pipes that rose in two levels above an enormous stage. Sunlight streamed through windows two-stories high and a painted blue sky with white clouds decorated the ceiling above a vast balcony that hung over the first floor on three sides. Thousands of people could fit inside this auditorium. I sat through my first concert dividing my attention between the music and the awesome surroundings. More than 40 years later, I was again in Woolsey Hall for the Baccalaureate service at Andy's graduation. Professors and administrators in a colorful array of academic robes and headgear filled the stage. The graduates in their black gowns filed into the front of the auditorium and took their seats. Behind were the guests. When the music began, I was ten years old again sitting next to my piano teacher on my first visit to Woolsey Hall. Parents came from all over the world to that graduation but, as far as I knew, I was the only one whose road traveled in a circle, bringing me back to where I had started.

Music provided a way for me to volunteer. By singing in the choir and writing for the ballet newsletter I was extending myself into areas that were not part of my life before my husband and son died. I devoted my time and money to benefit others, but one thing was still missing. I wanted to do something to celebrate Barry's life, to bring good from the tragedy that ended it. Women have become famous for their crusades following the deaths of loved ones. Candy Lightner founded Mothers Against Drunk Driving (MADD) after her daughter was killed by a drunken driver. Carolyn McCarthy won a seat in Congress, campaigning for stricter gun control after her husband was killed and her son critically wounded by a mad gunman on the Long Island Railroad. I wish I could be a crusader but I lack the confidence and the nerve. I would like to spread the word about heart attacks among young people. Cardiomyopathy, a disease of the heart muscle that killed Barry, affects 50,000 in the United States, most of them young. In 1994, the year Barry died, heart disease was the third leading cause of death of Caucasian men under 45. When famous young athletes die—a basketball player, an Olympic ice skater, the story is a news blip that engages our attention for a day or two before losing its place in the headlines. I hope that there will be more awareness and even a cure in the future, but my nature is not to be part of that mission.

My desire was to establish something small and local, a means to carry Barry's name forward with a memorial that will survive me and those of us who are still here to remember him. After considering several causes, I decided to create an endowment fund in his name to benefit a charity that would have been special to him. An organization in Highmount met my criteria. It is a center that was established 100 years ago to aid

European immigrants, helping them to learn the language and customs of their new land. It now serves primarily an African-American and Hispanic population with similar challenges, offering day care, after school programs, tutoring and college scholarships. It is the kind of place that Barry would have embraced—maybe even worked at. The center agreed to accept the endowment in Barry's name as part of their scholarship fund. I made a donation to start the fund and wrote to close relatives and Barry's friends who also contributed generously. Money from the fund is awarded annually to a college student to pay for books, fees, or other expenses that can make the difference between succeeding in school and having to drop out. One of the recipients who is studying to become a teacher wrote: "I feel honored to receive this award established in memory of a person whose genuine commitment to helping others is so apparent. I was inspired and reminded that we must see each day as an opportunity to succeed by helping others to succeed. The award will help me to achieve my dream which is to help people achieve their dreams also." By enabling needy students to graduate and begin a professional career, Barry's legacy will continue.

He has another living memorial in Washington, DC. In a city of great and small monuments, Barry's is a single flowering tree, a dogwood planted by his professors and classmates in the graduate psychology department. They dedicated it on a beautiful October Sunday, a day when Barry and Ellen might have played golf or walked along the canal in Georgetown. They spoke of Barry's commitment, intelligence and what he had brought to their lives. The tree stands in a busy courtyard where students scurry to and from class. Those who are there now and those to come will never know him, but I hope they pause to read his name.

Flying Solo

Where I live is as important to me as breathing. I know people who pay dearly to live in a specific zip code. I pay dearly to surround myself with space and a view. Before settling into this house, in this community where I have lived for so long, I moved every few years and always by choice. My moves were not dictated by corporate whim as were the frequent upheavals of many of my college classmates. I always had an eye out for a more commodious place, roomier and better situated. Once unpacked in the new spot, I rarely looked back. That I was once capable of such mobility now surprises me. Like a petrified tree, I have become calcified in place. I know I could give up some space but without my view, I would wither, like a houseplant too long away from the light. For eight years I worked in an office with a window that looked out on a brick wall. It was marginally better than having no window at all because by standing in the corner and twisting my neck, I could see a slice of sky. That piece of sky, no bigger than a bath towel, was my portal to the outside world. Without it, I might as well have worked in the basement. On the walls of my office, I created my view. I hung pictures from my travels—a little boy coming home from school in Les Baux, France, a motorcyclist passing through an ancient stone archway in Rhodes, old Dutch men sitting beside the road on the island of Marken, wearing their wooden shoes as required, to be photographed by tourists.

With a stubbornness that prevents me from relinquishing my dream, I have decided that my view requires either water or hilltop. A house in the woods would offer serenity but I would feel closed in. Too many shadows, not enough sunlight. Not enough open space for my spirit to explore. I moved with my husband to New Jersey when he came here to work. We chose an area between the buzz of New York City and the tranquility of Farmer Brown. For excitement and culture we visited New York but our milk came from a barn one town over. Living in a suburb was a new experience. The Connecticut town where I grew up was small and self-contained. Farms separated us from surrounding towns. Commuting was a rarity. People who lived in town worked there and the local economy filled our needs. Our vision was narrow. We were content where we were. South Hadley, Massachusetts where I went to college was even smaller. During freshman year, our departures from campus were sharply limited requiring a note from home when we wanted to escape. I viewed these restrictions as temporary and eventually learned to enjoy the pretty little town for the few diversions it offered.

Moving from South Hadley to Manhattan after college, I was in a world completely different from any I had lived in before. I was overwhelmed with its speed and the abundance of its offerings. I loved the subways and the escalators. In Meriden, we had no escalators. We didn't need them. The tallest buildings were two or three stories high and speed was no advantage in reaching an upper floor. As a child, I loved to go G. Fox and Co., a large department store in Hartford with escalators made of wide wooden slats. Moving stairs, people called them. When I got to New York, I was amazed to see people running up the escalators. I could not image why they would want to climb an escalator as if it were an ordinary flight of stairs when, by just standing there they could glide magically to the next floor. In Manhattan I could go out every night and with a different date if I wanted to. Compared with life at a woman's college, single men were everywhere, many of them with good jobs who could afford to take me to expensive restaurants, unlike the students I was used to dating. I became enchanted with the opera, ballet, restaurants that served food from all over the world and the beautiful department stores, nicer than any I had seen even in London and Paris.

I loved my three years living in Manhattan, but I began to feel crowded. I began to suspect that living in a big city was not what I wanted after all. I missed driving to the beach, which took hours in New York. I missed going to a grocery store where I could load my purchases into the trunk of my car and drive home. I missed the change of seasons.

From the window of my 17th floor apartment, I could see the Hudson River. In the morning, vast ocean liners, the Queen Elizabeth and the Queen Mary, nudged by their tugboats, slowly made their way up the Hudson River on the way to their berths on Manhattan's west side. I could see all of this, but I could not see a tree. Unless it snowed, summer and winter looked the same, all building, street and sidewalk.

In suburban New Jersey I found trees, highways and space. I accepted its congestion and its traffic as part of the price. I have lived here twice as long as I have lived any place else, but I am not a native like my husband and sons. My roots and mentality are elsewhere, in the New England of my youth which no longer exists. I cannot move back to the factory town where I grew up, now a bedroom community for those who work in towns nearby. My family left Connecticut long ago, our only legacy the red brick house with the white dormer windows that my parents built in 1948. When people ask what part of "Joisy" I live in, I try not to say I live near Route 80, although at times that is the best way to answer the question. We've all heard the standard joke, "New Jersey, which exit?" In New Jersey our highways define us. Tell me you live near the Garden State Parkway, exit 88, and I will know how close you are to the shore and how long it will take me to get to your house.

Long before the changes in my life occurred that made moving possible, I always believed that if I didn't have to live in this state I would be gone in a minute. I didn't want to live in a place that is as maligned as New Jersey is. I thought I could escape to a state that has a universally pleasant image, like Arizona or Utah. When friends told me to wait a year after Jay and Barry died before doing anything serious, such as selling my house, a year seemed about the right amount of time. "After that, I'm out of here," I told myself. No longer tied to career or family, I was free to depart. The problem was I hadn't the slightest notion of where I would go. A year went by, then two, then three. I have looked for places to live, from Cape Cod to Cape Fear. Too much choice is paralyzing. I have to narrow my search.

My search for what? An apartment or condo would be a logical choice, with no more yard work and house repairs to worry about. If Jay had outlived me, he would have sold the house within six months and all the contents as well. He would have moved to a one-bedroom apartment with a fold-out sofa for guests and found it adequate. Paring down my living to three or four rooms would be difficult at first but I could do it.

We were married for seven years before we bought a house. During those years I lived with my husband and son in apartments with two closets, one bathroom, one medicine cabinet and no garage. I had sufficient space for my wardrobe and possessions but my belongings have mushroomed since I have had space in which to keep them all. I inherited enough silver and china to entertain the Queen. I bought antiques that I fancied from all over the world. All that collecting, and for what? To find myself burdened with a lifetime of things that remind me of who I am and where I came from and are so difficult to part with. My things are my history, my life's archeology.

From my mother I inherited a love of clocks. My mother owned many clocks. Hers were delicate antique clocks in porcelain cases decorated with little pink flowers and gold trim. One of the exceptions and my favorite, a round clock set in a tiny blue enamel umbrella, is now on my bedroom dresser. My mother's clocks, most of them European, were merely ornamental. They had to be wound every day, but most of them didn't run anyway. Shortly after Jay and I were married I purchased my first antique clock from a dealer in Connecticut which was a clock-making center in the early nineteenth century. I wanted an American clock with a pendulum and a chime. Old clocks were easy to find but mine was special. A wooden steeple clock, so called because its pointed top had ornaments that resembled a church steeple, it had originally been a thirty-hour clock but had been rebuilt to run for eight days without winding. It kept perfect time, chiming sweetly on the hour and again on the half. The soft tick of its pendulum was the heartbeat of my home, wherever that home was. I loved that clock. After being a part of the household for many years, it died suddenly, or so I thought, in a fire that destroyed much of our home. Its glass was cracked, its wood was charred, its hands stopped at 3:15. I carried it to the basement and left it there.

For years I tried to replace the clock but the ones I bought didn't keep good time and frequently broke down. I hated them all. Living in New Jersey, I didn't have time to scour the antique shops in the hills of Connecticut where clocks like mine might still be found. Year after year, my ruined clock lay in the damp cellar. I despaired of finding another but couldn't bear to throw it out. I never lost faith that somehow, its brass works had survived and the rest could be fixed. Out of the blue came the answer to my prayers. Andy met a retired engineer in Virginia who repaired antique clocks. Mine was in such bad shape that I was embarrassed to send it, but I had nothing to lose. Imagine my delight to learn that it was reparable— for a sum that was 10 times what I paid for it. I didn't care. I would have scrubbed floors to repair that clock. The clock man and I communicated through e-mail. The brass works were still intact. He could get it to run. A woodworker would put on a new veneer, similar to what the clock wore when it was built years before the Civil War. The paper with the name of the clockmaker was still in place and readable behind the pendulum. It only needed some cleaning.

When the clock finally arrived in the mail, wrapped in plastic and nestled in styrofoam, I was so exited I could hardly open the box. I cut through layers of packing until I finally held it in my hands. Its case was a glorious cherry color, not the dull brown it had been when I purchased it. The gold decal on the glass was not as pretty as the one it replaced, but it was true to the period and fit the decor. I placed the clock on the mantle, attached the pendulum, gave it a gentle push and it began to tick. Once again, my house had a heartbeat. It is not often that a treasured possession that has been lost can be resurrected. I sat for an hour looking at it, listening to its beat and waiting for its chime. I thought about how happy Jay would have been to see the clock working once more. I marveled at the miracle of craftsmanship that had returned it to me. From now on, wherever I live, even if it is a room in a nursing home, my clock goes with me.

The piano is chancier. It has moved many times since my parents bought it for me. It is part of the baggage of my life that holds me hostage. I must find a way to take it to my next home. At Ellis Island in New York Harbor, where millions of immigrants first set foot on American soil, an exhibit called "Treasures From Home" displays items brought to this country by those who came to start a new life here. Most people arrived with a suitcase or two, many with their worldly gifts wrapped in a sheet or blanket but some brought steamer trunks. I was surprised to see the personal belongings they were able to transport on a voyage that may have started in a horse drawn wagon, continued by train and ended as their ship passed the Statue of Liberty. Most items were utilitarian, the symbols and necessities of home that they could use in the new land—brass candlesticks, Russian samovars, hand-embroidered linen tablecloths, down comforters. There were a few luxuries—a violin, a lace wedding gown, a box of military medals.

My grandfather, who came from Poland at 17, brought a handmade cowbell fashioned from a metal I cannot identify. It is small and round with a decorative design and the initials WB stamped into the metal. My grandfather's first name was Abraham. When he arrived at immigration, he took the last name of the most successful man in the village he had left. The initials mean nothing to me. During his life, he acquired many possessions but he never let go of the cowbell. My mother passed it on to me. It is my only link to him and his origins. He settled in Mississippi where he was a peddler in a small town along the Mississippi River, not far from Memphis. He married and after his wife died giving birth to their third son, he moved to New York to find a new wife and mother for his children. He found my grandmother, who was one of several sisters who had to be married off. If she had any choice in the decision, she never mentioned it. Her family was not wealthy in the old country but among their heirlooms were brass menorahs and candlesticks of such weight I wonder how they found their way to these shores. They, too, are among my baggage.

As soon as her divorce became final, a woman at my pool club sold her house and all of her furniture, packed her personal belongings into a few boxes which she stored in a neighbor's garage, and moved to Florida. Like the immigrants, she was ready to close her old life, taking little more than she could fit into her car. My problem is compounded. I trail behind me not only my by-gone life, but husband and dead son's as well. I know that Barry wanted to keep the things he left here when he moved out. I can't let them go now. They are all I have of him. They are small things and easily moved - pictures and key rings, his social security card, his childhood books that perhaps he hoped to read to his children. I will return Jay's college yearbooks and class banner to his alma mater but I will keep his framed diplomas, his appointment calendars with names of clients penciled in tiny script, his Army dog tags and the manila envelopes stuffed with yellowed newspaper clippings that described the milestones of his life. He would have taken these possessions with him to his one-bedroom apartment after selling the house.

"I wish I could press a button and find myself living someplace else," a widow said when we were comparing our housing situation. I suddenly understood why I have spent so long trying to leave my house. It is the leaving that is hard. Endings are difficult, transitions even worse. I know I could be happy in a completely different setting if only I had the courage to sell everything (except the clock and the piano), walk out the front door and never look back. A few years ago I almost bought a condo. Finding myself a little blue on a Sunday afternoon, I went to look at the model condominiums at a place called Eagle View, a development undergoing expansion in the next town. It was a cold, windy day in early December. Built on the site of a former pick-it-yourself strawberry farm, the models had British names like The Avon and The Sussex. The condos were two story town houses, spacious and quite luxurious. Poking around in one of them, I met a woman doing the same thing, but she wasn't interested in buying. She already lived in the complex and wanted to see what enhancements the new models offered. Her name was Cookie. She was a widow whose husband, a lawyer, had died about the same time as Jay did. She had sold her big house with the pool in the yard and bought one of the larger models at Eagle View. When we had finished admiring or criticizing the models—the dining room was too small, the master bath had no window, Cookie invited me to visit her condo. I told her I would stop by on my way home.

She greeted me at the door as if I were an old friend. Her condo was like a little house. It was alive with her present and her past. Her family was coming for dinner and a pot of spaghetti sauce simmered on the stove, filling the house with a zesty aroma I associated with my childhood. We lived on the second floor of a two-family house. Mrs. Pirillo downstairs cooked her sauce for hours. The smell filled the back hall and drifted upstairs when I came home from school. I longed for a plate of Mrs. Pirillo's spaghetti. My mother was a good cook but homemade tomato sauce was not part of her repertoire. Mrs. Pirillo's was among the best I've ever had, its virtue having increased with time. Cookie's home was warm, immaculate and attractively furnished. Snow-white plush carpeting covered all the floors except for the kitchen. If I had that carpeting, no one would ever be allowed to walk on it, certainly not in shoes. I would wear slippers but guests would have to hover above the floor, like angels in sixteenth century paintings. The Christmas decorations were all in place. The tree was lit. It was like an advertisement come to life—a real person had popped out of a glossy magazine to bring me the sounds and smells of home. The management should have hired her and paid her a commission on the sales. I had seen the "before," the professionally furnished models. They looked so stiff and un-lived in, with everything perfectly matched except for the family photographs provided by the decorator where no one resembled anyone else. In the models, not a stray piece of mail disturbed the marble kitchen counter. No newspapers cluttered the family room. I am sure that beautifully appointed model rooms sell houses and apartments, but they discourage me. I can't cope with all that perfection. A muddy footprint on the doormat, a stack of bills on the desk, a little dust here and there would make me feel right at home. Cookie's place was the "after" of the scenario. As she showed me each room, she told me how happy she was there. She knew that I would be too. "Turn the page," she encouraged me, "it's time to move on." Taking a final sniff of the sauce, I thanked her for the visit promising to contact her if I bought a condo there. She reminded me again to turn the page as I returned to the brisk night-time chill of the driveway.

On Monday morning, I called a realtor to inquire about purchasing the model that so excited me. It was currently under construction at the top of a hill with a view overlooking the valley. From the balcony I would be able to see sunsets beyond the ridge. The trees where I live now block out the afternoon sun. I miss the sunsets. The realtor told me she would work on it right away. The next day, I was so nervous about buying the place I forgot my business shoes when I went to a corporate headquarters to lead a workshop. In my dirty tennis shoes, I instructed people on how to dress for success in their interviews. Mortified, I apologized so many times they got tired of hearing it. "Forget about the shoes and get on with your work," their expressions seemed to say.

The following morning I woke up in a sweat, thinking that I had to sell my house. I was all excited about buying but leaving what I had was not going to be as easy as I thought. That night I called a friend in town, a widow, to tell her I saw a place I liked but was beginning to have second thoughts about moving. She asked me what I would miss about my house and my town. She told me that she would miss her big screened-in porch where she slept on warm summer nights. She would miss her garden. "I would miss everything," I moaned. I then realized that I didn't have to move if I didn't want to. I called the realtor and told her to forget the whole thing. I wasn't ready to turn the page. Maybe if Cookie had offered dinner, I would have reconsidered.

I am among the fortunate women who can choose my time to leave. A woman who lived in my neighborhood sold her house and was in a condo within three months of her husband's death. She barely had time to adjust to his absence and she was out of her house and into new surroundings. When I move I want to go to a new home that makes my heart beat faster just thinking about living there. I saw such a place in a seaside town in North Carolina. I flew there to check out the town because a popular television talk show listed it as one of the best places to retire. The newer developments were all gated golfing communities. I could throw away my old life and spend my days as a gated golfer. When not golfing, I would take courses at the university in town. I looked at houses in several communities. The one I loved was on a small lake about 10 minutes from the gorgeous ocean beaches. The house was open and airy, with a lovely garden. I tried to block out the fact that the town is a regular target for east coast hurricanes.

Before I went to North Carolina, someone who lived there told me that the people I meet would ask me two things: where do you come from and what church do you go to? Walking on the boardwalk outside my motel, I struck up a conversation with a friendly native. Following his retirement, he and his wife had moved from the mountains in the western part of the state to the coast.

"Where are you from?" he asked.

"New Jersey," I responded.

"I won't hold that against you," he continued. At least he didn't ask which exit. He told me how much he and his wife enjoyed their life in the small coastal town where they lived. Trying to place me into a frame of reference he could relate to, he then asked me what church I go to.

"I'm Jewish," I replied. His jaw dropped. He stared at me speechless. He seemed to be looking for little antennae growing from my head. Perhaps he had never before seen a Jew close up, much less spoken with one. Finally, regaining his composure, he said that he and his wife attended the Baptist church in town and I was welcome to go with them on Sunday. He seemed so sincere I had no doubt he would have picked me up and taken me there to worship if I had agreed. I thanked him for the invitation but told him I had other plans for Sunday.

I spoke with many southerners and northern transplants who lived in the area where I had found my dream house. The southerners said the summers weren't bad, there was always a breeze. They encouraged me to move down. The transplanted northerners all left for at least a month in the summer, saying the heat and humidity were unbearable. They told me not to be misled by the southern display of hospitality. The old time southerners and northern retirees didn't mix much. Southerners are polite and friendly when you meet them in the street or at the store, but they do not welcome Yankees, much less invite them to their home. I could see myself living in the house and loving it, but as a single woman, I wasn't so sure about making my home in the community. Golf would not be enough to fill my life. I would miss New York. My intuition told me I wasn't meant to be a southerner, even a pseudo one. I walked along the beach one more time and flew home.

Finding a place to live, like finding a mate, is for me a yes or no reaction. My initial response is the one I stick with. I don't easily tune in to the possibilities that someone or someplace might actually grow on me, that I could learn to love him or it. With a mate I'm a little vague about what I'm looking, for but I know what I will miss when I leave my house. I will miss sitting at the kitchen table with a cup of hot coffee, looking at the snow softly falling on the pines in the yard. The stream that runs by has a thin coat of black ice. The park just beyond has turned white. Squirrels chase one another endlessly from tree to tree and rock to rock. Cars, their sound muffled by the snow, are moving more slowly than the squirrels. The world is black and white. Like "The Wizard of Oz" my two-color winter world turns to Technicolor in the spring. Clumps of pale yellow daffodils line the stream. The crabapple is covered with dainty pink flowers. The leaves of the white birch are the softest green. Early fall is all reds, yellows and oranges, but I like late fall when some of the leaves are gone, opening up a view of the lake and sky. The first vibrant colors have become subtle brown and tan except for the Japanese maples which have suddenly turned auburn. Bright against the October sky, tiny red crabapples that look like strings of cranberries at Christmas cover the apple tree in front of the house. Out-of-towners who come to visit ask if I realize how beautiful it is where I live. "Of course I do," I tell them. "Why do you think I'm still here?"

I know this is an excuse. Fall is prettier in New England and so is winter. There are towns in New Jersey that have beautiful fall colors and sandy ocean beaches as well. The same is true of Delaware and Virginia. I'm here because I'm stuck. It's the base I cling to, the launch for my travel, the place to come back to. The home I would miss.

If there is one thing I am not ambivalent about, it is travel. Jay and I both loved to travel. We occasionally accompanied one another on business trips but most of our travel was selected for pleasure. We liked to fly to a city, rent a car and drive. Along the way, we drove on the highways and side roads, explored the cities and the villages. Where travel is concerned, there are movers and stayers. The stayers rent a farm or beach house and relax for a week or two. We liked to move on, two nights here, three there, and the next town or country beckoned. We stayed at small country inns and guest houses, searched for the diners, brasseries and bistros where the local people stopped for lunch, and followed the guidebooks to the not-to-be-missed museums, vistas, lookouts and monuments. In this way, we saw much of Europe and some of the United States. It was a style of travel that ended for me with Jay's death.

I cannot say that so much togetherness did not bring about disagreements and squabbles, even fights. When we argued in Communist Yugoslavia, I drove off, leaving him on a street corner and vowing never to return. I had the passports and visas, he had the money. I don't know who would have fared worse if I had kept my promise. In Nova Scotia I left him sulking in a motel room while I drove off to see Alexander Graham Bell's summer residence, an interesting excursion that he always regretted missing, although he wouldn't admit it. There are ways to make up when traveling with one's mate that are not available to friends and other relatives. Andy and I have traveled together. Most of our vacations have been ski trips where we see one another for breakfast and dinner but go our own way on the slopes. The exception was a trip to Eastern Europe. Stuck in a traffic jam in Bratislava, Slovakia, on our way to the airport, son calmed mother who was certain we would miss the plane. So the child became the parent. We get along because we know how to deal with the other's idiosyncrasies.

With a friend I would fear so much time together, just the two of us. I had to find a new way to travel. At first I visited all the friends who invited me. They gave me my own room and a sympathetic ear. They cooked my favorite dishes and took me to see the local sights. They were warm and understanding. I enjoyed these trips. I drove to see Andy who lived in Williamsburg, Virginia. Not wanting to be in his way, I stayed in a motel and spent my days visiting the tourist spots. For me, these were pleasant journeys when the two of us could spend time together as we tried to forge new lives. I flew to Florida to a convention where I knew I would see many professional colleagues, some of them old friends. They had called and sent notes when Jay and Barry died. This was our first time together since then. They made a fuss over me, giving me more attention than I deserved. The first night in the hotel, I suddenly remembered I hadn't called home as I would normally do on such a trip. Sadly I realized that no one was at home to answer. First denial, then awareness. From one part of the grief cycle to another.

In the meantime, I was searching for The Big Trip, a journey with a new group of people to a new destination. I had my choice from the multitude of travel brochures that arrived almost daily in my mailbox from academic institutions, professional associations, assorted organizations and tour companies. In glossy photos, happy couples smiled and waved to me from mountain tops, golden beaches, African safaris and treks in Napal. These journeys promised excitement, good fellowship, and excellent accommodations, per person, double occupancy. So I learned about another disadvantage of being uncoupled in a paired-up world: the single supplement. The financial penalty for traveling solo is steep. For comparable accommodations, an individual who wants a private room can pay half-again what someone pays who shares. Voyages involving a boat of any kind are the most egregious. A recent example came from a tour company touting a "CruiseTour to vibrant Singapore." For the cruise portion, they offered deluxe outside cabins featuring one or two beds, telephone, television, hair dryer, safe, marble bath with whirlpool tub and cabin doors that open onto the deck. The price for this luxury was $3595 per person, double occupancy. For the same price, a single person could obtain an inside cabin, with one bed and a private bath but without the marble whirlpool and television.

I imagined myself in my small single windowless room sitting in a stiff chair reading a book while couples relaxed in their whirlpool tub, watched a good movie on TV, then emerged from their room onto the deck in their glorious formal wear as people did on ocean liners in 1940's movies. The tour companies offer to pair singles up. I like to make new friends and can get along with most people but spending a few weeks with a roommate who snores would not be my idea of luxury. A quick poke to the ribs put a temporary end to my husband's nocturnal buzz saws but someone who has paid $3595 might not like to have her sleep disturbed, even though she was ruining mine. The fear that I too would snore and awaken her would keep me from sleeping, as well.

When a brochure arrived for a one-week trip to Portugal, I knew I had found a vacation I would love. Ever since seventh grade when my social studies project was a report on Portugal, I have wanted to see the places I had so carefully researched in my World Book Encyclopedia. Most tours go to Lisbon and the southern beaches, but this went to Lisbon and the north where we would stay in a hotel built as a hunting lodge for the last Portuguese king. When he lost his throne, the lodge, actually more of a castle, became a hotel. Best of all, for this trip, the single supplement was only a few hundred dollars. One week away was good for a starter trip. All the ingredients were right. I signed up immediately, but I almost didn't go.

A few months before my departure, I developed health problems that required having a hysterectomy. The surgery was scheduled for one month before my trip. The doctor told me to cancel my vacation. Four weeks would not be enough recovery time to travel to Europe. I was devastated. I had been dreaming about this trip for months. Determined to go, I didn't cancel. I had a difficult time anticipating this surgery. My coping skills were overtaxed, just a year after Jay and Barry's death. Although friends were wonderful, offering rides and other support, I felt so alone. Andy was in the process of studying for the written and oral exams for his degree. I didn't want to worry him so I decided I would call him from the hospital after the surgery was over. By then, his exams would be finished and he could come to help out. "You must tell him, he has a right to know," a woman told me. I waited until the night that he had finished his written exam and I called. He was angry that I hadn't called sooner. His professors granted him a postponement of his oral exams just as they had given him a postponement of his final term exams the year earlier when his father and brother died. He arrived from Virginia the night before the operation.

The next morning, we sat alone in a little room at the hospital chatting as if we were waiting for a train or bus. The room overlooked a hospital staff parking lot. For an hour, we watched doctors come to work in their Lexuses and BMW's. Finally, a "transport worker" came to take me to surgery. Fifteen months after his father had died in the same hospital, Andy was following behind the gurney as his mother was wheeled into the operating room for major surgery. The hospital had no place for me to leave my clothing. I cried the whole way down as I saw him walking along carrying a white plastic hospital bag containing the clothes I had worn to the hospital, my black coat over his arm. When we said goodbye at the door to the operating wing, I thought I would never see him again. The next thing I knew, I woke up six hours later full of tubes with

Andy's tall frame looking down at me from the foot of my bed.

As soon as I knew that I was alive, my only goal was to go to Portugal as I had planned. The nurses told me the key to a speedy recovery was to walk. From the first day, dragging my tubes and intravenous bag hanging from a pole, I walked. At first my legs could barely support me and the pain was considerable but canceling my trip would have hurt more. Each day, I walked a little more. From my bed, I read the travel brochure over and over. I saw myself strolling the grounds of the castle and eating in its formal dining room. I had many visitors during my hospital stay. They brought me frivolous magazines that I normally would not have time to read and other gifts but no flowers. My roommate received so many flower arrangements from her relatives that she could have opened a florist shop right there in our room. Her flowers lined the window sill and overflowed into the room. I sent Andy to the supermarket to buy me a bouquet and placed it on my table where I could look at it and think of the flowers of Portugal.

Three weeks later, a neighbor drove me to my follow-up visit with the doctor. He said I was almost healed. I asked the question I feared would end my dream.

"Is there any reason why I cannot go to Portugal next week?"

"Go and have a good time. You deserve it," he replied. I would have danced if I could have, but I was still too sore. A few days later, I decided to try to walk around the block. If I could not do that, how could I go to Europe? I would not make it to the airport gate. It was a lovely early spring day. The trees were getting ready to bud and the slightest hint of warmth was in the afternoon air. Halfway around, I was slow but still moving. I met neighbors also out for a stroll. I told them I was testing my ability to get to the plane the following week. I knew if I could get to the plane, I could enjoy Portugal.

"Isn't there any way you can get out of this?" my neighbor inquired.

"You don't understand," I told him. "More than anything else, I *want* to go."

By the next week I was ready. My travel companions were a congenial group. One of the women told me she didn't leave her couch for six weeks after her hysterectomy. My lack of mobility saved me money. While the others scurried off to shops as soon as we left the bus at one of our many shopping opportunities, I relaxed and read a book. Several of the people moved as slowly as I did. A woman with a bad knee sat with me in the back of a cathedral while the others climbed the stone tower. As the trip progressed, I got stronger. We spent several days in Lisbon before driving north. We reached the castle after dark. In the entry hall, the walls were covered with murals and fabulous woodcarvings. The dining room was elegant. Although my room was small, the bathroom was huge with ancient plumbing and a tub long enough to lie down in. The following morning, I drew back the curtains and pushed open the windows. The hotel was at the top of a hill. The morning dew sparkled in the sun. Two stories below me was a garden. Beyond that there were acres of forest. Extending outward for miles and miles were green hills and blue mountains. The view was so enchanting I thought I saw little elves peeking out from under their toadstools, but they were probably just frogs. I remembered the hospital, the pain and the tubes. I breathed in the fresh clean air. This was why I had fought so hard to come to Portugal. To look out this window and know a future.

The following year Andy and I traveled to Slovakia and Poland. People wondered why we would choose such places to visit. "Are you looking for your roots?" they asked. My roots were destroyed in the Holocaust, yet I wanted to see the country where much of my family lived for centuries. I planned the trip for six months. The Internet was not the force it is now. Obtaining bus and train schedules ahead of time required patience and detective work. For months before leaving home, I listened to German language tapes every time I got into the car because the guidebooks informed me that German would be more useful than English. It was a boring task, but my German saved us in some tight spots in train stations and on street corners when we were hopelessly lost.

We boarded a train in Vienna and set out for "The East," as the Austrians say, passing through the Czech Republic on our way to Poland. Along with us, thousands of others were coming to Cracow because our visit to the country coincided with that of the Pope. We were caught up in the frenzy that accompanies the return of Poland's native son and most famous citizen. Flags, banners and simple homemade signs were in every window. Bleachers were under construction. Our plans, made months before the Pope's schedule became public, called for us to visit Zakopane, a beautiful little ski resort high in the Carpathian mountains. We learned a few days before that the Pope would celebrate Mass on the day we planned to be there. In Cracow we were discouraged from going.

"Cancel everything," a tour guide told us. "You will not be able to get there and if you do, it will be a zoo."

After trying several bus companies, we made a reservation for the day before the mass. The bus was creaky, overcrowded, and hot. The only other American aboard was a woman who arrived with a 3-foot by 5-foot cardboard picture of the Pope which she wanted the driver to stow beneath the bus. He knew no English, but the woman managed to communicate her message. When she came down the aisle handing out cards with pictures of saints on them, we pretended to be Germans. Passengers and their luggage clogged the aisles, but the scenery distracted us from our discomfort. Leaving the congestion and bustle of the city, we were soon driving through a long green valley running parallel to snow-white mountains. An occasional ski slope appeared, its lone T-bar lift now stranded on a grassy hill. To the side of the road, a farmer loaded heavy logs into his horse-drawn wagon. Occasionally the bus stopped, and people with cumbersome packages and baskets of food left the bus with no indication in sight of where they might be heading.

Eventually, we stepped off the bus into the cool pine air of Zakopane. What a change from the heavy air of the city. I took a deep breath and was glad we came. Commercial vendors sold Pope souvenirs— tee shirts and hats, banners and flags. The local populace, seizing the opportunity, also sold their wares— embroidered tablecloths, hand-knit scarves and sweaters, knives with carved wooden handles, and handmade leather gloves. Small groups in colorfully embroidered local costumes gathered on corners. There were no crowds. We saw only a few people although more than 300,000 were expected for the mass the following day. Carrying our luggage, we walked down a wide, tree-lined avenue. On both sides were large old wooden houses that looked like illustrations from Grimm's fairy tales. Our hotel, with a view of the mountains, was in the center of town. A charming old pine building with a steep slanting roof, the place had painted flowers on its walls and large welcoming fireplaces. I have stayed in numerous ski lodges in New England that looked like this, but here was the real thing.

The next morning everything was closed— the bank, post office and all the shops. Our hotel served us stale rolls for breakfast because the baker had taken the day off. "Papa," the waitress explained in Polish. Remembering the extensive security and ticket frenzy surrounding the Pope's visit to Giants Stadium in New Jersey, I thought we would have no chance to get near the site at the bottom of the ski jump where the Mass was to take place. At the gate, we approached two soldiers, all gussied up in dress military uniforms. To our surprise, when we said we had no tickets, they handed us two and ushered us in. The crowds in the fields stretched beyond our view. A huge white cross rose into the sky above the ski jump. Spectators clung to the hill normally a vantage point for viewing the skiers. The Pope may have looked like a tiny doll from the perspective of most in attendance but among his people, he was larger than God.

The jubilation that accompanied this event was in sharp contrast to our visit to the death camps at Auschwitz and Birkenau only two days earlier. Andy and I knew the loss of two. In these unholy and awesome places we tried to comprehend the loss of millions. In a matter-of-fact tone he might have used to describe the state capital, our guide pointed out the railroad sidings installed to accommodate the daily arrivals of Jews from Hungary. The gas chambers have been destroyed but tourists can view the hellish barracks, outhouses and fields surrounded by barbed wire where the occupants lived their final days. It is all sanitized now. The sounds and smells are gone but the place is haunted by the ghosts of its hollow-eyed occupants. Groups of Polish school children made a mandated visit. Like us, they walked about seeing, weeping, trying to absorb the horror. At home in my synagogue, when I rise to pray for my dead, I picture one or two of the nameless thousands who perished at Auschwitz. I remember the little girls my age whose mothers braided their hair and hemmed their skirts. I say a prayer for them because the place where they died has become a tourist stop to enhance my experience. I gather them into my circle of loss. There is enough room.

My trip to Eastern Europe was good preparation for China. Not that they were similar in any way, but I regained the confidence I had as a 22-year-old wandering about Europe by myself. The spirit of adventure that had propelled Jay and me to so many places around the world had returned. A few years later, when a letter came announcing a three-week trip to China, I knew I had to go. It was an ambitious journey including nine flights, several riverboat cruises, a train trip and countless bus excursions. I wanted to do it while I still had strong legs and a good back. I immediately signed up, then started worrying about what could go wrong. Before I left home, I went to the cemetery to tell Jay I needed his help. I confessed I was nervous about going so far away, that I didn't know anyone in the group I was traveling with, that I wished he was going too but since he couldn't make it, I hoped he would look out for me. I figured he could see me in China as well as at home, so it shouldn't be too much of a challenge. In the last days before leaving, I was so excited I could barely function. Instead of looking forward to the wonderful sights I would see, I was apprehensive about getting a gall bladder attack on the four-day Yangzte River cruise. I worried about getting sick with no one to take care of me, or to stay behind with me if the group had to travel on without me. It never happened. From the minute the trip started and I was among other people, I stopped worrying.

My travel companions were my husband's college classmates, accompanied by spouses and friends, the ultimate off-shore reunion. We assembled in the Tokyo airport for the final leg to Beijing. I was the only one who came unconnected. They thought I was brave to do it. I didn't agree. I was with a group and all the arrangements were made for me. The only thing I had to do was show up. It was a life-changing journey, a view of a land and culture so remote from ours that we could have been on a different planet. Our guide, a forthright young woman, told us facts about life in China that are not in the newspapers. In the museums we saw thousand-year-old silk paintings of fishermen on tiny boats and farmers working the land with water buffaloes. Daily we photographed the descendents of the silk screen figures performing the same tasks, oblivious to a newer technology, unchanged by time. In a country of enormous contrast, I experienced a few. Our group stopped at a jewelry factory where workers strung pearl necklaces to order. When the order for one of our tour members was delayed, the factory offered to deliver it to our hotel. Leaving the factory, our bus drove down a narrow road lined with thatched-roof cottages and rice paddies where men bent over their crops and women bore heavy loads on poles that hung from their shoulders. Suddenly our guide received a call on her cell phone. The jewelry was about to be delivered. A few minutes later, a young man on a motorcycle overtook the bus. The jewelry had arrived.

In a hotel lobby I met a Chinese woman who symbolized the Chinese mentality. She was reading an English newspaper so I asked her how she learned English. She graduated from high school during the years of the Cultural Revolution when educated people were sent from the cities to live and work on farms in remote areas. More than a million died. Her dream was to learn English. Although she passed the examination for the university, she was sent away from her family to work on a farm. Ten years later, when the Cultural Revolution ended, she was considered too old to attend college. Back in the city, she did menial work while teaching herself English by reading text books that were available at the library and by listening to English language tapes. Eventually, she passed the examination to become an English language tour guide, one of the most prestigious jobs in China. Her tenacity and determination are typical of modern China. I thought of her when I visited the Great Wall. The small portion of the Wall that we visited contained thousands of steep stone steps leading from one guardhouse to the next. Climbing the steps reminded me of a camp song: "The bear climbed over the mountain, the bear climbed over the mountain, the bear climbed over the mountain and what do you think he saw? He saw another mountain, he saw another mountain and what do you think he did? He climbed the other mountain" and so on. I climbed from one guardhouse to another but there were always more stairs and another guardhouse in the distance. In China, the goal always appears to be beyond the next hill and the next hill is painfully far away.

The last stop on the trip was Hong Kong, a large modern city where the locals speak English. I was in my comfort zone. The first day, standing on the waterfront looking at the buildings and hills so familiar from movies and television, I wept tears of relief. I had come so far. I hadn't lost my passport, left any possessions behind or experienced any illnesses that a few pills didn't cure. Perhaps my traveling companions were right. I was brave to do it but if staying home was the alternative, I would do it again in a minute. I thought of Jay constantly on that trip. He would have loved it, but neither of us would have gone if he were alive. He would have tossed out the letter that so intrigued me. Except for attending football games, he had maintained few ties to his alma mater. The expense of the trip would have been considerable for two people. Ironically, his insurance paid my way and for my other jaunts as well. We would have continued to travel as we did when he lived, on our own to places not yet popular with American tourists. He would have been my companion to Eastern Europe. With more time available as our work loads decreased, we would have explored the parts of America we had not seen. Maybe we would have settled in a place that struck our fancy during our travels. Maybe we would have bought the house I loved in North Carolina. Jay would have liked the golf course. Our sons, daughters-in-law and grandchildren would have enjoyed the beach when they came to visit. In my mind, I see the life I might have had in North Carolina but alone I do not have the courage to build that life. At least not yet. But I rarely worry about traveling alone any more. Moving will be next. I'm almost ready.

14

All We Know of Heaven

When I was a teenager my family had a ping-pong table in the basement. I spent so much time playing ping-pong that I could beat all the boys who came to the house. My mother told me not to play so well because boys don't like losing to girls. I promised her that I would marry the first man who could beat me at ping-pong. Jay was that man. Of course, I didn't marry him for that reason. But on days when things were not smooth between us, I sometimes wondered why I did marry him. Recently, I was again reminded why. I was eating breakfast alone at an inn in Delaware when a song I had not heard in years came over the sound system. The room was noisy, and I couldn't hear the words, but I remembered most of them. My eyes filled with tears. Barbra Streisand sang:

"Why did I choose you? What did I see in you?
I saw a man I knew so well. I saw a quiet man
Who caught me in his spell.
Why did I want you? What could you offer me -
A love to last my whole life through.
And when I lost my heart so many years ago
I gave it lovingly and willingly to you.
If I had to choose again, I would still choose you.

Among our loved ones, our spouse is the only one we choose. I married Jay because he promised me a lifetime of love, and I believed he would make good on that promise. If he had told me that his lifetime would be shorter than other men I might have married, I would have chosen him anyway. Perhaps in the twenty-first century, people will choose their children. If all the babies were lined up, I don't know if I would have picked the bald baby boy whose feet pointed in the same direction, but I could not have done any better. He was all I ever wanted in a son.

More than five years have passed since they died. If I live out my statistically granted 78 years, I see my life dividing into three segments that will resemble a bell curve - 23 years single, 34 years married, 21 years widowed. As a TV sitcom, my life would be equal parts Friends, Home Improvement and Golden Girls. Well into the latter phase, I am seeking a way to carve out my niche. People who have lost loved ones told me that time would soften the edges of grief— like a piece of glass that washes up on the beach, smoothed by sand and water. Time has helped. Adversity has worn me down or maybe it's just age. I have stopped fighting my fate.

I often wonder how my life would have been different if both or either of them had lived. I suspect that Jay and I would have sold the house, as most of our neighbors have done. They have gone to warmer climates or assisted living accommodations. Ellen and Barry may have remained in the Washington, DC area where they had friends and work. When Andy, Barry and I sat on the living room sofa the morning that Jay died, Barry told me that he and Ellen would come to visit every weekend so I wouldn't be lonely. "No, I don't want you to do that, you have to live your own life," I answered, never imagining that his life would end the next day. Had he lived, I doubt they would have come every weekend, but we would have shared birthdays, holidays and special occasions.

What happens to those days— the wedding anniversaries and birthdays that are no longer cause for celebration? On Barry's birthday, I write him a letter telling him how much I miss him. I ask him what he hoped to be doing on that day, what plans he might have made for his future. I give a donation in his memory instead of buying him a gift that I would have spent hours choosing, hoping he would like it. On the other days that are now unmarked milestones, I walk around with a heavy heart missing the celebration I will never know again.

Last year, good news, I was able to add a happy occasion. Andy married Deborah, a college professor. She is tall, slim and smart. I have come to love her quiet confidence and strength. They met on a street corner in Philadelphia when she was roller-blading and he was walking home from the library. If she had been a faster skater, the story may have ended differently, but with his long stride, Andy was able to follow her home. Their wedding was a time for joy and reflection. Andy had spoken in the past about his disappointment that Deborah and Barry had never known one another. He introduced her to Ellen soon after they met, as the next best thing, the closest connection he could make to his brother. On the night before their wedding, as hostess of the pre-wedding dinner, I welcomed the long-distance guests and family who had come to Texas for the occasion, including my brother and sister-in-law from Israel, my friend Carol, who was a bridesmaid at my wedding, and several college friends with their husbands. To start my toast, which was light and humorous to fit the occasion, I told everyone that the day was special to me because it would have been Jay and my 39th wedding anniversary. There was an audible gasp. I knew they felt sorry for me but I was not seeking their pity. It was a wonderful occasion and I was as happy as everyone else.

At the wedding, Jay and Barry's absence was so palpable it became a presence walking among us. I missed them both so much, thinking of how handsome they would have looked in their tuxedos. How happy they would have been to share Andy's celebration. How witty Barry would have been toasting his "little brother" about to become a married man. I missed taking my husband's arm to walk down the aisle, but I walked with Andy instead. It was a good arrangement. The two of us who had endured such tragedy were now linked arm-in-arm in a joyous procession toward his new life.

My brother, who participated in the service, spoke of the significance of breaking a glass during the Jewish ceremony, the shattered glass reminding us that even on our happiest occasions, there is an element of sadness. By reciting the names of our lost loved ones, he brought them to us. Jay's brother Larry was best man, uncle, surrogate father and brother. Later, giving his toast, he spoke of them as well. So, we found ways to include them. And I was never sad. Not for a minute. I loved all of it, and I was so happy for Andy to have found a woman who could bring joy to his life. I ate and danced and of course I cried, but I cry at weddings even when I don't know the bride and groom. It was the best thing that had happened in four years and my tears were tears of gladness and thanksgiving.

Seeing me at the wedding, many would have wondered how I had reached that point. I appeared to be happy, organized, able to derive the best from my life. A woman I met a few years after my tragedy said I always seemed to be so competent. Assuming that I was shocked by my experience, she wanted to know how I went from "shocked person" to "competent." The answer is I didn't go from shocked to competent. I went from shocked and competent to resigned and competent, with a stop along the way at miserable and competent. I have been competent since I was three. During adversity, I revert to the behavior that is most familiar. I get the job done and, with a perverse stubbornness, I establish a new order out of chaos. I did this when a fire reduced our house to ruins the week before Andy's Bar Mitzvah, and I did it when death claimed half of my family. Competence is not a challenge for me. Competence keeps me going. I do the tasks that require doing, and doing them well brings me satisfaction. But don't confuse satisfaction with contentment. They're at a different level on the happiness scale. I know moreover that competence is not enough. It represents only part of the person I would like to become.

I recently met a woman, a friend of a friend, whom I hadn't seen in years. She said she remembered my being a working mother when it was an issue. I was surprised that people still hold that perception of me. Perhaps I didn't realize how unique I was. I think that psychologically my work prepared me for where I am now. Through my determination to "have it all," I acquired, along the way, the coping skills I could summon when tragedy in my life required them. To survive, I have had to be strong. I have had to create a shell to protect myself. With my armor in place, I face the world. I've had five years to learn how to handle my new life, and I can accept where I am. But like competence, acceptance isn't enough. I will have to learn to grow.

I will also have to learn again how to hope. I need a Dream, something so compelling that it will propel me steadfastly forward and upward to a new plateau. I encourage participants in my job search classes to pursue their Dream. I help them to write their resumes describing what they have done, but I urge them to reach out for what they can do. When I worked at the Career Center I had a client named Dorothy. She was memorable in several ways, not only for her attitude, but for her appearance. Most visitors to the Center, women and men, young and old, wore jeans or sweat suits. They saw us as another bureaucratic barrier on the road to their goal and dressing for a visit to our office was not high among their priorities. Dorothy came for her first visit in a striking orange linen suit with black trim. She wore orange leather high-heeled shoes and carried a matching orange bag. She looked smashing and I told her so. After she settled into the chair in my office, she told me why she had come.

"I have a Dream," she said. "I want to be a milliner. I want to make hats." I gasped, not too loudly, I hope. The government has rules, restrictions, road blocks. The government says it will pay for schooling to enter occupations currently in demand in New Jersey. There is a list: secretary, bookkeeper, heating/air conditioning mechanic, electronic technician, chef, truck driver, medical assistant. Jobs that could be learned in a year. But milliner? No one wears hats any more. She might as well have asked to be a shepherdess or a typewriter repairman. To complicate the issue, the only school that offered such a course was in New York. Not only was the school out-of-state, which created one set of problems, but it was part of a university, which created another. Universities discourage such students because of the government regulations and all the paperwork involved. People who want to take college courses become caught between two bureaucracies.

Six months passed from the time that Dorothy first entered my office until she received the funding to attend the course of her dreams. Every so often, she came back to visit bringing a big box of hats including some that she won awards for at school. She made hats for a wedding party, church hats, high fashion hats, stiff felt hats that perch on top of the head with little veils like my mother wore in the 1950's, and graceful wide-brimmed hats like the ones that adorn the beautiful wives and daughters of horse owners at the Kentucky Derby. All the women in the office tried them on. We loved them. At the time, I owned a plain broad-brimmed straw hat that Dorothy offered to decorate for me. I bought a few yards of deep blue satin ribbon, and she sewed it on making a bow with two long strands that trailed down the back. She changed my hat from merely utilitarian to simply elegant. I think of her each time I wear it. Dorothy was still in school when I left the Center and we lost contact. But I will wager she is making hats somewhere and bringing happiness to the women who wear them. She was a strong woman who didn't allow her Dream to escape.

My Dream involves a place and not a job. When I told the accountant years ago that I wanted a house by the water where I could write, I had a picture in my mind of a sunny cottage with flowers in the front yard. My office would look out on a bay or an inlet, maybe even a lake. I later saw that house on Cape Cod. It faced the afternoon sun. An English country garden grew out front with hollyhocks and delphinium, daisies and pink geraniums. I could say that if it had been for sale I would have bought it in a minute, but caution would have taken over and all the negatives would have jumped into my head. I have a house where I can look at water while I write. It's too big and worrisome but, all things considered, it is the best I can do right now. It was my dream house when I moved in but my Dream has changed. Sooner or later, the house will catch up.

If pursuing my Dream means going to a different state, I will be torn by my feelings of leaving my husband and son behind. I don't know who will visit their graves when I am gone. Bereavement books say one of the signs of improvement is visiting the cemetery less frequently. I used to visit almost every week but as time has passed, I go less often. Nevertheless, the cemetery is part of the anchor that keeps me where I am. I kneel on the coarse grass to be closer to the stones and I run my fingertips across the lettering, as a blind person would touch Braille. As I wiped Barry's face when he was a child, I wipe his stone when it becomes stained. I remove the offending leaf or piece of dirt, trying to make his place look good, as he always looked good.

I don't cry at the graves anymore. The surface wound has closed, leaving the pain deep inside. The first summer no grass grew over the raw brown dirt. The graves looked like unmade beds. I called Louis, the cemetery administrator, to ask when grass would be planted. "The grass will grow after a year," he responded. "It doesn't grow the first year. That's God's way. It is just another thing you will have to bear." It is also the cemetery's way of saving money. When the grass came, it was crabgrass and other hardy weeds, sent by God to cover the offending dirt. I planted flowers that withered in the summer sun. I attempted to water them but the cemetery faucets were not functioning. I complained to Louis. Nothing changed. Still, I plant flowers. I bring gallon jugs of water from home to pour on them. I want something to grow along with God's crabgrass.

Occasionally Jay and Barry visit me in my dreams. The first dream I had about them occurred a few months after they died. Barry came back and I was overjoyed to see him. I hugged him and my eyes filled with tears of happiness. He asked me for an orange. I called Jay from another room to tell him that Barry was back and that I had given him an orange. As they embraced I noticed that large bright red spots had suddenly appeared on Barry's white shirt and on the floor. Then my dream faded away. I awoke with my eyes still wet from the tears of joy in my dream. "Why did you return them to me only to take them away again?" I called to God in my anguish. "Now I have lost them twice." In subsequent dreams, Barry has come, but he always walks away at the end of the dream.

These dreams do not sadden me. He seems peaceful and the dreams are pleasant. I have become used to his leaving. Jay returned in a dream with an offer to help me clean out the attic. I appreciated that. He never offered when he was alive. After a long gap, I recently dreamed that I was in the lobby of a resort hotel trying to check out. Through the open doors, I could see people swimming and diving in a lovely blue lake. Suddenly someone tapped my shoulder. I turned around and there was Jay, young and handsome, wearing the tan plaid sport jacket he would have worn at a resort. "What are you doing here?" I asked in surprise as we hugged one another. I knew he was dead. I knew he was restored to me for only that moment. I think this represented progress because deep in my mind I have processed his death. He returns to me briefly in dreams as I remember him, but I know he will go away again and I am prepared.

Recognizing that I have changed is also part of the healing process. In a Compassionate Friends newsletter, Helen the chapter leader, wrote about a trip that she and her husband made to the national parks in Utah and Arizona three years after the death of her son. During part of their trip, they saw the results of a forest fire that had left the ground blackened with destruction. Only the charred remains of trees were visible. Helen contrasted this devastation with the vibrant grandeur of the Grand Canyon, with scenic mountains covered with lush green foliage and the unique beauty of the red rocks in Arizona. She suddenly realized that after the devastating loss of her son, she was learning to see color again, that slowly she was beginning to appreciate the beauty around her. Her experience reminded me of the movie "Pleasantville." Two modern teenagers are suddenly drawn into the black and white world of 1950's television in a town called Pleasantville. The citizens of Pleasantville are stereotypes, programmed to behave in a one-dimensional manner and limited by their prejudices. Gradually, the 1990's youngsters influence the people they meet. As the citizens of Pleasantville learn to accept new ideas and different behavior they turn to color. They could only appreciate the good things around them when they learned to change. Change is fearful, but it can't be worse than what I have already been through. The change I experienced was thrust upon me. Future change will have to be voluntary. Like the residents of Pleasantville, to improve my life I will have to choose to change it.

One sign of change is the ability to live with both good and bad memories of the past. For a long time, my happy memories of my family seemed to buried with my husband and son. The sadness weighed so heavily on my memories that it smothered them like a heavy blanket extinguishing a flame. Photographs of my son smiling in his graduation robe or dancing at his wedding evoked the most profound sorrow, even though he was most happy at those times. I eventually realized that his memory deserves those good days. They are part of his legacy. They were good days for me too and I had to learn to call them up without pain.

Barry and Ellen's wedding pictures, pictures of the Thanksgiving we all spent together two weeks before Jay and Barry died, bring sadness but not the sharp hurt they once did. I look forward to the time when they will blend into other memories, when I can look at them as reminders of the joyous days they were rather than forerunners of the tragic times that followed. I thought I would never again be able to visit some of the places that Jay and I traveled to together, but slowly they are looking attractive to me again. They are regaining their color. I am open to the possibility that one day I will be strong enough to go back.

One of my favorite places to return to is a spot that Jay never visited although I know he would have loved it. Every summer, like a Fresh Air Kid from the city, I visit my college classmate Pat and her husband high in the White Mountains of New Hampshire. Their house, which he rebuilt from an old farmhouse, is on a hill surrounded by green fields and unmown meadows. I sit on the deck and look out across the broad Connecticut River valley to the mountains of Vermont, miles in the distance. In the evening, my old friend and I put on warm sweaters to watch the sunset until the last vestiges of pink disappear in the west. The night sky is so broad and black that every star of the Milky Way is painted white against it. The setting is so lovely I never want to leave. On the way to Pat's house I pass a farm, its modest white farmhouse set far back up the dirt driveway. In front, out near the road, is a colorful hand-lettered sign: "Rainbow's End." It reminds me of the night before Jay died when I watched "Breakfast at Tiffany's" and Audrey Hepburn sang "Moon River:"

"Two drifters off to see the world
There's such a lot of world to see.
We're after the same rainbow's end
Waitin' round the bend.
My huckleberry friend
Moon River and me."

Forgetting how quickly rainbows disappear, I wondered while watching the movie whether Jay and I had found our rainbow's end. The rainbow we lived under then is gone, its color faded away, and I cannot return to the place where it was. I must seek a different end to my rainbow. It will be a mental rather than a physical place where I will no longer be just the woman-whose-husband-and-son-died-within-twenty-four-hours. I will emerge from the grief cycle to find that my rainbow's end will actually be a beginning. I am learning to create that beginning. I know that one day I will do it.

හගහගහගහ **Epilogue** ගහගහගහ

I n 2001, Deborah and Andy moved to the Midwest where they both found jobs. Suddenly my path became clear and I knew what I had to do. When I announced my plans to my friends, they were amazed. Knowing my attachment to New York, they questioned my resolve to move so far away - to a place that was so different from anywhere that I had lived before, where other than my two relatives, I knew no one. A short time later, I bought a house with a view of water and the big, midwestern sky. I sold my home of 25 years to a family who loved it and promised to care for it as I had done.

I thought there would not be a bucket big enough to hold the tears when the time came to leave my house for the last time. The movers came on a July day when the temperature hit 90 by 8 a.m. When I saw the moving van, my throat got tight and a few big tears rolled down my cheeks. This was the finality. I felt as if it was my last day on earth. All day long, my possessions slowly made their way onto the truck. By 6 o'clock the huge van was packed, the movers gone and I was alone in the empty house. I felt no sorrow, only an enormous experience of relief. The job of getting out that had occupied my time for months was completed. The house that had held so much of my life and the life of my family was vacant. It would soon no longer be mine. I packed my car to the last inch as I prepared to spend the night with a friend. Then, without shedding a tear, I turned the key in the lock and I left.

The following morning, before the sun came up, I pressed the "trip" button on my dashboard. Four zeros appeared. A blank slate. They symbolized the life I was about to begin. I headed for Route 80 and drove west.

APPENDIX

Where to Find Help

Support Groups

Several national organizations have long been a source of information and support for death and mourning. Many regional organizations exist as well. These groups offer individuals an opportunity to meet with one another within a small group, usually under the leadership of a professional, to air their concerns, share common needs and sometimes to meet a desire for social interaction. Many communities offer self-help groups sponsored by hospitals, religious and civic organizations and private agencies. The following large organizations, in addition to providing direct aid, can offer referrals to further resources.

AARP Grief and Loss Programs
601 E Street, NW
Washington, DC 20049
Call toll-free: 1-888-OUR-AARP (1-888-687-2277)
www.aarp.org/griefandloss/

An outreach service of the AARP Widowed Persons Service provides resourcesand information on grief. Services include online support groups, bulletin boards, articles and publications as well as the location of an AARP bereavement program in your area.

The Compassionate Friends (TCF)
P.O. Box 3696
Oak Brook, IL 60522-3696
Call toll free: 877-969-0010
FAX 630-990-0254
e-mail: nationaloffice@compassionatefriends.org
www.compassionatefriends.org

This is an active and long-standing national organization offering support to parents who have lost children. See the website for locations of local chapters and names of chapter leaders.

Mother's Against Drunk Driving (MADD)

MADD National Office
522 E. John Carpenter Frwy. Suite 700
Irving, TX 75062
TEL: 800 - GET-MADD
www.madd.org

The MADD website helps individuals to identify local chapters. It provides information on advocacy groups and research. E-mail MADD through its website by clicking on "contact us."

Parents Without Partners, Inc.

1650 South Dixie Highway, Suite 510
Boca Raton, FL 33432
TEL: 561-391-8833
FAX: 561-395-8557
e-mail: pwp@jti.net
www.parentswithoutpartners.org

An international organization with local chapters offering educational, family and social activities. Its website enables people to share ideas and participate in members-only forums.

Websites

A vast bereavement community exists on the Internet including bulletin boards and chat rooms facilitating communication among participants. Some of the most extensive websites are outgrowths of the regional and national organizations described above. The combination of traditional and electronic support groups, as well as the resources offered by both, provide mourners with an opportunity to obtain information and communicate with others.

Some of the popular Internet search engines offer hundreds of grief and bereavement related sites. With no attempt to provide a definitive list of grief support organizations or bereavement websites, or even to try to determine which is primarily one or the other, I offer the names of organizations and websites that have been helpful to me. Some of the sites are useful for their links to additional resources including on-line bookstores and the enormous body of literature related to death and dying.

Bereavement Magazine
Bereavement Publishing
4765 North Carefree Circle, Colorado Springs, CO 80917
Toll free: 1-888-604-HOPE
www.bereavementmag.com

A magazine and website founded by Andrea Gambill following the death of her 17-year-old daughter.

Counseling for Loss and Life Changes
e-mail: mail@counselingforloss.com
www.counselingforloss.com

A large website with many links and resources.

Crisis, Grief and Healing
Tom Golden
149 Little Quarry Mews
Gaithersburg, MD 20878
TEL: 301-670-1027
e-mail: wsgolden@webhealing.com
www.webhealing.com

Tom Golden is a licensed social worker, author and speaker who maintains a private practice in the field of death and dying. His site offers helpful links to bereavement groups and other websites.

Griefnet
www.griefnet.org

An internet community including e-mail support groups, many resources, and a bookstore. Griefnet, a non-profit organization, was founded and is directed by Cendra Lynn: cendra@griefnet.org.

Growth House, Inc.
TEL: 415-863-3045
e-mail: info@growthhouse.org
www. growthhouse.org

A San Francisco organization that provides information and referral services for agencies working with death and dying issues. The website has chatrooms and many helpful links to resources and support groups. Special pages address needs of bereaved families, natal and infant loss, helping children with grief and serious illness.

GROWW, Inc
11877 Douglas Road #102 PMB101
Alpharetta, GA 30005
www.groww.com
staff@groww.org

A large, well-organized website offering resources, chat rooms, bulletin boards, a library and other useful information.

BIBLIOGRAPHY

Bernstein, Judith R. 1997. *When the Bough Breaks*. Kansas City, MO: Andrews and McMeel.

Biller, Ray; Rice, Susan, <u>Health & Social Work</u>, Nov. 90, Vol.15, Issue 4, p283.

Diamant, Anita. 1997. *The Red Tent.* New York, NY: Picador.

Edelman, Hope. 1994. *Motherless Daughters.* MA, CA, NY : Addison-Wesley Publishing Co.p.5

Freud, Ernst L. ed *Letters of Sigmund Freud.* trans. Tania Stern and James Stern. NY: Basic Books.

Friedan, Betty. *The Feminine Mystique.* NY: Norton & Co., reprint 1997.

Jowell, Barbara Tom and Schwisow, Donnette. *After He's Gone: A Guide for Widowed and Divorced Women.* Secaucus, NJ: Carol Publishing Group, 1997.

Jurgensen, Genvieve, 1999. *The Disappearance.* New York, NY: W.W. Norton & Co. Inc.,. (English translation), pp. 146-147.

Kastenbaum, R.J. 1977. Death and development through the life span. In H. Feigel (ed.) *New Meanings of Life.* New York: McGraw-Hill,.

Kubler-Ross, Elizabeth MD 1969. *On Death and Dying.* New York, NY: Macmillan Co.,. Pp. 44, 152.

Kushner, Harold S. 1981. *When Bad Things Happen to Good People.* New York, NY: Avon Books.

Lamm, Maurice. 1969. *The Jewish Way in Death and Mourning.* Middle Village, NY: Jonathan David Publishers.

Leahy, Julia M, (National League for Nursing) "A Comparison of Depression in Women Bereaved of a Spouse, Child, or a Parent" *OMEGA:Journal of Death and Dying* 1992-1993. Vol. 26 (3), 201-217. P.207

Lieberman, Morton Ph.D. 1996. *Doors Close, Doors Open: Widows Grieving and Growing,* New York, NY: G.P. Putnam's Sons.

Plath, Sylvia. 1971. *The Bell Jar.* New York, NY: Harper & Row,.p.98.

Quindlen, Anna. 1988. *Living out Loud*, New York, NY: Random House, pp. 235-236.

Rando, Therese. 1988. *Grieving: How to Go on Living When Someone You Love Dies* Lexington, MA: Lexington Books,.

Rando, Therese, Ph.D. 1986 *Parental Loss of a Child,* Champaign, IL: Research Press.

Shaw, Eva. 1994. *What to do When a Loved One Dies.* Irvine, CA: Dickens Press. p.65

Strong, Maggie. 1988. *Mainstay: For the Well Spouse of the Chronically Ill.* Boston, MA: Little, Brown & Co.

Tolstoy, Leo. 1997. *Anna Karenina.* Barnes &Noble Publishing. Paperback Edition. p. 3.

Volkan, Vamik D. M.D. and Zintl, Elizabeth. 1993. *Life After Loss: The Lessons of Grief*. New York, NY: Charles Scribner's Sons, (Macmillan Publishing Co). p. 17, p.98.

When a Brother or Sister Dies. Oak Brook, IL: Published by The Compassionate Friends, 1993.

Wylie, Betty Jane. 1997. *Beginnings: A Book for Widows.* Toronto, Canada: McClelland & Stewart, Inc.

ACKNOWLEDGMENTS

Thank you to Jenna Laurent, Judy Levey, Harold Manchester, Inez Middlebury and Mirrell Walden for their advice, editing and encouragement; to Joann Herold who changed my life and made the world an emptier place by leaving it; to all the e-mail correspondents and others who described their losses in return for anonymity; to the late Judy Divers, the founder of GROWW, Inc.; to Melissa Rubins who believed in my story; to Deborah Houk Schocket for her support and to my son Andy who helped me to become a better writer.

Sandra Schocket

Photo by Sue Moesser

Sandra Schocket is a widely published freelance writer and author of the book *My Life Closed Twice: Surviving a Double Loss,* describing the loss of her husband and son within 24 hours, and her road to rebuilding a new life following this tragedy.

She has contributed articles to the *New York Times*, *Working Woman*, *New Jersey Star-Ledger*, *Trenton Times*, and *Boston Globe* as well as local and trade publications.

As a Board certified career counselor, Ms. Schocket draws on her experience counseling individuals who have suffered job loss to help her confront her own loss. In *My Life Closed Twice*, she explores the parallels between the stages of grief experienced through employment loss and those incurred through other major losses such as death and divorce.

Sandra Schocket is a graduate of Mount Holyoke College with a degree in psychology and economics. She holds a master's Degree in Education from Rutgers University.